Jim Buyens
Popular author, Web developer,
and programming expert

Beginning Programming

Take charge of Microsoft® Visual Basic®—
faster, smarter, *better*!

PUBLISHED BY
Microsoft Press
A Division of Microsoft Corporation
One Microsoft Way
Redmond, Washington 98052-6399

Library of Congress Cataloging-in-Publication Data
Buyens, Jim.
    Faster Smarter Beginning Programming / Jim Buyens.
        p. cm.
    Includes index.
    ISBN 0-7356-1780-5
    1. Computer programming.   2. Programming languages (Electronic computers)   I. Title.

    QA76.6 .B87   2002
    005--dc21   2002033765

Printed and bound in the United States of America.

1 2 3 4 5 6 7 8 9   QWE   8 7 6 5 4 3

Distributed in Canada by H.B. Fenn and Company Ltd.

A CIP catalogue record for this book is available from the British Library.

Microsoft Press books are available through booksellers and distributors worldwide. For further information about international editions, contact your local Microsoft Corporation office or contact Microsoft Press International directly at fax (425) 936-7329. Visit our Web site at www.microsoft.com/mspress. Send comments to *mspinput@microsoft.com*.

FrontPage, IntelliSense, JScript, MSDN, Visual Basic, Visual C++, Visual C#, Visual Studio, Windows, and Windows NT are either registered trademarks or trademarks of Microsoft Corporation in the United States and/or other countries. Other product and company names mentioned herein may be the trademarks of their respective owners.

The example companies, organizations, products, domain names, e-mail addresses, logos, people, places, and events depicted herein are fictitious. No association with any real company, organization, product, domain name, e-mail address, logo, person, place, or event is intended or should be inferred.

Acquisitions Editor: Danielle Bird
Project Editor: Sandra Haynes
Series Editor: Kristen Weatherby

Body Part No. X08-94873

*This book is dedicated to the
homeless mentally ill people of America.
Why do we lavish health care dollars on victims
of other, less debilitating illnesses, while condemning
these unfortunates to the streets and gutters?*

Table of Contents

Acknowledgments

First and foremost, I'd like to thank my wife Connie, my daughters Lorrill and Lynessa, and my son Justin for their continued love, patience, and understanding. Thanks as well to my parents, my brothers, and their families: Harold, Marcella, Ruth, Dave, Connie, Michael, Steven, Rick, Jenny, Matt, and Claire. Who'd have thought any of us would end up as we are?

At Microsoft Press, thanks to Danielle Bird, who handled all the business details, and to Kristen Weatherby, Dick Brown, and Wendy Zucker, who helped with initial planning. Thanks especially to Sandra Haynes, who as project editor kept the project on track and unified through completion.

Thank you also to Tempe Goodhue and all the other people at nSight who transformed a raw manuscript into the finished book before you now.

Most of all, thanks to you, the readers, who make an effort such as this one both possible and worthwhile. I hope the book meets your expectations and that we meet again.

Introduction

This Book Could Be for You

If you're an experienced PC user who's never delved into programming but now has the itch, this is the book that will get you started. It presumes you're proficient with Windows and Windows applications, but that you wouldn't know a line of code if it came up and bit you on the, uh, byte.

Chapter 1 explains the fundamental concepts behind all computer programming: the way computers store instructions in memory, the way they store data in memory, and the three logical constructs which, in combination, can express any procedure the human mind can conceive.

Of course you want to see how these concepts appear in programming statements, which requires a programming language to use an as example. In the case of this book, that language is Visual Basic .NET. Visual Basic traces its roots to the original BASIC language that John Kemeney and Thomas Kurtz developed in 1964 for teaching programming at Dartmouth College, and it's still one of the easiest programming languages to learn. It's also part of more Microsoft products than any other component, and it will serve you in good stead for writing macros, product extensions, and almost anything else not built into the products themselves.

Chapter 2 explains the fundamentals of Visual Basic .NET: how to obtain it, how to install it, and how to enter programming statements. Chapter 3 explains elementary data types and statements. Chapter 4 addresses operators and expressions, which calculate results in somewhat the same way as spreadsheet formulas.

Modern programming would be impossible without the means to divide large problems into smaller ones, to solve the small problems using small units of code, and finally to integrate many small units into a finished whole. Chapters 5 through 8 therefore describe functions, subroutines, classes, objects, modules, and forms. Each of these, in one way or another, make small, focused blocks of code available to other parts of a program.

Chapters 9 and 10 address specific issues of designing Windows forms; that is, of designing your own Windows user interface complete with drop-down menus, toolbars, buttons, and all the other gadgets and gizmos you're accustomed to finding in Windows programs. Chapter 11 introduces the topic of programming databases, and Chapter 12 concludes the book with instructions on how to construct programs that use an Internet browser rather than a Windows form as the user interface.

Programmers have been writing software for more than 50 years now, and even though the job gets easier with each new generation of tools, it remains an intricate and exacting task. Don't expect this book to make you a practiced or professional programmer, but do expect it to make you a fledgling one. From that starting point, you can pursue whatever direction your needs and interests demand.

System Requirements

Although you can profitably read this book without working the examples, truly learning to program—like learning to swim—requires physical practice. This, of course, means you'll need a copy of Visual Basic .NET. This comes with all versions of Microsoft Visual Studio .NET, and also with the stand-alone package sold as Microsoft Visual Basic .NET Standard. The Standard product usually costs less than $U.S.100 and is sufficient for all the examples in this book.

All .NET programming languages require the presence of the Microsoft .NET Framework and SDK (System Development Kit). The Visual Studio .NET or Visual Basic .NET setup program will install this for you, or you can download it free from Microsoft's Web site. (Chapter 2 provides more detailed instructions.)

As to operating systems, you'll need Microsoft Windows 2000, Windows XP, or later. If you want to program Web pages, as in Chapter 12, you'll also want to install Internet Information Services (IIS)—which includes Microsoft's Web server—on your PC. This rules out the use of Windows XP Home Edition, for which IIS isn't available. On Windows 2000, Windows XP Professional, or later, IIS is an option under Control Panel, Add/Remove Programs, Add/Remove Windows Components.

Support

The companion files for this book contain the source code for all the examples. To download these files, browse *http://www.interlacken.com/fsbp/* and select Request Companion Files from the main menu. This Web location also contains links for frequently asked questions, error corrections, and other news related to the book.

Please understand that the price of this book doesn't include any technical support or debugging assistance from Microsoft, the author, or anyone else. The Help files that come with Visual Basic are extensive and, once you grow accustomed to them, should answer many of the questions that come up. Additional information is available on the Microsoft developer network Web site at *http://msdn.microsoft.com*, on the Microsoft support Web site at *http://support.microsoft.com*, and on usenet newsgroups such as microsoft.public.dotnet.languages.vb.

Every effort has been made to ensure the accuracy of this book. Microsoft Press provides corrections for books at *http://mspress.microsoft.com/support/*. If you have comments, questions, or ideas regarding this book, please send them to Microsoft Press via e-mail to

mspinput@microsoft.com

or via postal mail to

Microsoft Press
Attn: Faster Smarter Series Editor
One Microsoft Way
Redmond, WA 98052-6399

You can also contact the author directly via e-mail (in English) at

buyensj@interlacken.com.

Please note that product support is not offered through the above addresses. To suggest enhancements to any piece of Microsoft software, send an e-mail to

mswish@microsoft.com

or browse the Web page at

http://register.microsoft.com/regsys/custom/wishwizard.asp

Chapter 1

Introducing Basic Concepts

Computer software is surely one of the most intangible commodities of our time. Nevertheless, it's also one of the most valuable. Of all the progress made during the past 50 years due to the use of computers, virtually 100 percent would have been impossible without someone having written the necessary software. A computer without software is like a rowboat without an oarsman: no objective, no plan, no activity, no progress.

Presumably, and for whatever reason, you've decided to learn how to write software of your own. The particular type of software you have in mind doesn't matter too much right now; first you need to learn the process of creating computer programs and fortunately, this is fairly universal.

Computer programming consists mainly of devising procedures capable of producing a given result, and then expressing those procedures in a way that the computer can understand. People often refer to programming as both an art and a science, and for good reason. Devising procedures that solve complex problems requires creativity, imagination, and insight. Articulating them for a computer, on the other hand, requires strict logic and attention to detail.

The earliest programmers created software using nothing more than paper, pencil, and switches on the computer console. Yecch. Nowadays, programmers automate much of their work by using existing software to create new software. In the case of this book, the existing software is Microsoft Visual Basic .NET.

- Visual Basic traces its roots to the BASIC language that John Kemeny and Tom Kurtz invented in 1964 specifically for teaching students at Dartmouth College how to program.

- Visual Basic is among the most widely used programming languages.

- Visual Basic .NET is the most powerful and easiest to use version of Visual Basic ever.

Chapter 2, "Introducing Microsoft Visual Basic .NET," explains how to install Visual Basic .NET and how to develop and run your first program. In the meantime, this chapter explains some basic concepts that'll significantly help you understand the material in Chapter 2 and the rest of the book.

How Program Code and Data Occupy Memory

A computer consisting of hardware only—that is, with no software—can do little more than hum and consume electricity. To do useful work, the computer requires a series of instructions that tell it exactly what to do; that is, the computer requires a *program*. The program and the computer hardware work together like this:

- Random Access Memory (RAM) holds in place the instructions and any associated data for use by the central processing unit (CPU).

- The CPU retrieves the instructions one by one, in order, and carries out whatever actions they specify. For example, it might copy data from one area of memory to another, perform arithmetic, compare one data value to another, or begin retrieving instructions from a different part of memory.

- Input/output devices—such as disks, printers, a console, and network adapters—provide various means of putting data into memory for processing and getting it back out for practical use. The CPU operates these devices by executing special instructions or manipulating special areas of memory.

Lingo   An *instruction* is any command that a computer's central processing unit can process directly. The term *machine instruction* is slightly more specific but both terms mean the same thing.

In modern computers, each character of memory has its own unique numerical address. The first character in memory has an address of 0, the second character in memory has an address of 1, and so forth. If you bought a computer with 128 bytes of memory, 0 would be the first memory address and 127 would be the last. If, more realistically, you bought a computer with 128 MB of memory, the last address would be $(128 \times 1024 \times 1024) - 1$, or 134,217,727.

Note   Because computers count by twos instead of by tens, they seldom use "nice" whole numbers like 10 or 1,000,000 for anything. Instead, the computer's idea of a "nice" number is any
power of two. This is why numbers like 2, 4, 8, 16, 32, 64, 128, 256, 512, and 1024 keep pop-
ping up in any discussion regarding computers.

A given area of memory can hold either instructions or data. There's no
physical difference between memory that holds instructions and memory that
holds data. When you load a new program into memory and start running it,
memory that previously contained data might now contain instructions, and
memory that previously contained instructions might now contain data.

Figure 1-1 shows some hypothetical data and instructions loaded into memory. Each instruction or element of data occupies one memory location. The
CPU knows that after processing each instruction, it should proceed to the next.

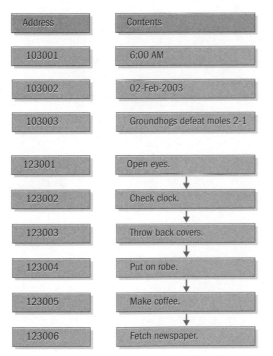

Figure 1-1   Computer programs are a series of instructions that the computer holds in memory and executes
one step at a time.

The diagram in Figure 1-1 is, of course, an oversimplification. The actual
instruction set of a typical CPU is much more cryptic and a single instruction or
data value can occupy several memory locations. The CPU knows how long
each type of instruction is supposed to be, and therefore how many bytes to
advance before retrieving the next instruction.

Lingo   A CPU's *instruction set* is the collection of all instruction types it can process.

Appreciating Data Types

Virtually all CPUs have instructions suited to specific kinds of data. Here are three of the most common:

- **Integer instructions**   These instructions add, subtract, multiply, divide, and otherwise manipulate whole numbers. Typically, these numbers are 8, 16, 32, or 64 bits in size. An 8-bit integer can hold values from 0 to 255 or from –126 to +127, depending on whether or not one of the bits indicates positive or negative.

Note   A bit is one binary digit: that is, a one or a zero.

- **Floating-point instructions**   These instructions operate on numbers having three parts: a sign, an exponent, and a mantissa. In a number such as 6.02×10^{23}, the sign is positive, the exponent is 23, and the mantissa is 6.02. In most cases, integers are better for counting things and floating-point numbers are better for scientific calculations. Table 1-1 summarizes the floating-point formats that Intel processors support.

Table 1-1   **Floating-Point Formats on Intel Processors**

Type	Bits	Exponent		Mantissa	
		Bits	Precision	Bits	Precision
Single	32	8	10^{38} to 10^{-44}	23	6–7 decimal digits
Double	64	11	10^{308} to 10^{-323}	52	15–16 decimal digits

- **String instructions**   These instructions operate on character data such as natural language text. On older computers, each character of text occupies 1 byte (8 bits) of memory. On newer systems, each character occupies 2 bytes (16 bits).

The reason for having these various data types is simple: efficiency. If your data is one of these types, the processor can carry out basic operations with a single instruction. This is very fast. Most programming languages support additional data types for dates, times, money, and so forth, but when you program an operation involving one of these types, the compiler must generate a series of instructions to do the job. This shouldn't be a deterrent toward using any data type your programming language supports, but it should be an incentive to use the correct type in all cases.

Chapter 3, "Using Elementary Statements," explains much more about data types and how to use them.

High-Level Languages

Nowadays, very few programmers deal directly with the individual instructions that a CPU processes. Instead, they code procedural statements in a special notation that a piece of software converts to machine instructions. This is much easier than coding the machine instructions directly. Over the years, computer scientists and developers have invented quite a few of these notations, each of which is a *programming language.* Programming languages and human languages are alike in that both have nouns, verbs, statements, punctuation, and rules governing what's correct and what's invalid. C, C++, COBOL, C#, Forth, FORTRAN, Java, JavaScript, Pascal, Perl, Python, and Visual Basic are all programming languages.

The lowest and most fundamental programming language of all is *machine language.* Writing programs in machine language means coding every one and zero in the entire program by hand. This is how the first programmers worked, but hardly anyone does this anymore. It's just too time consuming and error prone.

An *assembly language* is one with statements that correspond one-to-one with machine instructions. You write assembly language with a text editor, specifying cryptic abbreviations and decimal numbers rather than ones and zeroes. Also, in assembly language you can refer to locations in your program by name rather than by memory address. To run an assembly language program, you must save it as a text file and then convert it into machine language using a program called (what else?) an *assembler.* This is a huge improvement over coding machine language, but still quite time consuming and error prone. Also, if you want to run the same program on several different kinds of computers, you're out of luck. Assembly language programs are inexorably tied to a single type of CPU.

High-level languages have no relation to the instruction set of a specific CPU. Instead, they're designed primarily for ease in expressing whatever solution you've devised for the task at hand. C, C++, C#, JavaScript, Perl, and Visual Basic are all high-level languages.

Programs called *compilers* translate code from high-level languages to machine language. One high-level language statement typically results in several machine instructions. If compilers for the same language are available for different CPU types and operating systems, then running the same program on several different kinds of computers is a real possibility. Nearly all modern programming involves high-level languages.

High-level languages can be either procedural or nonprocedural. Using a procedural language, you must figure out the steps necessary to make the programs do what you want. In other words, your source code must supply a procedure for solving the problem. The term *third-generation language* (3GL) denotes a procedural high-level language. Visual Basic is primarily a 3GL: that is, a procedural high-level language.

Note   Historically, machine language was the first generation and assembly language was the second. However, no one used these terms until 3GLs came about.

Nonprocedural high-level languages don't require that you figure out procedures to accomplish your objectives. Instead, you specify what kinds of results you want and the high-level language figures out how to produce it. The terms *fourth-generation language* (4GL) and *specification-oriented language* both denote procedural high-level languages. The report writer feature of Microsoft Access is a 4GL, as is that of Crystal Reports. Visual Basic .NET includes graphical form designers for both interactive Windows applications and for Web pages; these designers, although not full 4GLs, are at least fourth-generation features.

Note   Although 4GLs provide more automation than 3GLs, they're less flexible, and this can lead to difficulty. The more you want to customize the results, the more you end up fighting or bypassing the 4GL.

Second-, third-, and even some fourth-generation languages require that you enter *statements* in an ordinary text file. Learning the format of these statements is a major part of learning to program, but generically they constitute your *source code*. The file that contains your source code is, of course, a *source file*. The assembler or compiler reads the source file and, if all goes well, produces an *executable file*, a file that the computer can load into memory and run.

Note   Many compilers and assemblers actually produce a sort of intermediate file called an *object file*. A program called a *linker* combines the object file with other prewritten software to produce the final executable. In most cases, however, the compiler runs the linker automatically, and you don't need to be aware of it.

Programmers tend to use the terms *code, source code, statements,* and *source statements* interchangeably. If someone asks to see your code, it means they want to look at your source statements.

Each line of text in a source file is one *line of code*. Experienced programmers usually code each program statement on a separate line but this isn't a hard and fast requirement. In most programming languages (as in most natural languages) one statement can span several lines and one line can contain several statements.

There are three fundamental types of statements:

■ **Data declarations**   These statements reserve areas of memory for use by data items. They also give the data item a name and specify its type: integer, floating point, string, and so forth.

Note   The word *variable* is another name for a named data item.

■ **Executable statements**   These statements cause things to occur while the program is running. For example, they perform arithmetic, evaluate decisions, execute loops, and get data into and out of the program.

■ **Control statements**   These statements provide information that the compiler uses while converting source statements to machine instructions. Unlike data declarations and executable statements, control statements directly add nothing to the final machine language program.

Tip   As you gain programming experience, you'll no doubt acquire the habit of formatting source statements so they're easily readable. This greatly improves the quality of life for you or anyone else who works on the program in the future.

One of the most important features of high-level languages, from second-generation assemblers on up, is that you can refer to memory locations by name rather than by number. The compiler then assigns numeric addresses to each name automatically. This has two advantages:

■ When you put some piece of information, such as your birth date, in memory, it's much easier to refer to that data element by means of a name (like *Birth_Date*) than by means of a memory address (such as *1785423*).

■ If you rearrange or otherwise modify your program, the compiler will figure out where your named data items end up and automatically assign new addresses to them.

You can name memory areas that contain instructions as well as memory areas that contain data.

The Concept of Layered Software

Early programmers, using machine language or assembler, wrote completely self-sufficient programs. As time passed and software became more complex, however, these monolithic programs became increasingly impractical. For one thing, with each program taking over the entire computer, it wasn't possible to run several programs at the same time. For another, the programs grew so large and complex that they nearly defied human understanding. Finally, many functions inside these large programs were essentially the same. There was no point in rewriting them for each program.

These are just a few of the reasons that operating systems exist. Today, most programs expect to run within the confines of an operating system such as Microsoft Windows and for the operating system to provide a variety of services that the program can use. One way of expressing this relationship is to say that programs run *on top of* Windows. Another way is to talk about an *operating system layer* and an *application layer*.

In fact, operating systems and applications both have layers within themselves. Every time one piece of software provides services and another piece of software uses them, you can speak of a layer existing between them. In general, you don't need to be concerned about how software at layers other than your own actually does its job. If, for example, you want Windows to open a file, read a few records, and then close it, you needn't concern yourself with details of how Windows does this. You only need to know how to request the service and retrieve the results.

Lingo   An *application programming interface* (API) is a mechanism through which software at one layer communicates with software at a different layer.

The Microsoft .NET initiative introduces a major new layer between applications and the operating system, namely the common language runtime (CLR) shown in Figure 1-2. When you compile a .NET program, the compiler doesn't produce executable code that uses the computer's native instruction set. Instead, it produces code in a format called Microsoft intermediate language (MSIL). The first time a .NET program runs on a given computer, the CLR compiles the MSIL code into the computer's native instruction set.

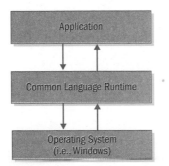

Figure 1-2   The CLR is a .NET layer situated between application programs and the operating system.

Here are some of the advantages that the CLR provides:

- The same ILC program can run on any processor or operating system for which a CLR is available. This provides a migration path from Pentium processors to the Itanium chip and the StrongARM processor in a Pocket PC.

- The CLR can perform memory management and other services that increase the reliability of both the application and the operating system.

- All programs that use the CLR use the same data types and the same interfaces to the operating system. This makes it much easier for programs written in different languages to interact.

Because Visual Basic .NET creates intermediate language code, any programs you write will only run on computers that have the Microsoft .NET Framework installed. (The .NET Framework includes the CLR). Furthermore, the framework is currently available only for Microsoft Windows 2000, Windows XP, and Windows .NET Server. If you or your users are still running Microsoft Windows NT, Windows Millennium Edition (Windows Me), Windows 98, or Windows 95, now is the time to consider an upgrade.

Note   If not already, then in the very near future, virtually all Windows software will be .NET software. The CLR will then be ubiquitous.

Structured Programming Constructs

Imagine a plate of spaghetti noodles, cooked and well tossed. Given enough time, you could draw a map showing where each strand begins and ends, but what a task! You might die of old age before you finished, even assuming the noodles never shifted around or grew brittle and cracked.

Believe it or not, programmers used to create programs using logic as convoluted as that plate of spaghetti. When it worked it was a miracle and when it didn't you either had job security for life or plenty of incentive to look for a new job.

Lingo   To this day, *spaghetti code* means source code so haphazard and disorganized that almost no one can understand it.

A technique called *structured programming* goes a long way toward preventing this sort of mess. The key concept is that you can write any program using only these three kinds of logical structures:

- **Sequence**   The computer will execute a group of statements in order. The statements in Figure 1-1 earlier in this chapter constitute a sequence.

■ **Decision** The computer will execute either one group of statements or another depending on some condition.

■ **Loop** The computer will execute a group of statements repeatedly until some condition is satisfied.

Figure 1-3 illustrates a decision. If today is Sunday, the procedure calls for visiting relatives; otherwise, it calls for going to work. In Visual Basic, you would code this as shown here:

```
If Weekday(Now()) = vbSunday Then
    Visit_Relatives
Else
    Drive_To_Work
End If
```

> **Note** In Visual Basic .NET, *Now()* is a built-in function that returns the current date and time. *Weekday()* is a built-in function that converts a date and time to a day-of-the-week code. The expression *vbSunday* is a built-in constant that always contains the day-of-the-week code for Sunday.

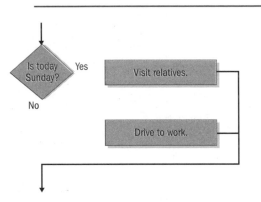

Figure 1-3 This flowchart illustrates a simple decision structure.

Both the *If* and the *Else* portions of a decision structure can contain zero statements, one statement, or several statements. Furthermore, these statements needn't be simple sequences; they can also be decisions or loops. For example, here's a decision structure that contains zero statements in the *Else* portion:

```
If Weekday(Now()) = vbSunday Then
    Visit_Relatives
End If
```

The next example shows nested decision structures; that is, one decision structure inside another. A corresponding flowchart appears in Figure 1-4.

```
If Weekday(Now()) = vbSaturday Then
    Clean_Yard
    Wash_Car
```

```
    If Month(Now()) > 8 Then
        Watch_Football
    End If
Else
    If Weekday(Now()) = vbSunday Then
        Visit_Relatives
    Else
        Drive_To_Work
    End If
End If
```

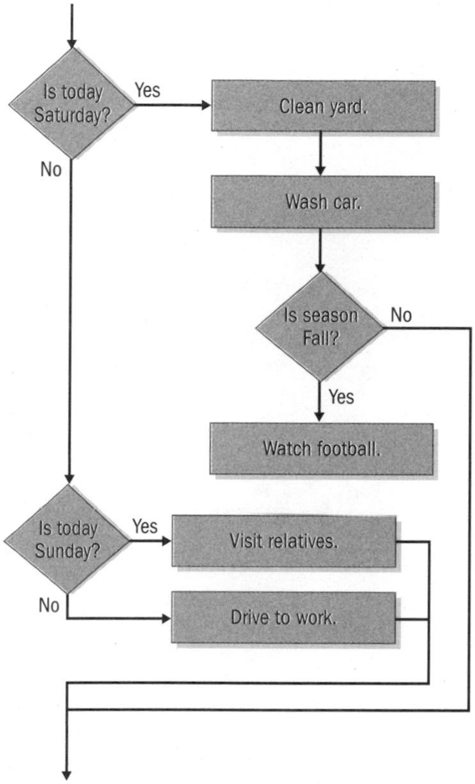

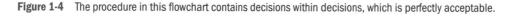

Figure 1-4 The procedure in this flowchart contains decisions within decisions, which is perfectly acceptable.

Note that in the previous code, the *Else* and *End If* for each decision appear directly beneath the corresponding *If*. Statements subordinate to an *If* or *Else* appear indented to the right. This alignment and indentation makes the code easy to read and easy to work with; easier, in fact, than the traditional flowchart. Virtually all experienced programmers indent their code this way.

Notice also that once the computer encounters an *If* statement, it'll always reach the *End If* statement. The flow of control never wanders out of the decision structure and into another piece of code. This sort of consistency makes structured programming so much easier to understand.

Figure 1-5 illustrates a simple loop structure. The actions *Go to sleep* and *Open eyes* will occur over and over again until the alarm starts ringing.

To describe this procedure in Visual Basic, you would write something like this:

```
Do
    Fall_Asleep
    Open_Eyes
Loop While Not Alarm_Ringing
```

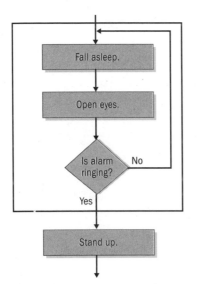

Figure 1-5   A loop structure executes one or more statements repeatedly until some condition is true.

As written, this code always falls asleep at least once, even if the alarm is already ringing. To allow the loop to execute zero times, you would put the condition at the top of the loop like this:

```
Do While Not Alarm-Ringing
    Fall_Asleep
    Open_Eyes
Loop
```

Again, note that the statement that ends the loop is aligned under the statement that starts it. Statements within the loop are indented to the right. This makes it easy to see at a glance where the loop begins and ends. These conventions are quite similar to those for decision structures.

You might wonder if loops and decision structures are permissible within loops. They are. Here's an example (Figure 1-6 shows the corresponding flowchart.):

```
Do While Not Alarm_Ringing
    Do While Not Aslecp
        Count_Sheep
    Loop
    Open_Eyes
    If Room_Is_Cold Then
        Pull_Up_Covers
    End If
Loop
```

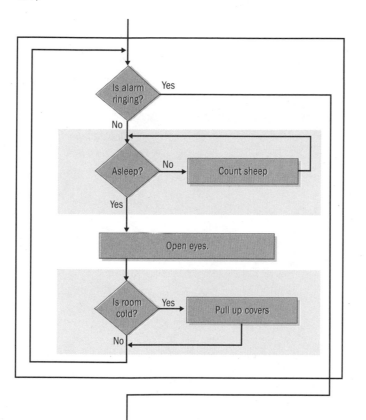

Figure 1-6 It's perfectly okay to code loops and decision structures inside other loops.

As with decisions, loops have only one way in and one way out. Even when you nest one loop inside another, executing the start of a given loop inexorably leads to that loop's one and only exit point.

Writing programs that consist solely of sequences, decisions, and loops requires a certain discipline and mindset. You might wonder, therefore, if there's another way to get the job done. There is, and it goes by the name *branch*, *jump*, or *go to*, depending on the programming language you're using.

A branch summarily tells the computer to start executing statements from some new spot in memory. At first this might seem to offer wonderful flexibility because you're no longer limited to single entry and exit points. In fact, programs that jump around from one spot to another are very difficult to get working properly in the first place and even more difficult to keep working as the need to make changes arises. As a result, modern programming languages no longer support branching except in a limited way; namely, you can branch to an exit point.

If you talk with experienced programmers for very long, you'll notice that they frequently speak about blocks of code. Sometimes the word *block* means any group of statements, but more often it means all the statements between the entry point and the exit point of a loop or decision. Why do you need to know this? Well, the limited form of branching that modern programming languages support is that of branching to the end of a block. This is quite handy when a statement in the middle of a block detects that running the remainder of the block would serve no purpose or generate an error.

Figure 1-7 illustrates a loop that counts how many cards in a deck precede the seven of clubs. The loop says to turn over the top card and then determine if it's the seven of clubs. If it is, you exit the loop. If not, you add one to the count of cards that weren't the seven of clubs, and then continue the loop. Of course, if you run out of cards before finding the seven, then you also exit the loop.

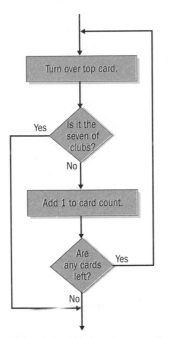

Figure 1-7   This loop has multiple paths to the exit point, but still only one exit.

Branching from the middle of a loop or decision to its normal exit point often simplifies your job as a programmer and leads to cleaner (that is, easier to understand) code. This technique, however, is easy to abuse. If you can figure out another way of doing the same thing, you're probably better off.

Top-Down Design

The flowcharts and code you've seen so far have all been simple. Hopefully, you understood them at a glance. Nevertheless, at some point flowcharts and program code grow so large and complex that no one—including the most talented and experienced programmers—can understand them. This would present a serious problem were it not for the concept of *modular design*.

The idea of modular design is to break large programs into smaller, more easily comprehensible modules, and then work on one small module at a time. If this sounds like a clear application of "Divide and conquer," you're right!

The design of a modular program usually begins with a so-called mainline. When you or your intended user loads the program into memory, the *mainline* is the first procedure to execute. A typical mainline

- First acquires and initializes any resources the program needs to operate: databases, files, network connections, and so on.

- Then runs a loop that receives input and creates output until no more input remains.

- Finally releases its resources and terminates the program.

The flowchart in Figure 1-8 illustrates this process.

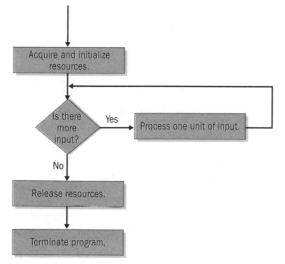

Figure 1-8 This flowchart illustrates the mainline flow of control in a typical program.

The block titled "Process one unit of input" is, of course, where all the interesting stuff happens. This code for this block typically contains a series of decisions that figure out what kind of input has arrived and what to do about it. If the purpose of the program is to update a database, there might be three kinds of input transactions: add a record, update a record, and delete a record. In Visual Basic, this block might look like this:

```
If Trans_Code = "Add" Then
    Add_Database_Record
Else
    If Trans_Code = "Update" Then
        Update_Database_Record
    Else
        If Trans_Code = "Delete" Then
            Delete_Database_Record
        Else
            Report_Invalid_Transaction
        End If
    End If
End If
```

The four statements *Add_Database_Record*, *Update_Database_Record*, *Delete_Database_Record*, and *Report_Invalid_Transaction* call upon other blocks of code (that is, other modules) that provide additional processing. If those modules turn out to be large or complicated, you would implement portions of them as still more modules. The result, if all goes well, would be a well-organized set of modules that solve a large, complicated problem in an orderly, methodical, and easy-to-understand way. (The next topic in this chapter, by the way, will explain how statements like *Add_Database_Record* call other blocks of code in your program.)

Top-down design is the name that describes this approach to designing programs. Top, in this case, means the most general, most obvious parts of the program. First you design the top module (the mainline), then any subordinate modules the mainline requires, then any modules those subordinate modules require, and so forth.

Tip   When deciding how to divide a problem into modules, try to design modules that perform single complete functions. Modules that do only one thing are easy to understand, and they're easy to reuse if a similar need arises again.

There's also such a thing as *bottom-up design*. In this mode you start by designing some low level module—usually one that performs an important or intricate function. Next, you write one or more modules that use that function.

Then you write more and more modules in an attempt to reach some high-level goal such as a user interface that makes the original, intricate function easy to use.

> **Tip**   Neither top-down nor bottom-up design is best in all cases. The best approach depends on the specific problem you're trying to solve.

Subroutines and Functions

There are several good ways of developing modules, but the use of subroutines and functions is among the most common and the best. Both of these structures are named blocks of code that are, to some extent, separate and isolated from other code in the same program.

No matter what programming language you're using, a subroutine tends to involve these elements:

- Special statements mark the subroutine's beginning and end.

- The statement that marks the beginning also specifies the subroutine's name and a list of *arguments*. Arguments are one of several ways that subroutines can receive input values and send back output values.

- Between its opening and closing statements, a subroutine can contain both data declarations and executable statements.

Perhaps an example will clarify these points. The following statements define a simple subroutine in Visual Basic:

```
Sub AddemUp (aintAlpha As Integer, aintBeta As Integer)
    Dim intAnswer as Integer
    intAnswer = intAlpha + intBeta
End Sub
```

> **Note**   The *Dim* statement in Visual Basic reserves memory for a data item. *Dim* was originally an abbreviation for Dimension, a statement that defined the size of an array. For example, *Dim X(5, 10)* created a two-dimensional array 5 cells by 10 cells.

The subroutine begins with the *Sub* statement and ends with the *End Sub* statement. The name of the subroutine is *AddemUp*, and it expects to receive two integer arguments: *aintAlpha* and *aintBeta*.

> **Note**   Many experienced programmers begin the names of variables with a one or three letter abbreviation that identifies the variable's data type. The additional prefix *a* identifies a subroutine or function argument.

The first statement inside the subroutine reserves memory of an integer data item named *intAnswer*. The second statement adds the two argument values and stores the result in *intAnswer*.

The arguments named *aintAlpha* and *aintBeta* are placeholders and not real data items. The code that calls the subroutine from elsewhere in the program specifies the actual data items that the subroutine will process. For example, if you coded

```
AddemUp(5, 6)
```

then the *AddemUp* subroutine would add 5 and 6. If another spot in the program called

```
AddemUp(2002, 3003)
```

then the subroutine would add 2002 and 3003. You can also specify data items as argument values. Here's an example:

```
Dim intRalph As Integer
Dim intRufus As Integer
intRalph = 500
intRufus = 700
AddemUp(intRalph, intRufus)
```

The first two statements declare integer data items named *intRalph* and *intRufus*. The next two statements assign the values 500 and 700 to these two variables, respectively. The last statement calls the *AddemUp* subroutine, telling it to process the values in *intRalph* and *intRufus*.

Functions work very much like subroutines except that they return a value. To appreciate the usefulness of this, consider that when your program calls the *AddemUp* subroutine, it has no way of getting the answer. Although the subroutine stores the answer in the *intAnswer* variable, that variable is inaccessible outside the subroutine.

Lingo   The *scope* of a variable describes which portions of a program have access to a given data item.

```
Function GetSum (aintAlpha As Integer, _
                 aintBeta As Integer) _
                 As Integer
    Return intAlpha + intBeta
End Function
```

Note   Don't be thrown by the fact that the *Function* statement just shown spans three lines. This is only because coding the entire statement on one line would make it too long to fit on the page. Whenever Visual Basic detects a space followed by an underscore, it ignores the underscore, the next line ending, and any leading spaces on the next line.

As you can see, the syntax for defining a function is very much like that for defining a subroutine. There are only two differences:

■   Instead of *Sub* and *End Sub* you code *Function* and *End Function*.

■   You must assign a data type to the function itself. This will be the data type of the value the function returns.

The *Return* statement on line 4 does three things. First, it adds the two argument values. Next, it assigns the result to the value of the function. Finally, it exits the function. To see how all this works together, consider the following statement, which you could code anywhere else in the program:

```
intTotal = GetSum(12, 34)
```

When this statement runs, the *GetSum* function adds the argument values 12 and 34, then returns the answer 46. The assignment operator = then stores this value in the variable *intTotal*.

Lingo   An *operator* is a special character or word that tells the compiler to perform some operation on one or more data items. Some common operators are addition (+), assignment (=), and joining two strings (&).

The self-contained nature of functions and subroutines and their ability to process any values you specify makes them perfect for any sort of processing you might need several times in the same program or, for that matter, in several programs. You code the function or subroutine just once and then use it many times.

Chapter 5, "Using Functions and Subroutines," has much more to say about functions and subroutines. For now, just remember that they exist and that their purpose is dividing large programs into smaller, easier-to-understand modules.

Note   Visual Basic uses the term *module* to mean a text file that contains the source code for one or more related functions or subroutines. This usage is more specific than the general term *modular design* and the general concept of modules themselves.

Processing Events

Unlike most other kinds of programs, programs that run on the Windows desktop go into a sort of "wait state" immediately after they start up and display their main window. The program is essentially at rest, waiting for the user to select a menu choice, click a toolbar button, manipulate a form control, resize the window, or the like. Windows calls each of these actions an *event*.

It's your job, as a programmer, to write an *event handler* for each event you want to process. Suppose, for example, that your main window contains a button named Button1. If you designate a subroutine in your program as an event handler for the *Button1.Click* event, that subroutine will run whenever the user clicks that button. If your program doesn't contain such a subroutine, clicking the button has no effect. Windows simply discards the event.

This mode of operation can be surprising at first. Your program doesn't seem to have a mainline at all; it just contains a bunch of event handler subroutines that you never write code to invoke. Instead, Windows invokes them if and when the user initiates the corresponding event.

In fact, such programs do have a mainline; it's called an *event loop*. Here's how this works:

1   The event loop receives one event.

2   It then tries to find an event handler.

-   If one exists, the event loop calls the event handler.

-   Otherwise, the event loop discards the event

3   The loop restarts at step 1.

Interesting as this is, the event loop isn't something you write yourself. Instead, it's part of the Windows operating environment. Your role is simply to write the event handlers your program needs and then trust Windows to run them when the necessary moment arrives. Later chapters provide many examples of event handlers.

Classes and Objects

Just as the concepts of structured programming once revolutionized software development, object-oriented programming (OOP) has revolutionized it again. Objects, in this sense, are software modules that group together all the data items and procedures necessary to represent some real or abstract entity. Suppose, for example, that you want to write programs that manage apartment leases. Associated with each lease are

-   Certain data items, such as the property location, the leaseholder's name, the monthly rent, the start date, the end date, and so forth. These are the *properties* of the lease.

-   Certain activities, such as initiating a new lease, printing it, receiving rent, creating an overdue notice if the rent is late, canceling the lease, renewing it, and so forth. These are the *methods* of the lease.

Obviously, it would be very handy to package all these properties and methods into a single module that you could incorporate into any program that needed them. This technology exists and the name for such a module is an *object*.

Curiously, though, programmers don't write objects; instead, they write *classes*. A *class* is a template for an object but it's not an object itself. To understand this distinction, suppose that a program needs to work with several leases at once. Perhaps it needs to work simultaneously with all leases in the same building, for example, or all leases with the same leaseholder. To do this, you would create one instance of the *Lease* class for each lease. This is very much like filling out one lease form for each lease.

Each instance of a class (such as the *Lease* class) is an object (such as a *Lease* object). Like a blank lease form, the class defines procedures and data structures but no specific data values. An object, however, does contain data values unique to a particular instance, and in this respect resembles a completed lease form. Generally the data values that pertain to each object (that is, to each instance) of a class will differ. All objects of the same class will, however, contain the same type of data.

Once again, an example clarifies these points. Here's some hypothetical Visual Basic code that loads two *Lease* objects into memory:

```
Dim Lease01 As Lease
Dim Lease02 As Lease
Lease01 = New Lease(2,107)
Lease02 = New Lease(2,108)
```

The first two statements reserve memory for two *Lease* objects. The third statement creates a *Lease* object that contains the current data for building 2, unit 107. The last statement creates a *Lease* object for building 2, unit 108. Both objects are *instances* of the *Lease* class. They both use the same code and the same data structures, just as two lease contracts would use the same lease form.

To code a class in Visual Basic, you start with a *Class* statement and end with an *End Class* statement. Between these, you code a function or subroutine for each method and either a data declaration or a property procedure for each property. (A property procedure is essentially a function or subroutine that runs whenever a program sets or requests a given class property.)

Chapter 7 explains classes and objects in more detail.

Key Points

■ Program code and data both reside at relatively random locations in the computer's main memory. There's no physical difference between memory that contains instructions and memory that contains data.

■ The process of running a program is that of fetching and executing instructions from memory in a prescribed sequence.

- Each type of processor has special instructions for dealing with data in certain formats. Compilers generally support the same data types as the processor, plus other types of their own.

- High-level languages are easier to use than languages that closely match the computer's native instruction set.

- Several conceptual layers of software generally exist between application programs and the computer hardware. The operating system and the .NET common language runtime (CLR) are layers, and have further layers within themselves.

- The fundamental programming structures are sequences, decisions, and loops.

- You can organize and simplify the job of programming by dividing each program into small modules, writing the main module (the mainline) first, and then writing whatever modules the mainline requires, and so forth, for as many levels as necessary.

- Subroutines and functions are named, free-standing blocks of code you can invoke from anywhere else in your program and they're an excellent tool for implementing modular design.

- Windows programs usually don't have a mainline. Instead, they contain a collection of event handlers that respond to menu selections, button clicks, and other events in the user interface.

- Object-oriented programming uses modules called classes that bundle together all the data items and all the processing methods for a single conceptual entity.

Chapter 2

Introducing Microsoft Visual Basic .NET

By its very nature, computer programming involves a myriad of highly interrelated concepts. This creates a very real problem for people learning to program, because you can't really understand one concept without understanding several others. And you can't understand those without understanding the first one.

People have struggled with this problem for years and inevitably, the best solutions involve learning by doing and learning incrementally. Learning by doing means that to learn programming, you must write programs. This in turn means that you need a programming language to learn with and—in the case of this book—that's Microsoft Visual Basic .NET. A large part of this chapter explains how to obtain and install Visual Basic .NET. The chapter continues with a bit of instruction on how to write Visual Basic .NET statements and concludes with step-by-step instructions for writing your first program.

Learning incrementally means that first you learn a little about several topics, then more about those topics, and so forth, in ever-increasing levels of detail. That's why, in the case of reading this book, you're likely to notice many of the same topics coming up repetitively. You're also likely to find missing ends and dangling issues after each discussion. To some extent this never ends; programmers and computer scientists with decades of experience are still learning nuances and refining techniques. To another extent, it means there's a reason to finish reading the book.

Preparing Your System

The information in this section explains the software and hardware requirements for developing applications in Visual Basic .NET. There are two quite different kinds of .NET applications—Windows and Web—each with requirements you need to consider separately.

Preparing for .NET Windows Applications

Visual Basic .NET programs only run on computers that have the Microsoft .NET Framework installed. This is a collection of software that you or anyone else can download and install at no charge from Microsoft's Web site. Several versions of the Framework are available but two in particular are important here.

■ **Microsoft .NET Framework SDK**   contains all the software you need to develop and run .NET programs, except for the Visual Studio .NET development environment. The Framework SDK requires one of these operating systems or later.

   ● Microsoft Windows 2000

   ● Microsoft Windows XP

■ **Microsoft .NET Framework Redistributable**   contains only the software your friends, your coworkers, or even your enemies need to run .NET software that already exists. The Framework Redistributable runs on these operating systems or later.

   ● Microsoft Windows 98

   ● Microsoft Windows NT 4.0 (SP 6a required)

   ● Microsoft Windows Millennium Edition (Windows Me)

   ● Microsoft Windows 2000 (SP2 Recommended)

   ● Microsoft Windows XP

   Installing the .NET Framework SDK on your own computer is no big deal; if it isn't installed already, the Visual Basic .NET setup program will install it from the product CD.

   If your friends, your coworkers, or even your enemies want to run your Visual Basic .NET programs on their computers, they won't need to install the development software, but they'll need to download and install the .NET Framework

Redistributable. Have them browse *http://www.microsoft.com/downloads/* and then, under Search For A Download, select .NET Framework Redistributable.

Of course, if there are any .NET Framework service packs available, you, your friends, and those other people should download and install them.

Preparing for .NET Web Applications

Chapter 12 of this book, "Programming Web Forms," explains how to write Visual Basic .NET programs that interact with the user through a Web browser rather than through the Windows desktop. This has the advantage that people using your program don't need to install your program files, don't need to install the .NET Framework, and in fact don't need to install anything except the browser itself. You, however, will need a Web server on your PC so you can develop and test these Web-based programs. This rules out Windows XP Home Edition because no Web server is available for it.

The bottom line: If you plan to skip Chapter 12, then Windows XP Home Edition will do. Otherwise, you'll need Windows 2000 or Windows XP Professional.

If you do want to try the Web exercises, you'll save steps by installing the Web server before you install Visual Basic .NET. Here's the procedure for Windows XP Professional (if you're using Windows 2000 the steps might vary slightly):

1 Open Control Panel.

2 Double-click Add Or Remove Programs.

3 Double-click Add/Remove Windows Components.

4 When the Windows Components Wizard dialog box appears, locate the list box titled Components and make sure the Internet Information Services (IIS) check box is selected.

5 Click Next and accept the defaults on any further dialog boxes.

To control or configure the Web server, choose Start, All Programs, Administrative Tools, Internet Information Services.

If the Start Program menu doesn't display an Administrative Tools option, either run Administrative Tools from the Control Panel or right-click Start, choose Properties, and then:

■ On Windows XP with the default Start menu in effect, choose Customize, then the Advanced tab, and then at the bottom of the Start Menu Items list, under System Administrative Tools, select Display On The All Programs Menu.

■ On Windows XP with the classic Start menu in effect, choose Customize and then, at the top of the Advanced Start Menu Options list, select Display Administrative Tools.

- On Windows 2000, right-click the taskbar, choose Properties, click the Advanced tab and then, at the top of the Start Menu Settings list, select Display Administrative Tools.

Sizing Your Computer

Microsoft recommends that Visual Studio .NET developers have at least a 450-Mhz Pentium-II class processor and the following amounts of RAM:

- Windows XP Professional, 160 MB

- Windows 2000 Professional, 96 MB

- Windows 2000 Server, 192 MB

For installing any Microsoft Visual Studio product with Standard in its name, you should have 2.5 GB of disk available, 500 MB of which must be on the system drive. Professional and Enterprise versions of Visual Studio require 3.5 GB of disk space, again with 500 MB on the system drive.

Microsoft also recommends at least a Super VGA (800 × 600) or higher video system that can display 256 colors. In practice, even a 1024 × 768 system is likely to feel cramped. Use the biggest monitor and best display card you can get.

Obtaining Visual Basic .NET

Microsoft distributes the Visual Basic .NET language and compiler without charge. You can obtain it by installing the .NET Framework SDK as the section "Preparing for .NET Windows Applications" earlier in this chapter described.

Note   If a copy of the Microsoft Web server—Internet Information Services—is present, installing the .NET Framework Software Development Kit (SDK) will also install Microsoft Active Server Pages (ASP) .NET. At that point, you could use Notepad, another text editor, or even Microsoft FrontPage 2002 to create ASP.NET pages.

What's missing from the .NET Framework SDK is an integrated development environment (IDE). An IDE is a cohesive set of development tools unified into a single graphical application; that is, into a single Windows application. Creating, testing, and running programs is much easier with an IDE than with just a text editor, and so this book assumes you want an IDE.

Tip   There is no need to download and install the .NET Framework SDK if you plan to install any Visual Basic .NET or Visual Studio .NET retail products. The product CD contains and installs the SDK.

The predominant IDE for Visual Basic .NET is Visual Studio .NET. If you buy a retail package with Visual Basic .NET in its name, you get a copy of Visual Studio that works with Visual Basic only. If you buy a retail product sold as Visual Studio, it works not only with Visual Basic .NET but also with Microsoft Visual C++ .NET, Microsoft Visual C# .NET, Microsoft Jscript .NET, and additional languages.

This book assumes you've purchased Visual Basic .NET Standard Edition because that's the cheapest way to get the Visual Studio IDE and the Visual Basic language. However, if you've already purchased a more advanced version of Visual Basic .NET or Visual Studio .NET, there's no need to uninstall it. You'll simply have more capability than you will with Visual Basic .NET Standard Edition, and all the examples will still work.

Installing Visual Basic .NET

Installing Visual Basic .NET Standard Edition isn't much different from installing any other Windows application. Here are the essential steps. Expect minor differences if you're installing a different Visual Basic .NET or Visual Studio .NET product.

1 Insert Disc 1 and wait for the Setup window shown in Figure 2-1 to appear.

Note In some cases, the installer might ask your permission to update software that the rest of the setup process requires. Permit this until the window shown in Figure 2-1 appears.

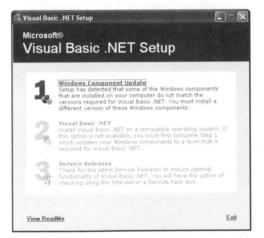

Figure 2-1 This menu presents the main options for installing Visual Basic .NET.

2 When you initially install Visual Basic .NET, all the options but one in Figure 2-1 will probably be unavailable. The one available option will be number 1, Windows Component Update. This option installs any service packs and fixes that Visual Basic .NET requires, as well as the .NET Framework SDK. Select this option and follow the instructions as they appear.

A typical result from running the Windows Component Update would be installation of the following components:

● Microsoft FrontPage 2000 Web Extensions Client

● Setup Runtime Files

● Microsoft .NET Framework

However, the exact components your system requires might vary.

3 When Windows Component Update finishes, option 2 in Figure 2-1 should be available. Select this option.

4 When the Options Page dialog box shown in Figure 2-2 appears, select the options to install and the disk location where you want them to reside. In most cases, you should install all the items and place them in the default locations.

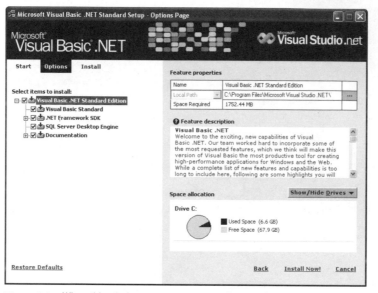

Figure 2-2 When this window appears, you can choose which Visual Studio options to install and see how much disk space they'll take.

5 Click the Install Now! link shown in Figure 2-2 and supply any additional CDs as required.

6 When you see a window titled Setup Is Complete, click Done.

7 When the Setup dialog box from Figure 2-1 reappears, option 3, Service Releases, will be available. Select this option to compare the software on your system to the most recent versions available on Microsoft's Web site. If this option recommends downloading and installing new versions of anything, you should almost certainly do so.

8   When the Service Releases option completes, click Exit to close the
Setup dialog box.

Easing into Visual Basic .NET

To get going with Visual Basic .NET, you must first start Visual Studio .NET. This
is true even if you installed Visual Basic .NET Standard Edition or some other
retail package with Visual Basic in its name. So, from the Start menu, choose:

■   Programs (or, on Windows XP, All Programs).

■   Microsoft Visual Studio .NET (the program group).

■   Microsoft Visual Studio .NET (the program item).

The first time Visual Studio .NET starts it always displays the Start page,
shown in Figure 2-3. The titles along the left edge are menu choices and Visual
Studio .NET helps you out by selecting the last one, titled My Profile. This option
affects the way Visual Studio .NET configures itself every time it starts. The four
drop-down lists above the line work together.

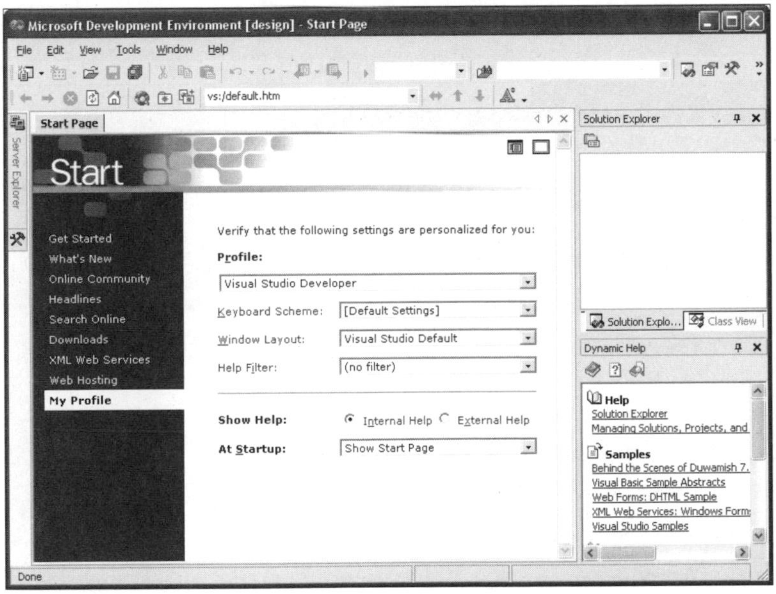

Figure 2-3   This panel appears the first time you start Visual Studio.

■   The Profile drop-down list selects a combination of choices in the next
three drop-down lists. For example, if you choose the Visual Basic Developer profile, Visual Studio sets the keyboard scheme to that of Visual
Basic 6, the Windows Layout to that of Visual Basic 6, and the Help Filter
to Visual Basic. However, for now, select a profile of (Custom).

■ The Keyboard Scheme drop-down list configures the keystrokes that
   correspond to menu options, toolbar buttons, and so forth. In past versions of Microsoft development tools, these keystrokes differed from
   one language to the next. This created endless confusion. Visual Studio
   .NET therefore uses the same keystrokes for all languages, but by
   default, it uses its own set.

   If you were a hard-core developer using one of those earlier products, you'd probably have its keystroke conventions wired into your
   brain and you'd probably want to keep using them. If you liked the
   Visual Basic 6 keystrokes, for example, you could choose the Visual
   Basic 6 keyboard scheme and feel right at home. As a new developer,
   however, there's no point in learning keystrokes from obsolete products. Therefore, choose Default Settings in this list box.

Note   All the keystrokes in this book are from the default set.

■ The Window Layout drop-down list controls which child windows
   Visual Studio displays when it starts up. Now, Visual Studio uses a lot
   of child windows, and unless you have an enormous monitor (and
   excellent long-distance vision) you'll probably open and close these
   windows frequently as you work. In fact, after a while, you probably
   won't care which windows are open on startup. For now, choose
   Visual Studio Default.

■ The Help Filter drop-down list affects the list of topics that appears
   when you search Visual Studio Help. If you choose No Filter, for example, then searching the Help for some keyword would return articles of
   all types. If you choose a Help Filter of Visual Basic, the search would
   return only articles that are applicable to Visual Basic.

   You can easily change this setting whenever you search for Help;
   as a result, its initial value isn't terribly significant. For now, choose
   Visual Basic and then move on.

■ The Internal Help and External Help choices affect the way Help windows appear. If you choose Internal Help, then help windows appear
   as child windows inside Visual Studio. If you choose External Help,
   then help windows appear in external windows. Either choice is fine.

■ The At Startup drop-down list configures what Visual Studio displays
   after the splash screen and the main Visual Studio window. The
   options are the following:

   ● Show Start Page displays—you guessed it—the Start page! This is
      the page that appeared in Figure 2-3 and that, most likely, currently

appears on your computer screen. The only difference is that Visual Studio selects the Get Started pane rather than My Profile. The Get Started pane has options for opening any project you worked on recently and for starting a new project.

Lingo   For now, think of a Visual Basic *project* as one Visual Basic program.

- Load Last Loaded Solution tells Visual Studio to load whatever solution was open when you last closed Visual Studio. In effect, this option tells Visual Studio to pick up where you left off. This is great if you work on one solution at a time, but a nuisance if you switch from one solution to another. (In the latter case, the most recent solution is frequently the wrong one.)

Lingo   A *solution* is a group of related projects (programs) that you work on simultaneously. Visual Studio always loads a solution, even if it contains only one project.

- Show Open Project Dialog Box displays an Open Project dialog box for finding and opening any project in your file system. This is essentially the same dialog box you'd use for opening a Microsoft Word or Microsoft Excel document except that in this case, it looks for file types that Visual Studio recognizes: projects, solutions, and so forth.

- Show New Project Dialog Box displays the dialog box for starting a new project. If you start a lot of projects and finish them at one sitting, this is the option for you. (Most projects aren't so simple and most programmers aren't so fast, but if this works for you, go for it.)

- Show Empty Environment tells Visual Studio to display nothing but the main window when it starts up. If you choose this option, then you'd typically use options on the File menu to open the project you want.

The Show Start Page option is probably the best choice for beginners because it helps you remember the last few projects you worked on and provides one-click access to the screen for starting a new project. Feel free, however, to choose any startup option you like. To display the Start page at any time, choose Show Start Page from the Help menu.

Tip   You can also change the At Startup option by choosing Options from the Tool menu. When the Options dialog box appears, open the Environment folder and then choose General. The At Startup option is in the top right corner.

Try This! If there's something about the Visual Studio environment that interferes with your normal way of working, you're in luck; just choose Options from the Tools menu. This displays the dialog box shown just below, which has options to change almost any setting that annoys you.

To change the At Startup option, for example, open the Environment folder and then choose General. The At Startup option is in the top right corner. To locate and modify other settings, open the applicable category by clicking it, then click the most likely subcategory.

Here are the high level option categories and their descriptions. If you need help understanding the options on a particular panel, just click the Help button.

■ **Environment**   sets default options for the integrated development environment (IDE).

■ **Text Editor**   changes the default settings for the Visual Studio text editor. These defaults also affect other editors based on the Text Editor, such as the Source view in HTML Designer.

■ **Database Tools**   changes the default settings for database projects.

■ **Debugging**   sets default options for interactively monitoring and debug programs as they run.

■ **HTML Designer**   controls options that pertain to any HTML, Active Server, and Web Form pages you open in the HTML Designer.

■ **Projects**   sets options for using Visual Studio to develop Web applications.

■ **Windows Form Designer**   changes the default grid settings for all visual designers within Visual Studio.

■ **XML Designer**   controls the default view when you open XML schemas and ADO.NET datasets.

Manipulating Visual Studio Windows

Figure 2-4 shows Visual Studio displaying the Get Started pane of the Start page. This is more or less how Visual Studio will look on startup if you chose the At Startup option Show Start Page. You have options to open the last four projects you worked on, to open any other project, and to create a new project.

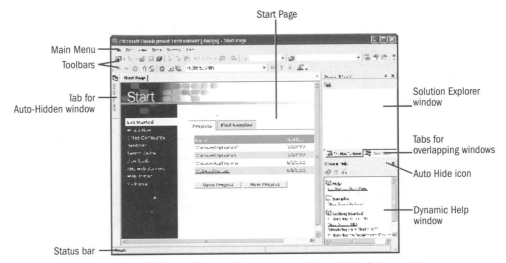

Figure 2-4   If you tell Visual Studio to display its Start page on startup, this is what you see.

The Visual Studio main menu, toolbars, and status bar work very much like those of other Windows applications. Of course, all the tasks and options pertain to programming rather than to creating textual documents, spreadsheets, presentations, or anything else.

All the child windows in Visual Studio are *dockable*. This means that by dragging their menu bars and dropping them near the main window border, you can affix them (that is, dock them) to that border. If you drag a docked window away from its main window border, it once again floats around the screen as a normal window. The Dynamic Help window in the bottom right corner of Figure 2-4 is docked. The same window in Figure 2-5 is floating. Try dragging and dropping this or any other child window around the Visual Studio main window until you develop a feel for this procedure.

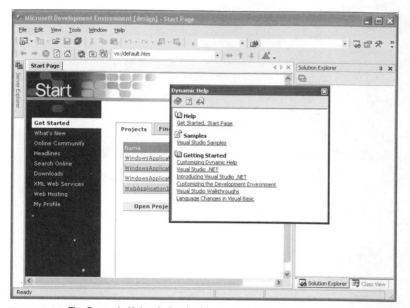

Figure 2-5   The Dynamic Help window in this screen shot is floating. In Figure 2-4 it was docked.

Note the two tabs that appear below the Solution Explorer window in both Figure 2-4 and Figure 2-5. Visual Studio displays such tabs whenever two docked windows occupy the same corner or edge. To bring any such window to the top, simply click its tab.

Tabs also appear for any window with Auto-Hide in effect. In both Figure 2-4 and Figure 2-5, for example, the Server Explorer tab along the left edge of the main window refers to an auto-hidden window. Auto-Hide means that the window is invisible until you click its tab, and then remains visible only while the mouse pointer remains over it. To activate this behavior for any window, click the Auto Hide button (the push pin) in that window. Auto Hide icons (push pins) appear in both the Solution Explorer window and the Dynamic Help window in Figure 2-4 and Figure 2-5.

If the window you want just doesn't seem to be open, open the View menu and select the window you want. The most often used windows appear directly on the View menu and more appear under the Other Windows choice.

Help, More Help, and Beyond Help

The Help database for Visual Studio is huge. Microsoft calls it the Developer Network Library and it covers nearly every topic related to programming in a Windows environment. This includes Windows itself, all the programming languages, the .NET Framework, database technology, Web server technology, browser technology, and a host of other topics. In short, finding Help articles that apply to a given question is seldom a problem. A more common problem is sifting through the hundreds of articles that match a given search.

Tip   The Microsoft Developer Network (MSDN) Library is also available on the Web. Browse *http://msdn.microsoft.com/library*.

There are two ways to search for Help. The first involves the Dynamic Help window you briefly noticed in the previous section (provided, of course, that you weren't asleep at the time). This window automatically displays a list of help topics that pertain to the current window or selection. So, whenever you need help with something, select it with the mouse and then check the Dynamic Help window. Chances are good that one of the links will suggest the correct topic.

Tip   If the Dynamic Help window isn't visible, choose Dynamic Help from the Help menu.

The second way to search for Help should be very familiar; it's the same procedure that almost every other Windows program uses. Just open the Help menu and choose Contents, Index, or Search.

■   **Contents**   displays a hierarchical table of contents. Clicking on any topic displays the corresponding article. Figure 2-6 provides an example. The Help system is in External Help mode.

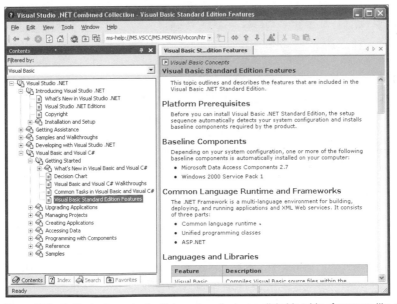

Figure 2-6   In Contents mode, the Help system displays a clickable table of contents like the one shown here at the left. Clicking any heading displays the corresponding article.

■ **Index**   displays list of keywords in alphabetical order. Clicking any keyword displays an Index Results window that displays the title of each matching article. Double-clicking any title displays the article itself.

To position the list of keywords, either use the scroll bars or type the first few letters of the keyword you want into the Look For text box. This box appears near the top of the Index window.

■ **Search**   performs a full-text search on the entire Developer Library for any word or words you want. To use this feature, enter the word or words you want in the Look For text box, then click Search. This displays a Search Results window that displays the title of each matching article. Double-click any title to display the article itself.

Tip   You can switch among Contents, Index, and Search modes by clicking the tabs at the bottom of the Help window.

Notice the Filtered By drop-down list in the top left quadrant of Figure 2-6. If you set this to No Filter, Help displays any matching articles in the entire Developer Library. If you set it to Visual Basic, Help only displays Visual Basic articles, and so forth. This is often quite useful for reducing the list of matching articles to a reasonable length. Although the figure shows Contents mode, this list box is available in Index and Search modes as well.

Understanding Visual Basic .NET Syntax

You're almost ready to code your first Visual Basic .NET statements, but first you need to understand a few rules. These are the beginnings of Visual Basic syntax. If you don't follow the rules, the compiler will reject your program and woe is you.

Lingo   In any language—programming, human, or otherwise—the rules that determine what's valid and what's not are its *syntax*.

As in most languages, the unit of code in Visual Basic is the *statement*. A statement is a command you give the computer to make it do something. The following statement, for example, declares a 32-bit integer named *intCount*:

```
Dim intCount As Integer
```

Lingo   A *declaration* is a statement that sets aside, names, and otherwise describes memory that you plan to use for some purpose.

The word *intCount* is an *identifier*; that is, a name that you choose yourself, and one that other statements can use in referring to the data item. The prefix *int* helps you remember that the variable is an integer; especially when you use the variable elsewhere in the program. The words *Dim*, *As*, and *Integer* are *reserved words*. This means that Visual Basic attaches special meanings to these words and you can't use them for anything else.

Lingo   The terms *identifier*, *element name*, and *variable name* all mean the same thing.

- *Dim* tells Visual Basic that it should set aside some memory, give that piece of memory a name, and also give it a type.

- *As* tells Visual Basic that the next word identifies a data type.

- *Integer* tells Visual Basic that this piece of memory will contain a 32-bit integer. Visual Basic uses this information to decide how much memory to set aside: 4 bytes in this case, because each byte contains 8 bits.

Assigning a type of *Integer* also tells Visual Basic that any value you put in this location must be a 32-bit integer. If you're copying another 32-bit integer into this location, you should have no problem. If you try to store any other type of data in this location, Visual Basic either converts the value to a 32-bit integer or, if that's not possible, blows up the program.

Lingo   The official term for blowing up a program is *throwing an exception*. Exceptions, however, only blow up the entire program if you let them. The alternative is to write an *exception handler* that takes corrective action depending on the type of exception.

Chapter 3, "Using Elementary Statements," has much more to say about data types and how to use them. The important task here is to understand the rules for coding statements, so here's another statement. This one assigns the value 0 to the variable *intCount*:

```
intCount = 0
```

Most Visual Basic statements occupy one line of text. The carriage return at the end of the line marks the end of the statement. There are no semicolons, periods, or other punctuation at the end of a Visual Basic statement.

Visual Basic ignores any spaces and tab characters that appear at the beginning and end of each line. Spaces or tabs separate the individual words and symbols in a statement, but the number of spaces or tabs makes no difference. The following statements are perfectly equivalent:

```
intCount = intCount + 1
    intCount    =    intCount    +    1
```

Blank lines are irrelevant except for readability.

Tip Experienced programmers invariably use indentation to indicate subordination. For example, if a given statement executes only if a prior decision statement is True, then the given statement would be indented more than the decision statement.

For all practical purposes, there's no limit to the length of a single statement. Statements that are hundreds or thousands of characters long, however, are extremely hard to read. For this reason, Visual Basic treats the underscore (_) as a *continuation character*. To break a statement across two lines, you end the first statement with a space and an underscore, and then resume the statement on the next line. Here's an example:

```
intCount = intChickens + intCows + _
        intHorses   + intHogs + intSheep
```

It's also possible to put two or more statements on one line. You simply code the first statement, then insert a colon, then the second statement, and so forth. Here's an example:

```
Dim intCount As Integer : intCount = 0
```

This technique is a carryover from the past. It's very much out of favor now, and you should avoid it at all costs. However, if someone else gives you code that contains multiple statements on one line, you should recognize what it's doing.

Comments are any sort of remark, description, explanation, or excuse you care to retain as part of your program. All good programmers add comments like these to their code. That way, when they work on the same program tomorrow, next year, or years from now, they have at least some clue about how the code works and what it's trying to accomplish.

With two exceptions, Visual Basic treats anything between an apostrophe and the end of a line as comments. In this code, for example,

```
intCount = intCount + 1 ' Increment count
```

the apostrophe (') marks the beginning of the comment. Visual Basic won't do anything with the words *Increment count* except store them as part of your code and display them when you view your code. There are, however, two situations in which you can't use an apostrophe to mark the beginning of a comment:

- An apostrophe enclosed in parentheses, as in this example, doesn't mark the beginning of a comment. Instead, the apostrophe is part of the data value:

  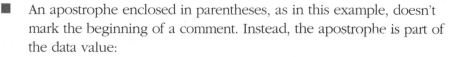

  ```
  strRefusal = "I'm sorry Dave, I can't do that."
  ```

To code a comment on this line, you'd have to put it after the second quotation mark like this:

```
strRefusal = "I'm sorry Dave, I can't do that."  ' Bummer.
```

> **Note** Many programmers prefix all their data names with a one or three letter abbreviation indicating the data type: *int* for *Integer, str* for *String*, and so forth.

■ You can't code comments after a continuation character. The following, for example, would be an error:

```
intCount = intMeats + intVeggies + _  ' No napping.
            intDairy + intRocks
```

To associate a comment with this statement, you must either put it on the last line or on its own line. Both of the following, for example, are valid:

```
intCount = intMeats + intVeggies + _
            intDairy + intRocks   ' No napping.

' No napping.
intCount = intMeats + intVeggies + _
            intDairy + intRocks
```

Each type of statement, of course, also has its own syntax. There's a syntax for writing statements that perform arithmetic, a syntax for manipulating character data, a syntax for coding decisions, a syntax for coding loops, and so forth. This reflects the fact that you must tell the computer what to do in terms it understands. Later chapters have much more to say about syntax but, for now, you're ready to code and comprehend your first program.

Writing and Running Your First Program

This exercise steps you through the process of creating the one-button calculator program shown in Figure 2-7. This is just about the simplest calculator you can imagine; it only knows how to add. The purpose of this example, however, isn't to attack the advanced scientific and financial calculator business. Its main purpose is to introduce the overall process of creating programs with Visual Basic .NET.

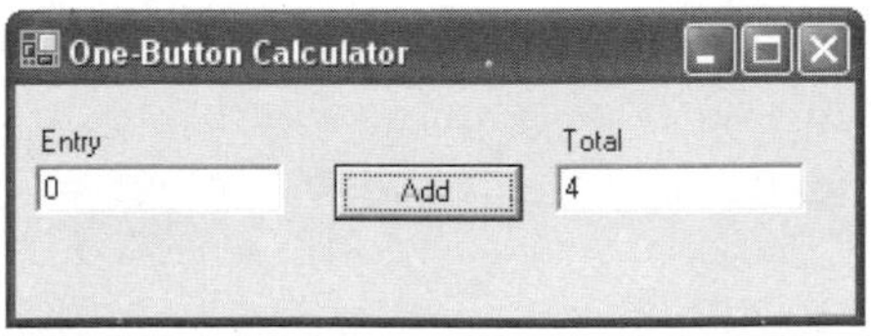

Figure 2-7 Clicking the Add button adds the number in the left box to the total in the right box.

To create this application, start Visual Studio and then proceed as follows:

1 Open the New Project dialog box shown in Figure 2-8. There are several ways to do this but the most common are these:

- In the Visual Studio Start page, click Get Started and then New Project.

- If the Start page isn't currently visible, choose New from the File menu, and then choose Project.

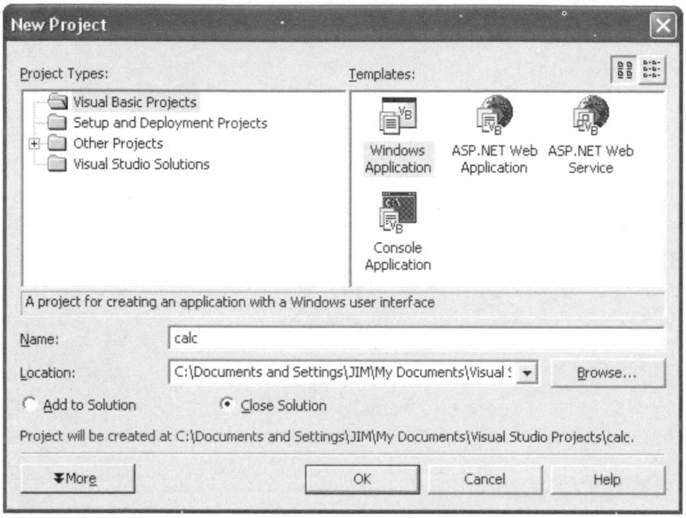

Figure 2-8   Use this dialog box to create a new Visual Studio project.

2 Select and fill out the New Project dialog box with these entries.

- **Project Types**   Select Visual Basic Projects

- **Templates**   Select Windows Application

- **Name**   Type *calc*

- **Location**   By default, this will be:
  C:\Documents and Settings\Jim\My Documents\Visual Studio Projects
  where Jim is your user name and
  C:\Documents and Settings\Jim\My Documents is the location of
  your My Documents folder. If you want to use a simpler path like
  C:\Source or a location on a network drive, feel free to do so.

3 Click OK. Visual Studio creates a new folder with the given name at the given location, populates it with a default set of project files, and opens the new files in Visual Studio. The Visual Studio window should then resemble Figure 2-9.

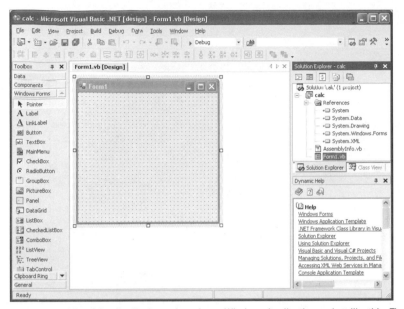

Figure 2-9   Visual Studio displays a brand new Windows Application project like this. The number and arrangement of child windows varies.

Notice the Toolbox window at the left of the figure. If this doesn't appear on your screen, choose Toolbox from the View menu.

Notice also that the Solution Explorer is no longer blank. It now displays a solution named calc that contains a project named calc. The calc project contains a list of references to .NET resources, an AssemblyInfo.vb file that describes the project and tracks its version, and a Form1.vb file that defines the blank form you see in the middle of the window.

4   The blank form titled Form1 will become the one-button calculator's main window. To give it a better title than Form1 follow these steps:

● Right-click the inside of the form (not the title bar or borders) and then choose Properties from the shortcut menu.

● A Properties child window should then appear. Property names appear in the left column of the scrolling list, and property values are in the right column.

● Scroll through the list of properties until you find the one named *Text*. This might be easier of you click the A-Z icon to put the list in alphabetical order.

● Select the value assigned to the *Text* property (most likely Form1) and change it to One-Button Calculator. Figure 2-10 illustrates this operation. The Properties window, the *Text* property, and the *Text* value all appear in the lower-right corner.

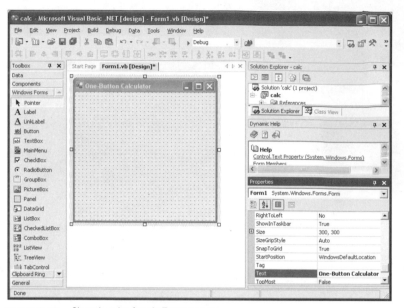

Figure 2-10   Changing the form's *Text* property.

Tip   Don't try to display the properties of a form control (that is, of a button, text box, or whatever) by double-clicking it. This action doesn't display the control's properties; it displays the code that responds to the control's events. If you double-click a form control by mistake, you can redisplay the form by clicking the Design tab at the top of the dialog box.

---

5   Add a TextBox to the form. This will become the Entry box shown in Figure 2-7. To add this element, follow these steps:

● Within the Toolbox window, click the Windows Forms heading. This should reveal a list of Windows form controls like the one in Figure 2-9 and Figure 2-10.

● Drag the *TextBox* control from the Toolbox and drop it near the left border of the One-Button Calculator form. A TextBox should now appear on the form and its properties should appear in the Properties window. The drop-down list at the top of the Properties window should say *TextBox1 System.Windows.Forms.TextBox*.

● In the Properties window, scroll down to the *Name* property and change its value from *TextBox1* to *txtEntry*. The prefix *txt* helps you remember that this name refers to a *TextBox* control.

● Without leaving the Properties window, scroll down to the *Text* property and changes its value from *TextBox1* to the number 0.

6 Add a second TextBox by repeating the procedure in step 5. This time, however, position the box near the right border and name it *txtTotal*. As before, set the *Text* property to 0.

7 Just as you dragged the two TextBoxes onto the form, drag a Button onto the form and drop it between the two TextBoxes. Change the button's name to *btnAdd* and its *Text* property to Add. The prefix *btn* helps you remember that this name refers to a Button control.

8 Align the *txtEntry* TextBox, the *btnAdd* Button, and the *txtTotal* Text-Box in a straight line across the form. You can drag these controls around just as you drag objects in a drawing program.

9 To provide a visible title over the *txtEntry* TextBox, follow these steps:

- Drag a Label control from the Toolbox and drop it just above the *txtEntry* TextBox.

- The Properties window should now pertain to a *Label1* control of type *System.Windows.Forms.Label*. If not, select the Label control you just dragged or right-click it and choose Properties.

- Set the *AutoSize* property to *True*.

- Set the *Text* property to *Entry*.

10 Provide a visible title for the *txtTotal* TextBox by repeating step 9. This time, however, drop the label control above the *txtTotal* TextBox and set its *Text* property to *Total*.

11 To satisfy your artistic nature, line up all the elements of the form and resize the form itself by dragging its bottom or left edge. The project should now look like Figure 2-11.

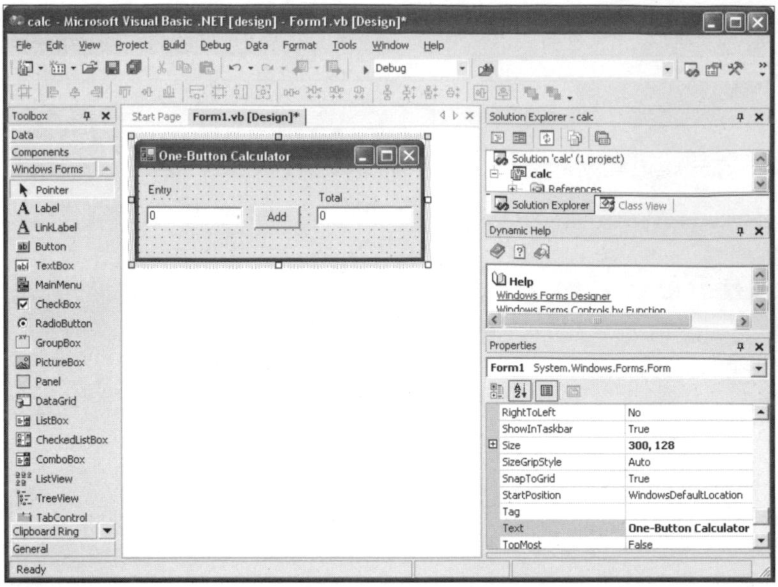

Figure 2-11 This is how Visual Studio displays the completed One-Button Calculator form.

12 Save your work by choosing Save All from the File menu.

Note The close box of a Windows form is the X icon that appears in its top-right corner.

At this point, you can run the program and see how your new form actually looks to a user. The procedure is simple; just press F5 or choose Start from the Debug menu. To stop the program, click the close box on the One-Button Calculator form or choose Stop Debugging from the Visual Studio Debug menu.

Lingo Visual Studio has two distinct operating modes: *design mode* and *run mode*, or *debug mode*. Design mode is for modifying forms and code. Debug (run) mode is for running programs and observing the results. You enter debug mode by running the current program, and you return to design mode by ending the program.

If you do run the program, you'll find that clicking Add doesn't actually add anything because you haven't written the code to make this happen. Fortunately, adding such code is simple. As proof, here's the procedure:

1 Make sure Visual Studio is in design mode.

- If the Visual Studio title bar begins Calc – Microsoft Visual Basic .NET [Design] then Visual Studio is in design mode.

- If the title bar begins Calc – Microsoft Visual Basic .NET [Run] then Visual Studio is in run mode. Quit the running program to return to design mode.

2 Double-click the *btnAdd* control. The window that previously displayed the form now displays the program code for events on the form.

3 Locate the subroutine that begins and ends with these statements. (In the code, the first statement will occupy one long line. The continuations are only for readability in the book.)

```
Private Sub btnAdd_Click(ByVal sender As System.Object, _
                         ByVal e As System.EventArgs) _
                         Handles btnAdd.Click

End Sub
```

Because you double-clicked *btnAdd*, these statements should already be visible in the Form1.vb window. If not, choose Form1 in the drop-down list at the top left of the window and *btnAdd* in the drop-down list at the top right.

4 Enter the following statement between the two statements you located in step 3:

```
txtTotal.Text = CDbl(txtTotal.Text) + CDbl(txtEntry.Text)
```

To understand this statement, you must first understand that the expression *txtTotal.Text* refers to the *Text* property of the *txtTotal* control. These are the same names you worked with when you designed the Windows form. The *Text* property contains the characters that are visible inside the TextBox.

Next, you must understand that data in the *Text* property of a TextBox has a data type of *String*. (In other words, the *Text* property always contains character data.) It makes no difference whether a *String* value contains letters, numeric digits, special characters, or a mixture; Visual Basic rejects any attempt to perform arithmetic on *String* values.

Fortunately, to resolve such problems, Visual Basic provides built-in functions that convert data from one format to another. One of these is the *CDbl* function, which converts values of almost any type into *Double* values. The statement:

```
txtTotal.Text = CDbl(txtTotal.Text) + CDbl(txtEntry.Text)
```

converts the *Text* property of the *txtTotal* control to *Double*, converts the *Text* property of the *txtEntry* control to *Double*, then adds the two results and stores the results in the *Text* property of the *txtTotal* control.

Note   The word *Double* is the official .NET name for double precision floating point. This is the most flexible and most general numeric format .NET offers.

This statement is worthy of three more observations. First, you might wonder what the *CDbl* function would do if you gave it a *String* value like "fred" rather than one like "98.6." Well, the *CDbl* function blows up the program. There are several ways to prevent this from happening; they appear later in the book.

The second observation is that although Visual Basic won't automatically convert *String* values to numeric format, it will convert numeric formats into *Strings*. That's why, after adding two *Double* values, you can just drop the result into *txtTotal.Text*.

Finally, you should be aware of IntelliSense. This is a feature of Visual Studio that displays pop-up selection lists as you type your code. In Figure 2-12, for example, the programmer typed `txtTotal` and a period; Visual Studio then displayed a drop-down list that includes the name of every property and method for that control.

Note   The hand-and-document icons in a code completion list denote properties. The purple cubes denote methods.

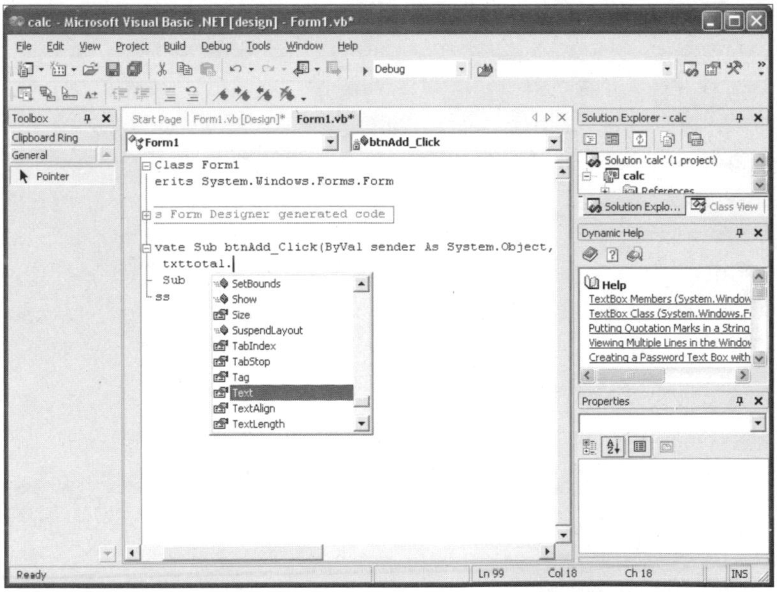

Figure 2-12   The IntelliSense feature of Visual Studio pops up selection lists of properties and methods whenever possible.

When an IntelliSense list appears, you can either ignore it and type the property or method name manually or you can select the name you want from the list and then press Tab.

5 Add the following statement just after the statement you added in step 4. This statement clears out the *txtEntry* TextBox now that you've added its value to the running total in the *txtTotal* TextBox.

```
txtEntry.Text = "0"
```

6 Figure 2-13 shows how the *btnAdd_Click* subroutine should look now that you've added two statements to those that Visual Studio provided. If any squiggly lines appear under terms you typed, they indicate spelling errors you need to correct.

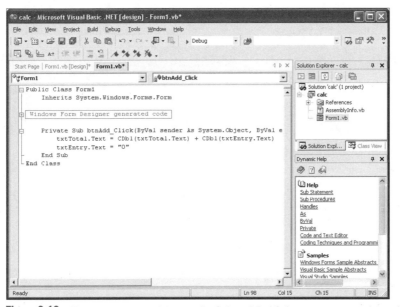

Figure 2-13 The two statements between the Sub and End Sub statements constitute all the code for the one-button calculator.

7 Save your work by choosing Save All from the File menu.

8 Press F5 or choose Start from the Debug menu. If your code contains any errors, Visual Studio displays a dialog box that says There Were Build Errors. Continue? If this happens, click No and then look for a window titled Task List – 1 Build Error Task Shown (Filtered). If you have two or more errors, the Task List window title of course indicates that. This window contains a list of error messages you need to resolve. To see which part of your code generated a particular message, double-click the message. Visual Studio highlights and positions the offending code so you can see it.

9 If you don't get any error message, the One-Button Calculator window should appear as shown previously in Figure 2-7. To add two numbers, type the first one in the Entry box, click Add, type the second one in the Entry box, and then click Add again.

Continue adding as many numbers as you like. To clear the Total box, select its contents and type zero.

10 To see the program blow up, enter something non-numeric in either text box and then click Add. The exact message will be this:

```
An unhandled exception of type 'System.InvalidCastException'
occurred in microsoft.visualbasic.dll
Additional information: Cast from string "s" to type 'Double' is not
valid.
```

Here, *s* represents the non-numeric string you entered. Click Continue to let the program finish blowing up or Break to halt the program and let Visual Basic show you the statement that failed.

The one-button calculator program isn't exactly a feature-rich, commercial-quality, awe-inspiring piece of software. It literally cries for Subtract, Multiply, and Divide buttons, for example, and a Clear button would be nice. The program shouldn't blow up so easily. Doing date arithmetic would be cool, as in, "Add 403 days to October 16, 1492," or, "What day of the week was October 14, 1066?" Such is the nature of programming; you never stop dreaming up enhancements. Fortunately, there are plenty of pages left in the book.

Key Points

■ You can only develop and run .NET programs—including Visual Basic .NET programs—on computers that have the .NET Framework installed. The framework requires Windows 2000, Windows XP, or later versions.

■ If you plan to develop Web applications, you should install Internet Information Services (IIS) before you install Visual Studio .NET or the .NET Framework. Web visitors, of course, will require no special software other than their browsers.

■ Microsoft Visual Basic .NET Standard is an inexpensive package that provides all the capability you need for the exercises in this book. However, if you own any version of Visual Studio .NET that includes Visual Basic, that's perfectly OK; the Visual Studio products have more functions, not fewer.

■ To install any Visual Basic .NET or Visual Studio .NET product, insert the first CD and follow the prompts.

■ Visual Studio uses a lot of child windows. To help you manage all these windows, you can configure Visual Studio to make windows visible, hidden, auto-hidden, docked, or free-floating.

■ All Visual Studio applications use an enormous Help database called the Microsoft Developer Network (MSDN) Library. Visual Studio can search this database in a variety of ways.

■ Visual Basic statements usually occupy one line. The line ending, rather than any special punctuation, separates one statement from the next.

■ To continue a line in Visual Basic, enter a space, an underscore, and then a line ending.

■ Apostrophes mark the beginning of a comment and line endings mark the end.

■ Creating Windows programs in the Visual Studio .NET development environment is fast and easy. You draw forms with a graphical editor and enter code with an advanced and highly intelligent editor.

Chapter 3

Using Elementary Statements

This chapter deals with three concepts applicable to almost any program you write in any language: variables, decisions, and loops. It's a safe bet that if you don't understand these concepts, your efforts at programming are doomed.

Variables are units of memory where your program stores whatever it needs to keep track of what it's doing. Whatever source of data a program uses, the program needs memory for receiving input, performing calculations, storing intermediate results, and sending the results into some sort of output channel. No variables, no memory, no program. It's as simple as that.

Decisions likewise are a critical component of every program. A program with no capability to compare values and take different actions depending on the results would be a very simple-minded program at best. That's why decisions are one of the key structures in any programming model including, of course, that of Visual Basic .NET.

Loops, of course, are another key programming structure. Loops control any process your program needs to run repetitively: repeatedly prompting for input; repeatedly reading records from a file or database; repeatedly fetching data from the network, or repeatedly doing anything at all. Only the simplest programs get away with not using loops so you might as well get up to speed. Are you ready?

Using Data Types

Most computers, and therefore most programming languages, provide a variety of data types, each uniquely suited for a different kind of data. The Pentium family of processors and Visual Basic .NET are no exceptions. You'll see in future chapters that Visual Basic .NET actually supports thousands of data types but this chapter concentrates on those in Table 3-1. These are the most basic data types and thus earn the name *elementary data types*.

Table 3-1 Elementary Data Types in Visual Basic .NET

Category	Type	Bits	Bytes	Enclosing Character	Appended Type Character	Typical Values
Character	*Char*	16	2	"	C	"A"C
	String			"	(none)	"Bits"
Date	*Date*	64	8	#	(none)	#2/13/2002#
Decimal	*Decimal*	128	16	(none)	D or @	5.00D
Floating Point	*Single*	32	4	(none)	F or !	5.123S
	Double	64	8	(none)	R or #	5.123R
Integer	*Byte*	1	1	(none)	(none)	0–255
	Short	16	2	(none)	S	5S
	Integer	32	4	(none)	I or %	5I
	Long	64	8	(none)	L or &	5L
Logical	*Boolean*	16	2	(none)	(none)	True False

The Category column in this table is strictly for your understanding and has no special meaning to the computer. The Type column is more significant; it contains the Visual Basic .NET reserved words you must use when declaring data items with these elementary types.

The Bits and Bytes columns show how many bytes of memory each elementary data type consumes. The *String* data type has no entry in these columns because strings can vary in size. The next section will explain Enclosing Characters, Appended Type Characters, and Typical Values.

Lingo   Programmers don't say they *define* data items; they *declare* them. A statement that defines a data item is a *declaration*.

The following data types warrant particular mention:

- ■ ***String*** This data type can accommodate strings from zero to 2 billion characters in size. (The precise maximum length is 2^{31}-1.)

- ■ ***Date*** All .NET languages store dates as 64-bit integers. A date value of zero means the stroke of midnight, January 1, year 1, at 0° longitude. A date value of 1 means 100 nanoseconds after that instant; 2 means 200 nanoseconds after that instant, and so forth. The maximum date value is December 31, 9999.

As you can imagine, dates in the twenty-first century are very large numbers indeed. There are a lot of nanoseconds between the year 1 and now. Fortunately, both Visual Basic .NET and the .NET framework provide convenient built-in functions that make it easy to work with dates and times in .NET format.

Note The *Date* data type stores times as well as dates.

- ■ ***Decimal*** This data type stores numbers accurate to about 29 digits left of the decimal place and 28 to the right. The most common use for the Decimal type is in handling currency, where accountants deal with numbers in the billions and expect accuracy to the penny.

- ■ ***Boolean*** When you assign other numeric types to a *Boolean* value, 0 becomes *False* and all other values become *True*. When you assign *Boolean* values to other data types, *False* becomes 0 and *True* becomes 1.

The importance of data types will become clear in the next three sections, which deal with literals, variables, and constants.

Using Literals

Like most programming languages, Visual Basic .NET supports the use of literals. A literal is simply a value, such as 417, 6.2, or "bonbon" that you code as part of a statement. Literal values are read-only. You can't change the value of 2 by coding a statement such as the following:

```
2 = 1 + 1 + 1
```

Literals in Visual Basic .NET have data types, just as variables do. If you don't specify a data type for a literal, Visual Basic .NET uses the rules in Table 3-2 to guess the data type you mean.

Table 3-2   Default Data Types for Literals

Type of Value	Example	Data Type
Integral numbers	15	*Integer*
Floating-point numbers	1.414	*Double*
True or False	True	*Boolean*
Character values	"nuisance"	*String*

Note   To include quotation marks in a string literal, code two quotation marks where you want one to appear. The following code, for example, is valid:

```
strText = "Tom said, ""Sorry,"" but Anne wasn't impressed."
```

It's seldom necessary to override the rules in Table 3-2 but if the need arises, there are two ways to do it. For some data types, you enclose the literal value with special *enclosing characters*. For others, you append a special *type character* to the value. Table 3-1 previously listed the enclosing characters and type characters for each data type. The literal 5S, for example, indicates a *Short* with a value of 5. The literals 125L and 125& both indicate a *Long* that equals 125.

Using Variables

Variables are locations in memory to which you assign a name and a type. To declare a variable, use the *Dim* statement, as shown in these examples.

```
Dim strDescription As String
Dim intQuantity As Integer = 0
Dim booAnswer As Boolean = False
```

Specifying a value, as in the second and third examples, is optional. If you don't assign a value when you declare a variable, Visual Basic .NET assigns an empty string, zero, or false, depending on the data type.

A variable name must conform to the following rules.

- It must be from one to 16383 characters in length. (Yes, this refers to the name, not to the data value.)

- It must contain only alphabetic characters, decimal digits, and underscores.

- The first character can't be a decimal digit. In other words, the first character must be a letter or an underscore (_).

- If a variable name begins with an underscore, it must contain at least one additional letter or decimal digit.

■   Variable names aren't case sensitive. If you define a variable named
    buckct, you can refer to it elsewhere as Bucket, BUCKET, bucKet, and
    so forth.

Each of the following is a valid Visual Basic .NET variable name. This
doesn't mean they're good programming style, it only means that Visual Basic
.NET will accept them.

```
X
intCount
That_Place_Where_I_Keep_The_Running_Total
_X__0__XX_0_X_
```

The following variable names are incorrect for the reasons given.

```
_Leading underscore not followed by letter or digit.
2003ProfitBegins with a digit.
Isn'tZeroContains a character other than a letter, digit, or underscore.
```

Naming is a key programming skill. Your names should clearly indicate the
variable's use, yet not be too long, too short, too cryptic, or too difficult to read.
Here are some rules of thumb.

■   Use variable names between about 6 and 15 characters in length.

■   Use common (or at least consistent) abbreviations. To abbreviate
    Address, for example, Addr is more common than Ad or Adrs.

■   Separate words in a variable name with underscores or initiation capi-
    talization. *HomeAddress* and *home_address* are both easier to read
    than homeaddress.

■   Assign a prefix to help you remember the variable's data type. It's easy
    to remember that the variable *strHomeAddr* is a string. Some additional
    common prefixes are *int* for *Integers*, *lng* for *Longs*, *sng* and *dbl* for
    Singles and *Doubles*, and so forth.

Tip   Capitalize carefully when coding variable names in *Dim* statements. No matter how you capitalize the same variable name in another statement, Visual Basic .NET will recapitalize it as you
did in the *Dim* statement.

You can declare several variables with a single *Dim* statement, as shown in
this example.

```
Dim strAlong, strCheese, strGuitar As String
```

If you do this, all the variables will be the same type. For example *strAlong*,
strCheese, and *strGuitar* will each be a string.

Tip   At the time you code a program, you have no way of knowing what physical memory location a variable will occupy. This doesn't matter, however, because you always refer to the variable by name. Windows assigns physical memory as it loads your program for execution.

If you declare a variable without specifying a data type, Visual Basic .NET makes the variable an *Object*. Later, when your code is running, an *Object* variable can become any other data type. This might seem like a real time-saver for you but it's time-consuming for the computer. Assigning or changing object types at run time (a practice called late binding or run-time binding) is a time-consuming operation. For this reason, it's best to use specific data types when declaring variables.

Lingo   *Late binding* (also called *run-time binding*) means declaring variables as general-purpose objects and converting them to specific data types at run time. The opposite of this practice is *early* (or *compile-time*) *binding*. Early binding is preferable, because the compiler can assemble much better code when it knows the exact type of each variable beforehand.

Using Constants

Constants are read-only named values. The following statement, for example, defines a constant named *PSWD* that's equal to *"sesame"*:

```
Const PSWD = "sesame"
```

Having coded this statement, you could use the name *PSWD* instead of the literal *"sesame"* in your code. This makes it easier to find and update the password when necessary. Constants are also a good solution when you use the same value several times in your code and it's important that you code this value exactly the same way in each instance.

The rules for naming constants are the same as those for naming variables. However, it's customary to name constants in all upper case. This distinguishes constants from variables when you use them in other parts of your code.

You can also use simple expressions to define the value of constants. The declarations below illustrate this:

```
Const ENOUGH = 100
Const TOO_MUCH = ENOUGH + 1
```

However, you can use only expressions that the compiler can evaluate *before* your program runs. The following declaration would produce a compiler error, because the compiler can't predict what the value of *Now()* will be at run time:

```
Const THE_DATE = Now()
```

Note *Now()* is a Visual Basic .NET built-in function that supplies the current date and time.

The default data type for a constant is the data type of its literal. However, you can code a specific data type if you want. The possibilities are *Boolean, Char, String, Byte, Integer, Short, Long, Date, Single, Double,* and *Decimal.* Here are two examples.

```
Const SPEED_OF_LIGHT As Single = 186287
Const START_OF_CENTURY As Date = #1/1/2001#
```

There are at least three reasons for explicitly coding a data type when you declare a constant:

- When you explicitly specify a data type, there's no doubt as to the result.

- Typed code is easy to read and maintain.

- When *Option Strict* is in effect, failing to declare a data type for a constant will produce a compiler error.

See Also *The next section in this chapter will explain more about Option Strict.*

Visual Basic .NET provides the built-in constants listed in Table 3-3. These are frequently useful when you need to include nonprintable characters in some output. The notation *Chr(13)* means ASCII character 13, the carriage return.

Table 3-3   Visual Basic .NET Print and Display Constants

Constant	Equivalent	Description
vbCrLf	*Chr(13) & Chr(10)*	Carriage return/linefeed character combination.
vbCr	*Chr(13)*	Carriage return character.
vbLf	*Chr(10)*	Linefeed character.
vbNewLine	*Chr(13) & Chr(10)*	New line character.
vbNullChar	*Chr(0)*	Character having value 0.
vbNullString	String having no value	Not the same as a zero-length string (""); used for calling external procedures.
vbObjectError	-2147221504	Error number. User-defined error numbers should be greater than this value.
vbTab	*Chr(9)*	Tab character.
vbBack	*Chr(8)*	Backspace character.
vbFormFeed	*Chr(12)*	Not useful in Microsoft Windows.
vbVerticalTab	*Chr(11)*	Not useful in Microsoft Windows.

Option Explicit and *Option Strict*

Visual Basic .NET has options that help you detect errors in your programs before they run. One of these is *Option Explicit*, which you code using one of these forms.

```
Option Explicit On
Option Explicit Off
```

If you code *On*, the Visual Basic .NET compiler will display an error message each time you try to use a variable name that you forgot to declare. These error messages are usually very easy to fix; simply code the required *Dim* statement and recompile!

If you code *Option Explicit Off* and try to use a variable name you didn't declare, the compiler will automatically declare a variable for you. At first this might seem like a wonderful laborsaving invention but it has two huge drawbacks.

■ The compiler declares any such variables with a type of *Object*. This makes your program run slower than if you'd explicitly declared a variable with the correct type.

■ If you misspell a variable name, the compiler simply declares a new variable with the misspelled name and continues blithely on its way. You, however, might spend hours figuring out why your code doesn't work. Consider, for example, the following code.

```
Dim decDiscntPct As Decimal = 0.1
Dim decDiscntAmt As Decimal = 0
Dim decFullPrice As Decimal = 10.0
Dim decSalePrice As Decimal = 0

decDiscntAmt = decFullPrice * decDiscntPct
decSalePrice = decFullPrice - decDiscmtAmt
```

If you code *Option Explicit Off*, you'll find that this code never takes a discount. The reason is that, in the last line, you misspelled the variable name *decDiscntAmt* (the first letter *m* is supposed to be *n*) and so Visual Basic .NET set up a new variable with the misspelled name and a default value of zero. Thus, the last line of code subtracts *decDiscmtAmt*, which is always zero, rather than *decDiscntAmt*, which contains the calculated discount.

In a large program, tracking down misspelled variable names can be a nightmare. Visual Basic .NET therefore makes *Option Explicit On* the default. If you want to override this, place an *Option Explicit Off* statement at the very top of the file that contains your code.

Option Strict is another feature that helps find errors in your code. If this option is *On*, the compiler will display an error message anytime you try to copy data from one variable to another variable of lesser capacity. Suppose for example, that you declared a 16-bit number (a *Short*) named *srtQty* and that it contained the value 500. Suppose further that you tried to copy this value into an 8-bit number (a *Byte*) named *bytAmt*. Here's how this would look in code.

```
Dim srtQty As Short = 500
Dim bytAmt As Byte
bytAmt = srtQty
```

If *Option Strict* isn't in effect, the compiler will accept this code as written. (Also, by the way, the compiler will automatically generate code that converts the *Short* value into *Byte* format.) If the *Short* variable *srtQty* contains a number between 0 and 255, the code runs fine. If it contains a negative number or a number greater than 255, the programs halts with a *System.OverflowException*. To resolve this, you would need to take one of these actions.

- Stop values outside the range 0–255 from getting into the *Short* variable *srtQty*.

- Change *bytAmt* from type *Byte* to something larger. (Type *Short* would work, of course, but so would type *Integer, Long, Single, Double*, and *Decimal* because all of these can contain any value that a *Short* can contain.)

- Add code that tests the value of *srtQty* and takes some other action of the value is outside the range 0–255. Here's an example.

```
If srtQty < 0 Then
    bytAmt = 0
Else
    If srtQty > 255 Then
        bytAmt = 255
    Else
        bytAmt = srtQty      End If
End If
```

The real point however, is that you discovered the need for one of these solutions only by receiving (and painfully debugging) an exception when the program ran. If *Option Strict On* had been in effect, you would have discovered the need when you compiled your program.

Many experienced programmers dislike getting all the error messages that occur when *Option Strict* is set to *On*. These programmers are very accustomed to thinking about data type issues whenever they copy data from one variable to another and don't feel they need the helping hand. Furthermore, to satisfy this faction, Visual Basic .NET defaults to *Option Strict Off*. Don't this dissuade you from turning it back on, however; there's much to be said for getting all the assistance you can. Simply add the following line at the top of the file that contains your code.

```
Option Strict On
```

This statement, by the way, also sets *Option Explicit* to *On*. As a result, there's no need to put two *Option* statements in the same file.

Working with Arrays

An array is a series of variables, each identified by the same name but a different index number. Arrays make it very easy for a program to process sets of related variables. Suppose, for example, you wanted to accumulate totals by month. To declare all twelve variables—one for each month—you could code:

```
Dim decMonTot(11) As Decimal
```

This reserves memory for 12 numbers of type Decimal. To access the total for January, you would code decMonTot(0). The total for February would be in decMonTot(1) and so forth. If you try access a subscript that doesn't exist (outside the range 0–11 in this case) the program will fail.

Lingo The word *subscript* means the numeric index of an array. If you specify a subscript larger than the array's allocated size, you'll get a *System.IndexOutOfRange* exception.

If you have the month number in a variable, such as the *intMon* variable shown below, you can use that variable as the index for the array.

```
Dim decMonTot(11) As Decimal
Dim intMon As Integer = 5
Dim decCurAmount As Decimal = 15.00

decMonTot(intMon) = decMonTot(intMon) + decCurAmount
```

In Visual Basic .NET, the first element in an array always has the subscript zero. Therefore, the statements above add 15.00 to the total for June.

Visual Basic .NET initializes arrays with the default value for the given type. If, for example, you declare an array that has a numeric type, all the elements will contain zero. To initialize an array with any other values, code a comma between each value and put curly braces around the whole list. Here's an example.

```
Dim strSize() As String = {"Small", "Medium", "Large"}
```

Notice that in this declaration, there's nothing between the parentheses. This is usually where the maximum subscript goes. In fact, the array will contain as many elements as you specify values. The *strSize* array, for example, will contain three elements numbered 0, 1, and 2.

Tip   Visual Basic .NET allocates memory for all possible elements at the time you define an array. Therefore, don't make arrays grossly larger than necessary.

Visual Basic .NET arrays can have from one to sixty dimensions. You can think of a two dimensional array as a checkerboard or grid. The array

```
Dim strSquare(8, 8) As String
```

for example, represents a grid with eight elements on a side. The array

```
dim intRoom(10, 15, 20) As Integer
```

represents a cube with 10, 15, and 20 cells on its side. As such, it might represent an office building with 10 floors, 15 cubicles from north to south, and 20 cubicles from east to west.

The number of dimensions determines the array's *rank*. An array of rank 3 would have three dimensions, like the *intRoom* array. Most arrays have one dimension, and arrays of more than three dimensions are extremely rare.

Visual Basic .NET arrays are variable-length. However, this *doesn't* mean that Visual Basic .NET automatically enlarges arrays to accommodate any subscript you specify. Instead, it means you can use a statement called *ReDim* to make any array larger or smaller whenever you want. If, as before, you declared an array as

```
Dim decMonTot(11) As Decimal
```

then the following statement, coded elsewhere in the program, would enlarge the array to 24 elements.

```
ReDim Preserve decMonTot(23)
```

Preserve is a keyword that tells Visual Basic .NET to retain any values that were in the array before the *ReDim* statement executes. If you don't specify *Preserve*, Visual Basic .NET discards any existing data and initializes each element of the array to zero or an empty string. There are three additional restrictions:

- You can't use the *ReDim* statement to initially declare an array. Use *Dim* to declare the array and *ReDim* to modify it.

- You can change the length of any dimension you want, but you can't change the data type or the number of dimensions.

- If you want to preserve existing data in the array, you can only resize the last dimension.

Tip   Whenever your code executes a *ReDim* statement, it first creates a completely new array, then copies over any existing array elements, and then deletes the first array. This is so expensive, in terms of resources, that you should avoid executing *ReDim* statements often. For example, don't *ReDim* an array one element larger every time you want to store another value.

Scoping Out Variables

In the early days of programming, each variable a programmer declared was available to the entire program. This had the benefit of simplicity, but only for a while. As software became more and more complex, one part of the code would inevitably modify variables in ways and at times that other parts of the code didn't expect. Chaos and midnight debugging sessions were the result.

The solution to this problem was a concept called *scope*. In all modern programming languages, including Visual Basic .NET, variables are only available to limited parts of a program. If you declare a variable inside a function or subroutine, for example, then it won't be available to code outside that function or subroutine. The *scope* of such variables is limited to the subroutine that contains them.

Of course, there may be times that you *want* the same variable to be available to several subroutines. The solution is to put the *Dim* statements that declare such variables *outside* any function or subroutine that needs to use them, but *inside* the next higher structure.

As you saw in the One Button Calculator example, each event that occurs on a Windows form hooks up to a corresponding subroutine that you code as part of the form. To make a variable available to any of these subroutines, you must code its *Dim* statement between the *Class* and *End Class* statements that define the form, but not within any of the subroutines themselves. Schematically, here's how this looks.

```
Public Class Form1
    Dim ...  ' This variable would be available to every
             ' subroutine and function in the Form1 class.
    Sub ...
    End Sub
    Sub ...
    End Sub
End Class
```

Scoping is a complex topic that will come up again in Chapter 7, "Creating Classes and Objects." The *Public* keyword on the *Class* statement just above defines the scope of the class, for example. For now, just remember that variables you declare with *Dim* statements are only available to code within the same function, subroutine, or class.

Writing Decision Statements

Visual Basic .NET supports only two decision statements: *If* and *Select Case*. Here's the general format of an *If* statement:

```
If [condition] Then
'    Statements to execute if condition is true
Else
'    Statements to execute if condition is false
End If
```

The *Else* and its following statements are optional. The *End If* terminator and the line ending after *Then* are required.

Visual Basic .NET doesn't care where the keywords *If*, *Else*, and *End If* begin on their respective lines, nor where any statements subordinate to the *If* and *Else* begin. It's customary, however, to left-align the *If*, *Else*, and *End If* keywords uniformly, and to indent any subordinate statements further to the right. This makes complex *If* statements much easier to read. Here's an example.

```
If intCount = 0 Then
    strMessage = "No units found."
Else
    strMessage = intCount & " units found."
    intCount = 0
End if
```

Visual Basic .NET also supports a form of the *If* statement that uses the keyword *ElseIf* instead of *Else*. This is useful when you need to test a series of conditions until you find one that's true. Here's an example.

```
If strEntree = "Pancakes" Then
    strTopping = "Syrup"
ElseIf strEntree = "Potatoes" Then
    strTopping = "Gravy"
ElseIf strEntree = "Salad" Then
    strTopping = "Dressing"
ElseIf strEntree = "Spaghetti" Then
    strTopping = "Sauce"
ElseIf strEntree = "Tacos" Then
    strTopping = "Salsa"
Else
    strTopping = "Air"
End If
```

In such cases, using the *ElseIf* form can be much easier to read and understand than a nested series of *If...Else...End If* statements like this (which, by the way, is equivalent).

```
    If strEntree = "Pancakes" Then
        strTopping = "Syrup"
Else
        If strEntree = "Potatoes" Then
            strTopping = "Gravy"
        Else
            If strEntree = "Salad" Then
                strTopping = "Dressing"
            Else
                If strEntree = "Spaghetti" Then
                    strTopping = "Sauce"
                Else
                    If strEntree = "Tacos" Then
                        strTopping = "Salsa"
                    Else
                        strTopping = "Air"
                    End If
                End If
            End If
        End If
    End If
End If
```

The *Select Case* statement provides another way to test a series of conditions until one is true. The *Select Case* statement has this general form:

```
Select Case [expression]
    Case [condition]
'        Statements to execute if condition is true
    Case [condition]
'        Statements to execute if condition is true
    Case Else
'        Statements to execute if no preceding condition is true
End Select
```

You can code as many *Case* statements as you like, and the *Case Else* statement is optional. The format of the *Case* conditions is very flexible. The following statement, for example, is completely valid:

```
Select Case lngAge
  Case < 1
    lblDesc.Text = "Infant"
  Case 1 To 5
    lblDesc.Text = "Toddler"
  Case 6, 8
    lblDesc.Text = "Even Child"
  Case 7, 9
    lblDesc.Text = "Odd Child"
  Case 10 To 12
    lblDesc.Text = "Pre-teen"
  Case Else
    lblDesc.Text = "Trouble"
End Select
```

Writing Loops

A loop is a series of statements that executes repetitively until some condition is true. Coding a loop requires a statement that marks the loop's beginning, another statement that marks its end, and a condition that controls whether the loop keeps executing or stops.

Visual Basic .NET supports three basic constructs for writing and controlling loops: *Do...Loop*, *For...Next*, and *While...End While*. In each case, the keyword before the ellipsis defines the start of the loop and the keyword after the ellipsis defines its end.

Coding Loops with *Do...Loop* Statements

The code for a simple *Do* loop appears below. The *Dim* statement isn't part of the loop; it's only there for your information.

```
Dim intCount as Integer = 0
Do
    intCount = intCount + 1
Loop
```

Unfortunately, this loop contains a critical flaw—it never ends! To make the loop end when the count is 10, add a condition as shown below.

```
Do While intCount < 10
    intCount = intCount + 1
Loop
```

If the value of *intCount* starts out as zero, this loop executes 10 times. (Note that the value of *intCount* increases by one during each iteration.) If the value of *intCount* starts out as 11, the statements between *Do* and *Loop* never execute at all.

Note   In a real program, other statements would no doubt appear between the *Do* and *Loop* statements. Otherwise, this is a terribly inefficient way of making a number equal at least 10.

If you want the loop to execute once, no matter what the starting value of *intCount* happens to be, code the condition on the *Loop* statement. Here's an example.

```
Do
    intCount = intCount + 1
Loop While intCount < 10
```

Most programmers try not to use this form for reasons of clarity. When they see a *Do* statement, they immediately want to know what result the loop is striving to attain. The condition that makes the loop end is a key piece of information in understanding this, so they like having the condition right there on the opening *Do* statement.

A *Do* loop with a *While* keyword will execute as long as the condition is *True*. If you'd rather have the loop execute as long as the condition is *False*, code *Until* instead of *While*. These two loops are equivalent.

```
Do While intCount < 10
    intCount = intCount + 1
Loop

Do Until intCount > 9
    intCount = intCount + 1
Loop
```

If, during execution of a *Do* loop, you detect a condition that requires immediately escape, code:

```
Exit Do
```

This statement immediately jumps out of the loop, regardless of whether the loop condition is *True* or *False*. The following loop, for example, runs until the *intMon* variable reaches 12 or until the corresponding element in the *decMonTot* array is greater than 1000. Regardless of why the loop ends (*intMonth* reaching 12 or the *Exit Do* firing) execution would continue with the first statement after the *Loop* statement.

```
Dim decMonTot(11) As Decimal
Dim intMon as Integer = 0

Do While intMon < 12
    If decMonTot(intMon) > 1000 Then
        Exit Do
    End if
  intMon = intMon + 1
Loop
' Additional application code would go here.
```

Coding Loops with *For...Next* Statements

Instead of beginning a loop with a *Do* statement and ending it with *Loop*, you can begin it with *For* and end it with *Next*. However, *For* loops and *Do* loops provide somewhat different features.

As with *Do* loops, there are two types of *For* loops. The first is specifically for loops that vary a number from a starting value to an ending value. Here's an example.

```
Dim intCount as Integer = 0
```

```
For intCount = 0 To 11 Step 1
'    Statements to process each value of intCount go here.
Next
```

This is exactly equivalent to the following code, which uses the *Do* loop syntax you already understand.

```
intCount = 0
Do While intCount < 12
'    Statements to process each value of intCount go here.
     intCount = intCount + 1
Loop
```

As you can see, the *For...Next* syntax saves you two lines of code: the line that initializes the value of *intCount* and the one that increments the value of *intCount*. The *For...Next* syntax is simply another end to the same means. Here are some more important facts about *For...Next* loops.

- The counter (*intCount* in the example) can be any elementary numeric type that supports the greater than (>), less than (<), and addition (+) operators. An *Integer* is the most common choice because Pentium processors can perform arithmetic on Integers faster than on any other type.

- The expression *Step 1* specifies how much to change the count variable for each pass through the loop. If you omit this expression, the default increment is 1. To decrement a counter for each integration, specify a negative number, as in

  ```
  For intCount = 11 To 0 Step -1
  ```

- To immediately exit a *For* loop, code an *Exit For* statement.

The second form of the *For...Next* loop executes a series of statements once for each element in a collection or array. During each iteration, a so-called *element variable* points to a different element. Here's an example.

```
Dim decMonTot(11) As Decimal
Dim intMon as Integer = 0

For Each intMon in decMonTot
'    Statements to process each value of intMon go here.
Next
```

During each iteration of this loop, the *For Each* statement supplies a different subscript of the array decMonTot. In other words, it supplies the numbers 0 through 11. A *For Each...Next* loop, however, can do much more than iterate through the subscripts of an array. It can also iterate through all the files or subfolders in a folder, through all the fields in a database record, and through all the elements of many other collections of items.

This, of course, raises questions of how to access these other kinds of collections, and what kind of element variable to use for iterating through them. These are interesting questions indeed but unfortunately, the answers involve concepts from later chapters. For now, just remember that *For Each…Next* loops can iterate through many kinds of collections other than arrays.

Coding Loops with *While…End While* Statements

A *While…End While* loop executes a series of statement repeatedly until some condition is true. Compared to a *Do* loop, this offers absolutely nothing more. The following loops accomplish exactly the same result.

```
While intCount < 10
    intCount = intCount + 1
End While

Do While intCount < 10
    intCount = intCount + 1
Loop
```

There's no such thing as an *Until* loop that corresponds to the *Do Until* structure. Also, you can't code a condition on an *End While* statement the way you can on the *Loop* statement.

Because *While* loops offer no advantages over *Do* loops, you might wonder why Visual Basic .NET even supports *While* loops. In fact, *While* loops are historical baggage. They've been part of Basic for a long time and exist primarily so that old code keeps running. Most programmers now avoid *While* loops and just use *Do* loops instead. However, if you come across a *While* statement in somebody's code, you should know what it is. And if you feel like using one, go for it. It's still a supported part of the language.

Example: Writing a Tape Calculator

This chapter has touched upon quite a few different concepts. Presenting a single example that uses all these concepts yet avoids any concepts from future chapters is a practical impossibility. As a result, this example concentrates mainly on illustrating *Dim* and *If* statements. Literals, of course, are ubiquitous. Examples in later chapters will duly illustrate arrays and loops.

Figure 3-1 shows the example program running. As you can see, it's another calculator like the one in Chapter 2, "Introducing Microsoft Visual Basic .NET." This one, however, has both Add and Subtract buttons, a tape that shows a history of what you entered, and a Clear button. Also, if you try to add or subtract something that isn't a number, this calculator displays a dialog box rather than blowing up.

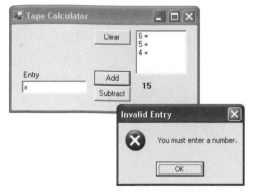

Figure 3-1   This calculator has several improvements over the one in Chapter 2. For one, it doesn't blow up because of an invalid entry.

To develop this calculator, make sure you have Visual Studio running and then proceed as follows.

1   Open the New Project dialog box just as you did in Chapter 2. For example, click the Get Started option and then the New Project button on the Visual Studio Start Page, or choose New and then Project from Visual Studio's File menu.

2   Select and fill out the New Project dialog box with these entries, and then click OK.

Project Types	Select Visual Basic Projects.
Templates	Select Windows Application.
Name	Type calc2.
Location	Use the same location that you used for the example in Chapter 2. Visual Studio will have remembered this.

3   Select the default form and set its *Text* property to Tape Calculator.

4   Add a *TextBox*, three *Buttons*, two *Labels*, and a *ListBox* to the form. Arrange them as shown in Figure 3-2.

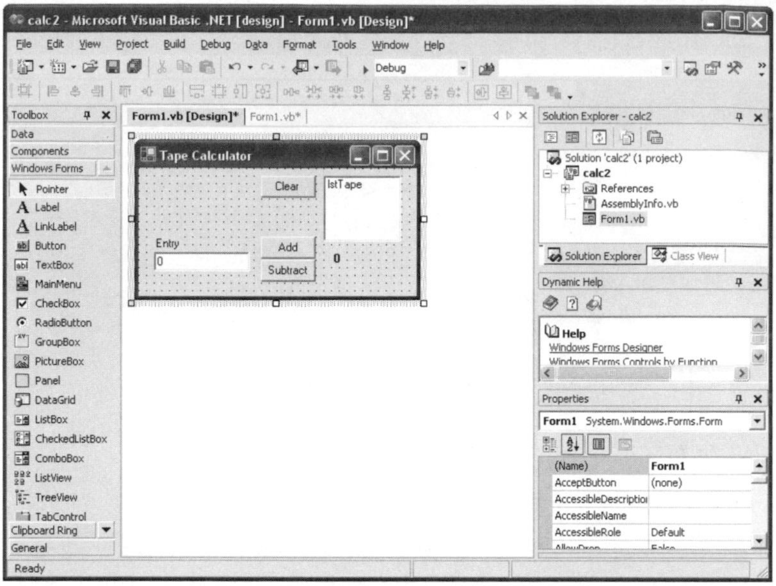

Figure 3-2   Arrange the elements on the Tape Calculator form like this.

5   Set the *Name* and *Text* properties of the following controls as indicated.

Name	Text
lblEntry	Entry
txtEntry	0
btnClear	Clear
btnAdd	Add
btnSubtract	Subtract
lstTape	(no text)
lblTotal	0

6   Set the *Autosize* property of the *lblEntry* and *lblTotal* labels to *True*.

7   Set the *TextAlign* property of the *lblTotal* control to *TopLeft*, and the *Bold* property to *True*. (To set the *Bold* property, you'll first have to expand the *Font* property. To do this, click the Plus icon that precedes *Font* in the property list.)

8 Double-click the *btnClear* button. When the Visual Studio code editor appears, scroll to the top. The following code should be visible.

```
Public Class Form1
    Inherits System.Windows.Forms.Form
+ Windows Form Designer generated code
    Private Sub btnClear_Click( _
            ByVal sender As System.Object, _
            ByVal e As System.EventArgs) _
            Handles btnClear.Click

    End Sub
End Class
```

The *Private Sub btnClear_Click* statement shown here on four lines will actually appear on one line. If a minus icon appears in front of the line "Windows Form Designer generated code," change it to a Plus icon by clicking it.

9 Add the following statement just before the *Private Sub btnClear_Click* statement you located in step 8. This will define a variable for keeping the calculator's running total.

```
Dim dblTotal As Double = 0
```

To check your work, compare it to the code that appears in Figure 3-3.

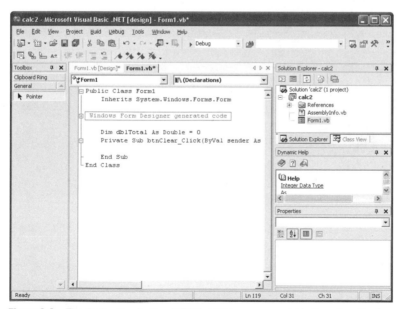

Figure 3-3 The declaration for the *dblTotal* variable appears outside the subroutine for any form element. This makes it available to any such subroutine.

10 Between the *Private Sub btnClear_Click* and *End Sub* statements, enter the code that you want to execute when the user clicks the Clear button. Here it is.

```
lstTape.Items.Clear()
dblTotal = 0
lblTotal.Text = "0"
```

The first statement clears all the items in the *lstTape* list box, which serves as the calculator tape. The second statement sets the *dblTotal* variable you declared in step 9 to 0. This clears the running total. The third statement displays a zero in the *lblTotal* literal, which displays the running total to the user.

11 Create a blank subroutine that will run when the user clicks the Add button. To do this, click the Form1.vb [Design] tab and then double-click the *btnAdd* button.

12 Between the *Private Sub btnAdd_Click* and *End Sub* statements, enter the code that should execute when the user clicks the Add button. To begin, enter this code.

```
Dim dblEntry As Double                   ' Current entry

If IsNumeric(txtEntry.Text) Then        ' Is entry valid?
'    Code to process a valid entry will go here.
Else
'    Code to report an invalid entry will go here.
End If
```

The *Dim* statement provides a variable to temporarily store the current entry as a *Double*.

The *If* statement uses a Visual Basic .NET built-in function called *IsNumeric* that returns *True* if Visual Basic can convert a given expression to a number and *False* if it can't. The first expression below, for example is *True* and the second is *False*.

```
IsNumeric("98.6")
IsNumeric("zero")
```

The earlier *If* statement uses the *IsNumeric* function to decide whether the text that the user typed into the *txtEntry* TextBox is, in fact, a number. If it is, some statements after the *If* will process the addition. If it isn't, a statement after the *Else* will display an error message.

13 Replace the comment that appeared in step 12 after the *If* with the code shown below.

```
dblEntry = CDbl(txtEntry.Text)     ' Convert entry
lstTape.Items.Add(dblEntry & " +") ' Update tape.
dblTotal = dblTotal + dblEntry     ' Calc new total
lblTotal.Text = dblTotal           ' Display total
txtEntry.Text = ""                 ' Clear entry box
```

The first statement converts the text in the *txtEntry* TextBox to *Double* and stores the result in the *dblEntry* variable. *CDbl* is a built-in Visual Basic .NET function that converts the contents of any data type into a value of type *Double*. Of course, the given contents must be numeric.

The second statement adds an item to the *lstTape* list box. This item contains the value in the *dblEntry* variable, a space, and a plus sign. The expression *lstTape.Items.Add* invokes the *Add* method of *Items* collection of the *lstTape* list box. This simulates printing the tape.

Tip The *Items* collection of any ListBox contains one entry for each line the ListBox contains.

The third statement adds the value in *dblEntry* to the running total in *dblTotal*.

The fourth statement copies the running total in *dblTotal* to the *Text* property of the *lblTotal* label. This displays the total for the user to see.

The last entry clears the user's entry in the *txtEntry* TextBox. This makes it easier to enter the next value.

14 Enter the following statement between the *Else* and the *End If* in step 12.

```
MsgBox("You must enter a number.", _
      MsgBoxStyle.Critical, _
      "Invalid Entry")            ' Error message
```

MsgBox is another built-in Visual Basic .NET function. It displays (what else?) a small dialog box containing a message. The first parameter, "You must enter a number.", specifies the message text. The second parameter, *MsgBoxStyle.Critical*, specifies a standard windows icon for critical messages. The third parameter, "Invalid Entry", specifies the window title.

15 Save your work by choosing Save All from the File menu.

16 Press the F5 key to run the program.

- If you enter a number in the *txtEntry* text box and click Add, the number should appear in both the *lstTape* list box and the *lblTotal* label.

- If you enter a second number and click Add, two items should then appear in the *lstTape* list box, and a new total should appear in the *lblTotal* label.

- If you enter a non-numeric value and then click Add, you should get a message box like the one in Figure 3-1.

- If you click the Clear button, the *lstTape* list box should turn empty, and the *lblTotal* label should display zero.

  If you get a compiler error or if something doesn't work properly, check your typing.

17 To quit the Tape Calculator program, click the Close box in the top-right corner of its dialog box.

18 To make the Subtract button work, repeat step 11. This time, however, select *btnSubtract* in the left list box or double-click the *btnSubtract* button.

19 Copy all the code inside the *btnAdd_Click* subroutine and paste it inside the *btnSubtract_Click* subroutine. (Don't copy the *Sub* and *End Sub* statements.)

20 Within the *btnSubtract_Click* subroutine, locate the line

```
lstTape.Items.Add(dblEntry & " +")
```

and change the plus sign to a minus. Then, in the next line

```
dblTotal = dblTotal + dblEntry
```

change the plus sign to a minus as well.

21 Save your work by choosing Save All from the File menu.

22 Press F5 to test the program. The Subtract button should now work just as well as the Add button.

Try This! To create a subroutine that runs whenever any control on your form detects an action you care about:

1 Switch to the code editor.

2 Select a control in the top left drop-down list box.

3 Select an event in the top right drop-down list box.

This procedure creates an empty subroutine (or, as hard-core programmers would call it, a *stub*). It's your job to supply specific code that does what you want.

By now, you should start to realize that Visual Basic .NET, the .NET Framework, and Windows itself are providing most of the code that makes a program work. This is as it should be. If Microsoft or anyone else can write a piece of code once and then millions of programmers can use it, that's a millionfold increase in productivity!

At the same time, you should realize that organizing all these resources into a cohesive solution requires both knowledge of the resources themselves and careful, line-by-line programming. The next chapter will concentrate on knowledge of Visual Basic .NET built-in functions, which are some of the most useful resources you'll find.

Another point you should recognize is the "divide and conquer" approach to successful programming. (Those people who call it "dying by degrees" are just sourpusses.) You start with a large problem but break it down into several medium sized problems. Then you break the medium sized problems into smaller ones, then repeat the process until the individual problems are small enough to think about and code easily. If you do this properly, the components of your problem will parallel the components of the original problem, and your program will be easy to develop, modify, and keep working over time.

Key Points

- Visual Basic .NET, like most programming languages, provides a variety of data types that are suited for different kinds of data.

- Literals are values that you supply directly as part of program statements; 17, 62.5, and "shovel" are all literals.

- Variables are named areas of memory that contain data of a specific type. Because you always refer to variables by name, their physical memory locations aren't important.

■ Constants are, in essence, read-only variables. Declaring a given value as a constant makes your code easier to read and guarantees uniformity.

■ The setting *Option Explicit* Off tells the Visual Basic .NET compiler to create any variables you forget to declare. This usually causes more problem than it solves. *Option Explicit On*, the default, is usually the better choice.

■ An array is a collection of variables that you can process as a set. A numeric index (or subscript) identifies each element of an array.

■ In Visual Basic .NET (and most other modern programming languages) variables are only accessible within the subroutine, or function, that declares them. To give a variable greater scope, you must declare it within some larger structure (such as a class). Chapter 5, "Using Functions and Subroutines," will have more to say about classes.

■ Visual Basic .NET provides two decision statements: *If* and *Select Case*.

■ Visual Basic .NET provides three looping constructs: *Do...Loop*, *For...Next*, and *While...End While*.

■ As time passes, operating systems and high-level languages provide more and more services. This makes programs of given complexity easier and easier to write.

Chapter 4

Using Operators and Expressions

This chapter introduces two of the unsung heroes of nearly every computer language: operators and expressions. Contrary to some reports, operators aren't people who control mechanical equipment. Instead, they're special symbols or words that specify an operation or an action that you want to occur between two or more values. Addition signs and subtraction signs are some of the most common operators, but there are many more. This chapter will get you up to speed. Expressions, likewise, aren't something you practice in the mirror before a date or a job interview. In programming languages such as Microsoft Visual Basic .NET, they're combinations of operators and values that the computer can evaluate. For example, 1 + 1 is a simple expression.

Operators and expressions are hardly the glamour features of any programming language. They've been around so long that differences in the way they work from one language to another are usually minor. The reason for this ubiquity, of course, is utility. No programmer could get along without operators and expressions and so, most likely, neither can you. Are you ready?

Introducing Operators

In computer programming, an *operator* is a symbol that tells the computer to perform a specific type of processing. The plus sign, for example, is an operator that tells the computer to add the number that precedes it and the number that follows it. Here's an example.

```
intSum = intChickens + intCows
```

The variables *intChickens* and *intCows* are *operands*. This is because the plus sign operates on the *intChickens* variable and the *intCows* variable. The plus sign is a binary operator because it operates on two operands. *Unary* operators, by contrast, work on just one operand. The minus sign in the code shown here is a unary operand:

```
sngLowTemp = - 20.0
```

Both of these statements, by the way, also use the *assignment operator*— the equal sign. The assignment operator evaluates the expression at its right and assigns the result to the variable at its left.

In fact, Visual Basic .NET provides six kinds of operators: arithmetic, assignment, comparison, concatenation, logical, and miscellaneous. The following sections explain each kind.

Forming Expressions

Taken together, an operator and its operands form an *expression*. The following, for example, is an expression:

```
intWins + intLosses
```

Evaluating an expression always returns a result. The data type of that result depends on both the operator and the data types of the operands. The preceding expression, for example, returns an *Integer* value because each of its operands is an *Integer*.

Note   Especially in documentation, the term *expression* usually includes single variables, properties, literals, and constants. So, if you look up how to do something and the documentation tells you to provide an expression, it's acceptable to code a variable, property, literal, or constant.

It's perfectly fine to use the result of one expression as the operand of another. Here's an example that does this:

```
curBalance + curInterest + curPurchases - curPayments
```

The first plus sign adds the first two operands, then the second plus sign adds that result and *curPurchases*, and finally the minus sign subtracts *curPayments*. Each of the three operators produces a *Currency* result because all the arguments are *Currency*.

The next example joins three strings together; that is, it *concatenates* them. The ampersand (&) is the concatenation operator and it always returns a string, no matter what data types its operands might be. In this example, the first ampersand concatenates *strFirstName* and a space; the second concatenates that result and the variable *strLastName*:

```
strFirstName & " " & strLastName
```

When an expression contains multiple operators, Visual Basic .NET evaluates them in order using these rules:

- First evaluate any expressions that are inside parentheses. This rule should be familiar if you've ever studied mathematics or written spreadsheet formulas. This expression

  ```
  10 - 4 - 3
  ```

  equals 3 because Visual Basic .NET first subtracts 4 from 10, and then subtracts 3 from 6. If this isn't what you want, you can code

  ```
  10 -(4 - 3)
  ```

  Visual Basic .NET doesn't process the operators in this expression in strict left-to-right order as it did in the previous expression. Instead, it starts with the operator inside the parentheses. To be precise, it first subtracts 3 from 4, and only then subtracts the resulting 1 from 10.

- Next, evaluate operators in the order shown in Table 4-1. To appreciate this rule, try to guess the value of this expression:

  ```
  10 + 4 * 3
  ```

  Did you guess 22? According to Table 4-1, the multiplication operator (*) has precedence over the addition operator (+). Therefore, Visual Basic .NET performs the multiplication first, as if you'd coded:

  ```
  10 + (4 * 3)
  ```

  If the list of operators in Table 4-1 seems confusing, take heart. The rest of this chapter explains them.

- If neither of the preceding rules applies, evaluate operators from left to right.

Table 4-1   Operator Precedence in Visual Basic .NET

Category	Operator	Symbol
Arithmetic	Exponentiation	^
Arithmetic	Negation	-
Arithmetic	Multiplication and floating-point division	*, /
Arithmetic	Integer division	\
Arithmetic	Modulus (remainder)	Mod
Arithmetic	Addition and subtraction	+, -
Concatenation	Concatenation	&
Logical	Relational	=, <>, <, >, <=, >=, Like, Is, TypeOf...Is
Logical	Conditional NOT	Not
Logical	Conditional AND	And, AndAlso
Logical	Conditional OR	Or, OrElse
Logical	Conditional XOR	Xor

In fact, most programmers neither try nor succeed at memorizing these operator rules. It's much more accurate to code what you want by using parentheses. For proof, compute the value of this expression:

```
5 + -3 * 4 ^ 3
```

Not so easy, right? Did you get –187? Now try this one, which—as far as Visual Basic .NET is concerned—is perfectly equivalent to the previous one:

```
5 + (-3 * (4 ^ 3))
```

Arithmetic operators are notorious for producing unexpected results when you code several of them in the same expression. This occurs because invariably, Visual Basic .NET doesn't process the operators in the sequence you expect. There are two choices for dealing with this issue:

- Scrupulously memorize and apply the rules of precedence given in Table 4-1.
- Use parentheses to indicate the order of evaluation you want.

Using Arithmetic Operators

Table 4-2 lists the arithmetic operators that Visual Basic .NET supports. None of these should be surprising until you get to division, of which there are two kinds.

Table 4-2 Visual Basic .NET Arithmetic Operators

Operator	Symbol
Addition	+
Subtraction	–
Multiplication	*
Floating-point division	/
Integer division	\
Integer remainder	*Mod*
Exponentiation	^

- **Floating-point division**   This type of division always returns a *Double* result. (Recall that *Single* and *Double* are both floating-point formats.) If you use the / operator to divide the Integer 7 by the Integer 2, you get the Double value 3.5.

- **Integer division**   This type of division always returns an *Integer* result. If you use the \ operator to divide 7 by 2, you get the Integer 3.

The *Mod* operator returns the remainder from an *Integer* division. The expression *17 Mod 5*, for example returns a value of 2 because 17 divided by 5 is 3 remainder 2. To get both the quotient and the remainder of an *Integer* division, you must code two distinct statements as shown here (the *Dim* statements are only for clarity):

```
Dim intDivisor As Integer = 5
Dim intDividend As Integer = 12
Dim intQuotient As Integer
Dim intRemainder As Integer

intQuotient = intDividend / intDivisor
intRemainder = intDividend Mod intDivisor
```

The exponentiation operator raises a number to a power. The expression *4 ^ 3* equals 64 because 4 cubed is 64. The result of an exponentiation is always a *Double*.

Converting Numeric Types

Numeric operations involving mixed data types are permissible and generally produce the result you want. This is possible because of some details Visual Basic .NET handles behind the scenes. Specifically, Visual Basic .NET:

1 Decides what the data type of the result should be.

2 Converts each operand to that type.

3 Performs the operation.

This, of course, begs the question of what type the result should be. Here are the rules.

- The result of an exponentiation is always a *Double*.

- The result of a floating-point division is always a *Double*.

- The result of any other numeric operation is the widest type of either operand. Widest, in this sense, means the operand data type with the greatest range. Here are the numeric types in order of range: *Byte, Short, Integer, Long, Decimal, Single, Double. Byte* is the narrowest type and *Decimal* is the widest.

If you add a *Byte* and a *Short*, the result will be a *Short*. If you add a *Short* and an *Integer*, the result will be an *Integer*. If the operands are a *Long* and a *Decimal*, the result will be a *Decimal*. The data type that can hold the largest number will be the data type of the result.

Using Assignment Operators

The assignment operator assigns a value to a variable. In Visual Basic .NET, as in most programming languages, the assignment operator is the equal sign. Here's a very simple example that uses the assignment operator. It assigns the value 42 to the variable *x*.

```
x = 42
```

The left operand receives the value of the right operand, and must be a single variable name or property. The first statement shown here is valid because it assigns a value to a property. The second is unacceptable because the value on the left isn't a single variable name or property.

```
lblTotal.Text = dblTotal
intEcks + 5 = intWye - 3
```

The right operand can be any literal, variable, expression, or function that returns a value, as in this example:

```
sngTravelTime = Math.Abs(sngEnd - sngStart) / sngSpeed
```

Note   *Math.Abs* is a .NET method that returns the absolute value of an expression.

Using Compound Operators

A high percentage of assignment statements mention the same variable on both sides of the assignment operator. Here's an example.

```
intCount = intCount + 1
```

To save you some typing, Visual Basic .NET provides a special operator, +=, that combines the functions of the addition operator and the assignment operator. The following statement is equivalent to the previous one. In normal language, it reads, "Add one to *intCount*":

```
intCount += 1
```

> **Lingo** *Concatenation* means joining two strings. When you concatenate *up* and *shot*, you get *upshot*.

Operators that combine assignment with arithmetic are available for all the arithmetic operators and also for the String concatenation operator. Visual Basic .NET calls them *compound operators*. Table 4-3 provides a complete list.

Table 4-3 Visual Basic .NET Compound Operators

Compound Operator	Means Assignment Plus:
^=	Exponentiation
*=	Multiplication
/=	Floating-point division
\=	Integer division
+=	Addition
-=	Subtraction
&=	Concatenation

Understanding Type Conversion

In any assignment statement, the receiving variable must be capable of receiving the value you want to assign. You can't, for example, assign a *String* value like "Medieval History" to an *Integer* variable. This would produce this error message:

```
Cast From String "Medieval History" To Type 'Integer' Is Not Valid.
```

> **Lingo** In programming, *casting* means converting a value from one data type to another.

If the assigned value and the receiving variable are the same type—and if that's a value type—you're home free. You can always assign an *Integer* value to an *Integer* variable, a *String* value to a *String* variable, and so forth.

Two Types of Types: Value and Reference There are countless differences among the many data types that Visual Basic .NET supports; otherwise, they wouldn't exist. One of the most fundamental, however, is that some types are *value types* and the rest are *reference types*.

■ With value types, the value you store in a variable resides at that variable's own memory location. Boolean, Char, Date, and all numeric data types are value types.

■ With reference types, any values you store become part of a more complex structure that resides somewhere else in memory. The variable for a reference type doesn't contain the data itself; it contains the address of the more complex structure. Strings, arrays, and class types are all reference types.

To find out whether a specific type is a value type or a reference type, look it up in the MSDN Library (that is, in Visual Studio .NET Help).

If the assigned value and the receiving variable are different types, Visual Basic .NET might attempt *type conversion* on your behalf. Suppose, for example, that you try to store an *Integer* value in a *Long* variable. Visual Basic casts the *Integer* value to a *Long* value and then stores the *Long* value.

Numeric type conversions can be either widening or narrowing. A *widening conversion* means that the data type of the receiving variable can hold a larger number than the data type of the value you're trying to store. If, for example, you assign an *Integer* (32-bit) value to a *Long* (64-bit) variable, a widening conversion takes place. Widening conversions are always acceptable.

A *narrowing conversion* means that the data type of the receiving variable can't hold numbers as large as the data type of the value you're trying to store. Suppose, for example, you assign an *Integer* (32-bit) value to a *Byte* (8-bit) variable. Any one of three things can happen:

■ If *Option Strict* is in effect, you'll get a compiler error such as this:

    Option Strict On Disallows Implicit Conversions From 'Integer' To 'Byte'.

■ If *Option Strict* is off and the given value fits into the narrower data type, the statement executes normally. There would be no problem, for example, storing an *Integer* value between 0 and 255 into a *Byte* variable.

■ If *Option Strict* is off and the given value won't fit into the narrower data type, an overflow exception occurs. Attempting to store an *Integer* value of 1024 into a *Byte* variable causes the program to fail with this error message:

An Unhandled Exception Of Type 'System.OverflowException' Occurred.

Additional Information: Arithmetic Operation Resulted In An Overflow.

Lingo   *Overflow* means that a variable is physically unable to store a value that your program tries to assign.

In the following numeric data types—*Byte, Short, Integer, Long, Decimal, Single, Double*—conversions in a left-to-right direction are widening. Conversions in a right-to-left direction are narrowing.

Tip   Even though a widening conversion will never cause an overflow, it can lose precision. A conversion from *Decimal* to *Single*, for example, is a widening conversion even though it might discard some low-order digits. Because of such issues, you should approach all data conversions carefully.

Assigning Reference Variables

The assignment operator might surprise you when you try to assign one reference variable to another. To understand why, recall that reference variables don't actually contain data. Instead, they contain a pointer to the data.

Lingo   A *pointer* contains the address of something else in memory. A *String* variable, for example, doesn't itself contain a string. Instead, it contains the memory address where the data actually resides.

Consider, for example, the *String* data type. From moment to moment, the value of a *String* variable might be 0 bytes in length, 1 byte in length, or thousands of bytes in length. How much memory should Visual Basic .NET reserve when you declare a *String*? There's no way to tell!

The solution to this dilemma is ingenious. Suppose that you declare a variable as follows:

```
Dim strMessage As String = "No problems found."
```

The literal "No problems found." contains 18 characters, so Visual Basic .NET asks the operating system for 36 bytes of memory, stores the given value there, and stores the address of the 36 bytes in the *strMessage* variable. Later, however, you change the value of the *strMessage* variable by coding:

```
strMessage = "Regrettably, the hippopotamus has run amok."
```

Lingo   All .NET programming languages use a double-byte character set called *Unicode* to represent strings. *Double-byte* means that each character occupies 2 bytes of memory. A *character set* is a specific collection of letters, numbers, and symbols, with a different number to identify each one. A double-byte character set can represent 65,535 different letters and numbers. This is more than enough to represent all the letters, numbers, and symbols in all the written languages on earth.

The new value is 43 characters long and therefore requires 86 bytes of memory. This won't fit in the 36 bytes currently allocated, so Visual Basic .NET asks the operating system for 86 more bytes of memory, stores the new value there, stores the new address in the *strMessage* variable, and finally gives the original 36 bytes back to Windows.

Note   Actually, the memory structure for storing a string includes more data than just the string itself. Storing a 43-character string therefore takes more than 86 bytes of memory. The important point is that the amount of memory a *String* variable requires can change as your program executes.

Is this perfectly clear? *String* is a reference type because a *String* variable doesn't actually contain the *String* value; it contains an address that refers to the actual *String* value. What happens when you assign the value of one reference type to another? In the case of strings, Visual Basic .NET:

1   Asks Windows for enough memory to accommodate the new value.

2   Stores the new value in the new memory location.

3   Stores the address of the new value in the receiving variable.

4   Gives memory that contained the old value back to Windows.

However, *String* is one of the few reference types that work this way. For most reference types, including arrays, the assignment operator simply copies the pointer value. Can you see the implications of this? Suppose that you declared two arrays like this:

```
Dim strTools() As String = {"Auger", "Blowtorch", "Chisel"}
Dim strFruit() As String = {"Apricot", "Banana", "Cherry"}
```

The *strTools* variable would point to a structure that contained various information about the array—it's data type, its rank, and the maximum subscript in each dimension, for example—plus an array of pointers to *String* values. The *strFruit* variable would point to a similar structure. Now, suppose that you code this statement:

```
strTools = strFruit
```

When this statement executes, it copies the pointer in the *strFruit* variable into the *strTools* variable. This means that the *strTools* variable will point to exactly the same memory location as the *strFruit* variable. *strTools*(0) and *strFruit*(0) will both equal Apricot. *strTools*(1) and *strFruit*(1) will both equal Banana, and so forth. This is probably what you expected. Suppose, however, that you proceed by coding this statement:

```
strTools(0) = "Drill"
```

Would you expect *strFruit* to equal Drill as well? Well, it does. Any change you make using the *strTools* variable will show up when you access the array using the *strFruit* variable (and vice versa). This is because *strTools* and *strFruit* both point to the same array.

Lingo   When two reference variables point to the same memory location, each is an *alias* of the other.

The point of all this is to be very careful when using the assignment operator with other than elementary data types. Having two variables point to the same object in memory is sometimes useful, but other times it's definitely not what you want.

Incidentally, the following statements will truly copy the *strFruit* array to the *strTools* array:

```
Dim intPos As Integer

ReDim strTools(UBound(strFruit))
For intPos = 0 to UBound(strFruit)
    strTools(intPos) = strFruit(intPos)
Next
```

See Also   *For more information about arrays and about* For...Next *loops, refer to Chapter 3, "Using Elementary Statements."*

Here are the salient points regarding this code:

- The *ReDim* statement assures that the *strTools* array contains the same number of elements as the *strFruit* array.

- *UBound* is a built-in function that returns the maximum permissible subscript for a given array.

- The *For* statement controls a loop that varies the *intPos* variable from zero to the maximum permissible subscript for the *strFruit* array.

- The next-to-last statement assigns each *String* value in the *strFruit* array to the corresponding *String* value in the *strTools* array.

   Note that because this statement is assigning *String* values and not entire arrays, it copies the value and not the reference.

Most data types have built-in methods that carry out common operations. These vary depending on the data type, but one-dimensional arrays have a method for copying themselves. Here's an example.

```
strFruit.CopyTo(strTools, 0)
```

See Also   *For more information about using methods, refer to Chapter 7, "Creating Classes and Objects."*

This statement copies all the elements of the *strFruit* array into the *strTools* array, starting at position zero of the *strTools* array. To search for methods that operate on a given data type, follow these steps:

1   In Microsoft Visual Studio .NET, select Index from the Help menu.

2   In the Filtered By drop-down list, select .NET Framework SDK.

3   In the Look For text box, type the name of the data type (**array**, in this case).

4   In the list of topics, look for the name of the data type followed by the word *class* (Array Class, for example).

5   Beneath the class title, click the topic titled Members or All Members.

6   The main Help window displays a list of all properties, methods, and events for the given data type.

Using Comparison Operators

Visual Basic .NET supports the comparison operators listed in Table 4-4. If both operands are numeric, Visual Basic .NET compares them numerically. If one or both are characters or strings, Visual Basic .NET compares them as text.

Table 4-4   **Visual Basic .NET Comparison Operators**

Comparison Operator	Description
=	Equal
<>	Not equal
<	Less than
>	Greater than
<=	Less than or equal
>=	Greater than or equal
Like	Matches pattern
Is	Returns *True* if both operands point to the same object

Comparing Numbers

The rules for comparing two numbers are essentially the same as those for performing arithmetic on them. If the numbers have different data types, Visual Basic .NET temporarily converts the narrower type to the wider one.

If you compare two numbers, Visual Basic .NET compares them numerically. That's no surprise. If, however, you compare a numeric data type to a string, Visual Basic .NET converts the number to a string and then performs a string comparison, explained in the next section.

Comparing Strings

When comparing two strings, Visual Basic .NET starts by comparing the first character of each operand, then the next character of each operand, and so forth, until it finds two unequal characters or until one string runs out of characters.

■ If it finds two unequal characters, the result of comparing them becomes the result of the entire operation. For example, the string "abcDEF" is less than "abcXA" because D (Unicode 0044) comes before X (Unicode 0058).

■ If one string runs out of characters before the other, the longer string is greater. Thus, "abcd" is greater than "abc". The string "abc " (which includes a trailing space) is also greater than "abc".

■ If both strings run out of characters at the same time, then they are equal.

Text comparisons can be either case-sensitive or non-case-sensitive, depending on the current *Option Compare* setting, as follows:

■ ***Option Compare Binary***   This setting compares strings based on the binary number that represents each character. Here, for example, are the numbers that represent certain characters in the Unicode character set:
A   0041
B   0042
a   0061
b   0062
With *Option Compare Binary* in effect, the letters *A* and *a* wouldn't be equal because 0041 doesn't equal 0061. Furthermore, *B* would come before *a* because 0042 is less than 0061.

■ ***Option Compare Text***   This setting compares strings based on a sort order that the computer's locale identifies. This sort order isn't case-sensitive and, as a result, *B* and *b* would be equal and *a* would come before *B*.

Note   The *locale* for a given computer is a Language setting in the Regional and Language Options portion of Control Panel. There's no guarantee that everyone who runs your program will have the same locale settings as you.

Option Compare Binary is the default. To override this, add the following line at the top of the file that contains your code:

```
Option Compare Text
```

Be aware, however, that this setting affects every *String* value comparison in the file that contains it. As a result, most programmers allow *Option Compare Binary* to remain in effect. If they need to perform a case-insensitive comparison, they temporarily convert both strings to the same case. Here are two examples. (*UCase* is a Visual Basic .NET built-in function that converts a string to uppercase. Similarly *LCase* is a built-in function that converts *String* values to lowercase.)

```
Dim strItem1 As String = "fishLINE"
Dim strItem2 As String = "FISHline"

If UCase(strItem1) = UCase(strItem2) Then
'    This comparison returns True because
'    "FISHLINE" equals "FISHLINE"
End If
If LCase(strItem1) = LCase(strItem2) Then
'    This comparison returns True because
'    "fishline" equals "fishline"
End If
```

Using the *Like* Operator

The *Like* operator compares a *String* to a pattern. If the two match, the comparison is *True*; otherwise, of course, it's *False*. If both the *String* and the pattern are empty, the result is *True*. If only one is empty, the result is *False*. Table 4-5 lists the available patterns.

Table 4-5   Patterns for Comparisons Using the *Like* Operator

Characters in Pattern	Matches in String
?	Any single character
*	Zero or more characters
#	Any single digit (0–9)
[charlist]	Any single character in charlist
[!charlist]	Any single character not in charlist

Using the *Like* operator requires knowing its quirks and peculiarities. Here are some tips:

■ Visual Basic .NET compares a bracket expression in the pattern—no matter how long—to exactly one character position in the comparison String. The expression

```
"abc" Like "a[xyzb]c"
```

is true because a matches a, b matches one of the characters in xyzb, and c matches c.

■ To match the left bracket ([), question mark (?), number sign (#), and asterisk (*), enclose them in brackets. In the following example, the first expression is *True* because the asterisk matches any character. The second is *False* because "X" doesn't equal the specific character *.

```
"aaXaa" Like "aa*aa"
"aaXaa" Like "aa[*]aa"
```

■ To include a range of characters within the brackets, code the character with the lower sort order, a hyphen (-), and then the character with the higher sort order. The following expressions are equivalent:

```
"A" Like "[0-9A-F]"
"A" Like "[0123456789ABCDEF]"
```

■ If you code a hyphen as the first or last character within brackets, it matches only another hyphen character. The following expression is *True* because the hyphen is one of the characters in the first group and A is one of the characters in the second group.

```
"-A" Like "[-02468][A-Z]"
```

■ An exclamation point (!) at the beginning of a bracketed group matches any character except those in the group. The first of the following expressions is *True*, whereas the second is *False*:

```
"void" Like "[!a-u]oid"
"-oid" Like "[!-ad]oid"
```

■ Outside of any brackets, an exclamation point matches itself.

■ An empty group ([]) signifies an empty string ("").

■ You can't use the right bracket (]) to match itself inside a group, but you can use it outside of a group as an individual character. The pattern ac[em]or]uv doesn't match ac]uv, for example, because [em]or] isn't a group that matches e, m,], o, or r. The pattern ac[em]or]uv does match aceor]uv because [em] matches e.

Getting It Together with Concatenation Operators

You can concatenate strings using either the plus (+) operator or the ampersand (&) operator. The following statements are equivalent:

```
strResult = "Welcome to " + "my circus."
strResult = "Welcome to " & "my circus."
```

Experienced programmers, however, never use the plus (+) operator for joining strings. There are two very good reasons for this:

■ It's very easy to code an expression such as a + b that you think will concatenate the variables *a* and *b*. However, if the variables are numeric, this expression actually adds them. The expression a & b always performs a concatenation.

■ Visual Basic .NET halts with a compilation error if you use the plus (+) operator to concatenate a mixture of *String* variables and numeric variables. The ampersand (&) operator, however, does the same job without complaining at all.

In the end it comes down to this: Use the concatenation operator (&) for concatenating and the addition operator (+) for adding. What could be easier than that?

When you concatenate (that is, join) *Strings*, you must always include spaces around the & operator. If you try to code an expression such as a&b&c, the compiler will report a syntax error and halt. You must instead code a & b & c.

Using Logical Operators

Logical operators work strictly with Boolean (that is, *True/False*) operands. The *And* operator, for example, is useful for determining if two *True/False* conditions are both *True*. Table 4-6 lists the complete set of logical operators that Visual Basic .NET provides.

Table 4-6   Visual Basic .NET Logical Operators

Operator	Mode	Result
Not	Unary	True if operand is False False if operand is True
And	Binary	True if both operands are True False if either operand is False
Or	Binary	True if either operand is True False if both operands are False
Xor	Binary	True if exactly one operand is True False if both operands are True or False
AndAlso	Binary	Same as And but short-circuited
OrElse	Binary	Same as Or but short-circuited

With the exception of *Not*, all of these operators require two operands as shown here. Note that each operand is an expression that evaluates to *True* or *False*.

```
(lngOrderQty > 0) And (lngOnHandQty > 0)
```

If you supply a numeric argument where Visual Basic .NET expects a Boolean argument, Visual Basic .NET converts the argument for you. A zero value is *False* and all nonzero values are *True*. The following *If* statements are equivalent:

```
If lngOrderQty <> 0 Then
    MsgBox("Order quantity is non-zero")
End If

If lngOrderQty Then
    MsgBox("Order quantity is non-zero")
End If
```

Using Short-Circuited Operators

To understand the difference between *And* and *AndAlso*, consider the following expression:

```
IsNumeric(strQty) And (CLng(strQty) > 0)
```

IsNumeric is a built-in function that returns *True* if the value you supply is a number, or if Visual Basic .NET can convert it to one. *CLng* is a built-in function that converts a value to a *Long*. Here, then, is how Visual Basic evaluates the expression:

1 The *IsNumeric* function returns *True* if Visual Basic .NET can convert the value in *strQty* to a number, and *False* otherwise.

2 The *CLng* function returns the value in *strQty* as a *Long*. The > operator compares this result to zero. If the result is greater than zero, the comparison returns *True*. If it's less than or equal to zero, the comparison returns *False*.

3 The *And* operator examines the results from steps 1 and 2. If both are *True*, the *And* operator returns *True*. Otherwise, it returns *False*.

Do you see the problem here? If *strQty* contains a nonnumeric value such as "xyz", executing the expression *CLng(strQty)* will throw an exception because there's no way of converting a string like xyz to a number. One way of avoiding such an exception is by nesting two *If* statements, like this:

```
If IsNumeric(strQty) Then
    If (CLng(strQty) > 0) Then
'        (Code that does the work goes here.)
    End If
End If
```

But the new *AndAlso* operator provides a more elegant solution:

```
If IsNumeric(strQty) AndAlso (clng(strQty) > 0) Then
'   (Code that does the work goes here.)
End If
```

This tells Visual Basic .NET that if *IsNumeric(strQty)* turns out to be *False*, it shouldn't bother evaluating *(CLng(strQty) > 0)*. After all, if the first operand of an *And* expression is *False*, the entire expression will be *False*, no matter the state of the second operand. Therefore, Visual Basic .NET skips (short-circuits) evaluating the second operand.

Similarly, the *OrElse* operator short-circuits the second operand if the first operand is *True*. If the first operand of an *Or* expression is *True*, the entire expression will be *True* no matter the state of the second operand.

Using Bitwise Operators

The *Not*, *And*, *Or*, and *Xor* operators have a second use: they can manipulate the individual bits of integer values. An integer value, in this case, means a value of type *Byte*, *Short*, *Integer*, or *Long*.

When you apply the *Not* operator to an integer value, it changes all the 0 bits to 1 and all the 1 bits to 0. Consider, for example, the following variable:

```
Dim srtStack As Short = 1
```

In binary, this variable would contain the bits 0000 0000 0000 0001. Executing the following statement would transform this value to 1111 1111 1111 1110 which, on an Intel processor, is equal to −2:

```
srtStack = Not srtStack
```

And, *Or*, and *Xor* perform bitwise arithmetic when you code them with integral operands. This applies the operator to the first bit of each operand, then to the second bit of each operand, and so forth. In the following code, the *Or* operator sets each bit in the result to 1 if the corresponding bit in either argument is 1:

```
Dim intBits As Integer = 3    ' 0000 0000 0000 0011
Dim intBats As Integer = 14   ' 0000 0000 0000 1110
Dim intHits As Integer
Dim intHats As Integer

intHits = intBits  Or intBats ' 0000 0000 0000 1111
intHats = intBits And intBats ' 0000 0000 0000 0010
```

The fact that *Not*, *And*, *Or*, and *Xor* are logical operators in some situations and bitwise operators in others can be confusing, especially if you get in the habit of coding numeric values where Visual Basic .NET expects Boolean ones. An expression like

```
(intBits <> 0) Or (intBats <> 0)
```

always returns *True* or *False*. The following expression, however, can return millions of different values:

```
intBits Or intBats
```

Using Miscellaneous Operators

The *AddressOf* operator returns the address of a subroutine or function. This is useful in certain situations where you must supply the address of a procedure that Visual Basic .NET calls when a specific event occurs.

The *GetType* operator returns the type object of the specified type. The expression *GetType(Integer)*, for example, returns the base object that defines the entire *Integer* class. This can be useful for obtaining information about the type, such as its properties, methods, and events.

Testing Operators and Expressions

Reading about operators and expressions might be great fun, but the real excitement comes from coding and testing them. The purpose of this exercise, therefore, isn't to mimic a small fraction of a real program's capabilities. Instead, the purpose is to show you how to run experiments and test your work. Are you ready? Follow these steps:

1   Start Visual Studio, open the New Project dialog box, and create a new project named expressions.

2   Select the default form and set its *Text* property to Expression Test.

3   Add a button to the form. Set its name to *btnTest* and its *Text* property to Test.

4   Double-click the button. Your screen should now resemble Figure 4-1.

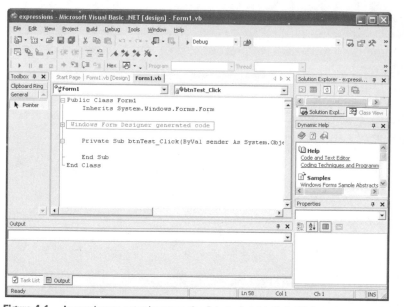

Figure 4-1 Any code you enter between the *Private Sub btnTest_Click* statement and the *End Sub* statements will run whenever you click Test.

5 Between the *Private Sub btnTest_Click* and *End Sub* statements, enter this statement:

```
MsgBox()
```

6 Inside the parentheses you entered in step 5, enter any expression you want to test. If your expression requires any variables, add *Dim* statements just above the *MsgBox* statement to declare them. For example, type the following:

```
Dim intStart As Integer = 125
Dim intFinish As Integer = 300
Dim intTime As Integer = 135
MsgBox((intFinish - intStart) / (intTime / 60))
```

7 Press F5 to run the program. If Visual Studio displays the message box

There Were Build Errors. Continue?

this means that the Visual Basic .NET compiler has detected an error in your program. Click No, locate the Task List window, and resolve each message you find there. Double-clicking any message highlights the word or statement that caused the error.

8   If the run-time version of your form appears, click Test. A message box displays the results of evaluating the expression you put inside the *MsgBox()* parentheses.

9   If your expression fails, Visual Studio displays a message that begins this way:

An unhandled exception of type...

Visual Studio also displays Break, Continue, Ignore, and Help buttons. Click Break.

Contrary to what you might think, the Break button doesn't smash, crash, destroy, or otherwise abuse your program. Instead, it breaks into the normal flow of execution and freezes your program in its tracks.

10   After you click Break, Visual Studio displays the portion of your source code that caused the error. The statement that caused the error is highlighted in green. To try this, change the code you entered in step 6 as shown here (the changed portions appear in bold):

```
Dim intStart As Integer = 125
Dim intFinish As Integer = 300
Dim strTime As String = "none"
MsgBox((intFinish - intStart) / (strTime / 60))
```

If Visual Studio won't let you update this code, it's because your program is still running. Click your form's close box (the X in the top-right corner) and then try changing the code again.

11   Press F5 to run the program, then click Test to cause an exception. If you copied the code in step 10, the exception will be this:

An Unhandled Exception Of Type 'System.InvalidCastException' Occurred In microsoft.visualbasic.dll

Additional Information: Cast From String 'None' To Type 'Double' Is Not Valid.

12   In addition to the highlighted source code, Visual Studio displays a Command window. This is the long window that occupies the bottom of Figure 4-2. To display the value of any variable or expression, type a question mark (**?**), a space, and the name of the variable or the expression, and then press Enter.

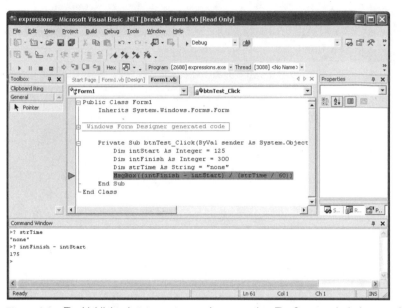

Figure 4-2   The highlighted statement caused an exception. The Command window can display
the value of any variable or exception.

13 The Debug menu provides additional commands you can use after
breaking into your program. Four of the most useful are the following:

- Continue (F5)—This command tells Visual Studio .NET to continue running your program at full speed (that is, with no more
interruptions). Of course, if you haven't fixed the cause of an
exception, the exception will occur again.

- Step Into (F11)—This command executes the next line of code.
This provides a way to watch your program run in slow motion.
Each time you press F11, you execute one more line of code. If
the current statement calls a subroutine or function, Visual Studio
.NET runs the first statement in that subroutine or function.

- Step Over (F10)—This command works like Step Into except that
if the current statement calls a function or subroutine, Visual Studio .NET runs the whole function or subroutine without stopping.

- Step Out (Shift+F11)—This command is useful when the current
statement is inside a subroutine or function. In that case, pressing
Shift+F11 finishes running the function or subroutine without
interruption and then halts after the statement that called the subroutine or function.

Being able to inspect and diagnose a program that throws an exception is a valuable capability, but wouldn't it be great if you could break into a program anywhere you wanted and look around even if it isn't throwing exceptions? Well, you can. Just select the statement where you'd like execution to stop and then press F9. Visual Studio .NET highlights the statement in dark red and halts the program whenever that statement is about to run. Visual Studio .NET calls this *inserting a breakpoint*. You can also do it by right-clicking the line of code and choosing Insert Breakpoint from the shortcut menu.

To remove a breakpoint, either select the line and press F9 or right-click it and choose Remove Breakpoint from the shortcut menu. To clear all breakpoints in a program, choose Clear All Breakpoints from the Debug menu.

Visual Studio offers many additional debugging and diagnostic tools. You can explore these as your proficiency grows, but the information in this exercise should at least get you started.

Key Points

- Operators are symbols that tell Visual Basic .NET to perform some action on one or two operands.

- Expressions are combinations of variables, properties, literals, constants, and operators that the program will evaluate as it runs.

- Arithmetic operators perform mathematical operations on one or two numbers.

- The assignment operator copies the value of an expression into a variable or property.

- Comparison operators return *True* or *False* depending on the relative values of two expressions.

- Concatenation operators join two expressions as strings. The ampersand (&) operator is preferable to the plus (+) sign as a concatenation operator because the ampersand can't accidentally perform arithmetic.

- Logical operators manipulate the results of one or two Boolean expressions. The *And* operator, for example determines if both of its operands are *True*.

- Bitwise operators manipulate the individual bits of integral values.

- Visual Studio .NET provides testing and debugging commands that are powerful and easy to use.

Chapter 5

Using Functions and Subroutines

Writing programs to solve everyday problems would be nearly impossible without the ability to divide them into small, relatively independent units. This is the ability that functions and subroutines provide.

Microsoft Visual Basic .NET provides hundreds of built-in functions. The Microsoft .NET Framework provides thousands more in the form of methods (which are functions you access as part of an object). If none of these functions serves your purpose, you can, of course, write your own. After all, that's why people want to learn programming; they want their own custom program rather than a prepackaged, generic solution.

Introducing Functions and Subroutines

If you've ever written spreadsheet formulas, you've probably used one or more of the functions built into Microsoft Excel. If cell A1 contained some mixed-case text and you wanted some other cell to contain an uppercase version of the same text, you would put the function *=UPPER(A1)* in that other cell.

Functions in programming languages work very much the same way. Suppose, for example, that a variable named *strMixed* contains some mixed-case text.

To get an uppercase version of the same text, you could run it through the *UCase* function that comes with Visual Basic .NET. Here's how this would look in code:

```
strWhatever = UCase(strMixed)
```

In programming lingo, the *UCase* function accepts one *String* argument and produces a *String* return value. An argument, in this sense, is a value that you supply to the function as input. The return value contains a single result that the function produces as output. A function can produce many other kinds of results as well. For example, it can display something on the screen, read or modify files or databases, modify variables passed as arguments, and, in some cases, modify other variables in your program.

Based on task they perform, some functions have no need to produce a return value. In such cases, it's better to create a subroutine. A subroutine can do anything a function can do except produce a return value. To call a subroutine, you simply code its name as a statement. Here's an example.

```
MkDir("C:\temp\myfolder")
```

> **Note**   *MkDir* is a built-in subroutine that comes with Visual Basic .NET. It creates new folders and doesn't provide a return value; it either works or throws an exception.

Functions and subroutines can require zero, one, or many arguments. The arguments go inside the parentheses that follow the function or subroutine name. If there's more than one argument, separate them with commas.

Both arguments and return values have types, just as variables do. If the argument you specify is of a different type than a function or subroutine requires, Visual Basic .NET converts the value, if possible.

Coding Your Own Functions and Subroutines

Just as you must declare variables before using them, you must declare functions and subroutines as well. In its simplest form, a subroutine declaration looks like this:

```
Sub name ()
End Sub
```

In place of *name*, of course, you would code whatever name you want your subroutine to have. Between the *Sub* and *End Sub* statements you would code whatever statements are necessary to make the subroutine do its work.

> **Note**   You don't need to declare the built-in functions and subroutines that come with Visual Basic .NET or with the .NET Framework. You only need to declare functions and subroutines you write yourself.

A function declaration is slightly more complex because you must identify the data type of the return value. Here's the requisite form. In place of *type* you would code *Integer*, *String*, or whatever type you decide to use.

```
Function name () As type
End Function
```

The rules for naming subroutines and functions are the same as those for naming variables. It isn't customary to begin them with *sub*, *fun,* or any other prefix, but it is customary to name them with verbs. If your subroutine is going to shuffle a deck of cards, you might name it *ShuffleCards*.

See Also *For more information on the rules for naming variables, refer to the section titled "Using Variables" in Chapter 3.*

One function or subroutine can't reside within another. Therefore, to add a new function or subroutine, you must code it just before or just after an existing one. You can declare functions and subroutines in any order you like because Visual Basic .NET executes them by name and not in the order in which they appear.

Declaring Arguments

If your function or subroutine needs to receive input values from the code that calls it, you must declare an argument for each value. The following statements declare a subroutine that accepts two arguments:

```
Sub DisplayMsg (astrMsg1 As String, astrMsg2 As String)
End Sub
```

As you can see, each argument declaration begins with a name, then the word *As*, then the name of the data type you expect to receive. Many programmers prefix all argument names with the letter *a* (as shown in the previous example), but this is entirely at your discretion. You can name the arguments after the inhabitants of your fish tank, if you like.

Arguments are *positional*. The first argument you declare in a function or subroutine receives the first value you specify in the calling statement, the second argument receives the second value, and so forth. There's no requirement that the variable names you specify in the calling statement match the argument names you assign in the *Function* or *Sub* statement.

Lingo *A calling statement is one that calls (that is, uses) a function or subroutine.*

To call a function, you simply code its name and any arguments in an expression. The following statement calls the *TwistInsideOut* function using one argument and stores the return value in a variable named *intResult*.

```
intResult = TwistInsideOut("T-shirt")
```

To call a subroutine, simply code its name and arguments as a statement. Here's an example.

```
SpreadHappiness("Everywhere")
```

If you like, you can precede the subroutine with the word *Call*, as shown next, but this is entirely optional:

```
Call SpreadHappiness("Everywhere")
```

If you need to call a function but don't care about the return value, you can invoke the function as if it were a subroutine. However, if you do this, there's no way to get the return value later.

Passing Arguments by Value

By default, arguments in Visual Basic .NET receive a copy of any argument values the calling statement specifies. The term for this is receiving an argument *by value*. Suppose, for example, you wrote a subroutine named *ZeroOut* that contained this code:

```
Sub ZeroOut(intArg As Integer)
    intArg = 0  ' Zero out first argument
End Sub
```

So far, so good. Now suppose that you called the subroutine with this code:

```
Dim intCount As Integer = 5
ZeroOut(intCount)
MsgBox("The count is " & intCount)
```

If you ran this code, you'd find that the value of *intCount* remains 5 even though you passed it as the first argument to the *ZeroOut* subroutine, and even though the *ZeroOut* subroutine zeroes out the first argument! This is because the *ZeroOut* subroutine only receives a copy of the original data item. The subroutine can modify the copy, but when the subroutine ends, Visual Basic .NET discards the copy without updating the original variable.

To help you remember that passing arguments by value is the default, Microsoft Visual Studio adds the *ByVal* keyword in front of each argument you declare unless, of course, you specify *ByVal* or *ByRef* yourself. An example that specifies *ByVal* appears below. (The next section of this chapter explains *ByRef*.)

```
Sub ZeroOut(ByVal intArg As Integer)
    intArg = 0  ' Zero out first argument
End Sub
```

If this seems too simple to be interesting, life is about to improve for you. Recall that for reference types, the variable you code in your program doesn't contain the data, it contains a pointer to the data. If you pass a reference type to a *ByVal* argument, the function or subroutine receives a copy of that pointer. The function or subroutine can't modify the original pointer, but it can modify the data that the pointer identifies. To illustrate this, here's an example:

```
Dim strNames(2) As String
strNames(0) = "Muriel"
strNames(1) = "Maureen"
ZapFirst(strNames)
MsgBox(strNames(0) & vbCrLf & UBound(strNames))

Sub ZapFirst(ByVal astrNouns() As String)
    astrNouns(0) = "Madeline"
    ReDim Preserve astrNouns(5)
    astrNouns(0) = "Malinda"
End Sub
```

The first block of code declares an array named *strNames*, then stores the name Muriel in the first element and Maureen in the second. Next, it calls a subroutine named *ZapFirst*, passing the entire array as an argument. (Note the lack of a subscript after the variable name *strNames* on line 4.) Finally, the code displays the name of the first element in the array and the size of the largest permissible subscript.

The second block of code declares the *ZapFirst* subroutine. The subroutine expects to receive a *String* array as its only argument. The parentheses indicate that the argument is an array but don't specify how many elements the array should contain. This varies, depending on the array that the calling statement specifies. If the subroutine needs to know how many elements the *Array* argument contains, it can use the expression *UBound(astrNouns)*.

The code inside the subroutine stores the name Madeline in the first element of the array and then redimensions the array so that it contains five elements. Finally, it again changes the first element of the array, this time to Malinda. What do you think the resulting message box will display? Figure 5-1 shows the actual result.

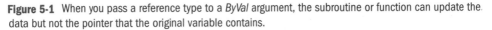

```
ByRefArray - Microsoft Visual Basic .NET [run] - Form1.vb [Read Only]

File  Edit  View  Project  Build  Debug  Tools  Window  Help

Debug

Start Page | Form1.vb [Design]  Form1.vb

Form1                              ZapFirst

        Private Sub btnTest_Click(ByVal sender As System.Object
            Dim strNames(2) As String
            strNames(0) = "Murial"
            strNames(1) = "Maureen"
            ZapFirst(strNames)
            MsgBox(strNames(0) & vbCrLf & UBound(strNames))
        End Sub
        Sub ZapFirst(ByVal astrNouns() As String)
            astrNouns(0) = "Madeline"
            ReDim Preserve astrNouns(5)
            astrNouns(0) = "Malinda"
        End Sub

Command Window

Build succeeded                              Ln 68    Col 12    Ch 12    INS
```

Form1

    Test

ByRefArray

    Madeline
    2

        OK

Figure 5-1 When you pass a reference type to a *ByVal* argument, the subroutine or function can update the data but not the pointer that the original variable contains.

The *ZapFirst* subroutine can change elements in the array because the *astrNouns* argument points to the same array as the original *strNames* variable.

Recall, however, how redimensioning an array works. The *ReDim* command creates a new array structure in memory, then stores the new memory address in the *Array* variable, then discards the original array structure. When the *ZapFirst* subroutine does this, it only updates the copy of the original *strNames* variable that the subroutine knows as *astrNouns*. Thereafter, any changes *ZapFirst* makes to the *astrNouns* array will affect only the new 5-member array. The *strNames* variable in the calling code will still access the original 2-member array. The name Malinda appears in the 5-member array that Visual Basic .NET discards once the subroutine stops executing.

Note   Every time a function or subroutine finishes executing, it discards any variables or reference types that it created.

The moral here is to be very careful when updating reference types that your subroutines and functions receive by means of a *ByVal* argument.

Passing Arguments by Reference

The alternative to passing arguments by value is passing them *by reference*. This gives the function or subroutine full access to the original data item rather than access to a copy. To receive an argument by reference, begin its argument declaration with *ByRef.* Here's an example.

```
Sub ZapFirst(ByRef astrNouns() As String)
    astrNouns(0) = "Madeline"
    ReDim Preserve astrNouns(5)
    astrNouns(0) = "Malinda"
End Sub
```

When a *ByRef* argument receives a value type, updating the argument updates the original variable. When a *ByRef* argument receives a reference type, it can reliably delete and re-create the entire structure as well as its properties. Rerunning the previous example with *ByRef* in effect produces this output:

Because *ByRef* variables seem more predictable, you might wonder why Visual Basic .NET doesn't make them the default. In fact, *ByRef* was the default in previous versions of Visual Basic. The reason for changing is that in Visual Basic .NET, it's very easy to get two or more subroutines or functions executing at exactly the same time. This could result in two or more processes making changes to the same variable at the same time, a situation much akin to (but much less enjoyable than) a three-ring circus. Passing arguments by value minimizes the risk of this.

You should be aware that in some cases, VisualBasic .NET passes arguments by value even though you specify *ByRef* on the *Function* or *Sub* statement. One such case occurs when you specify a literal or constant as an argument value like this:

```
ZeroOut(1)
```

```
Sub ZeroOut(ByRef aintArg As Integer)
    aintArg = 0   ' Zero out first argument
End Sub
```

This code doesn't throw an exception, but neither does it update the value of 1 because Visual Basic .NET sets up a temporary data area that contains the *Integer* 1 and passes that address to the *ZeroOut* subroutine. Within the subroutine, *aintArg* behaves like an ordinary variable and not a literal.

ByRef arguments also receive arguments by value when Visual Basic needs to perform a type conversion. Consider, for example the following code:

```
Dim strOne As String = "1"
ZeroOut(strOne)
MsgBox(strOne)

Sub ZeroOut(ByRef aintArg As Integer)
    aintArg = 0   ' Zero out first argument
End Sub
```

Visual Basic .NET accepts and runs this code even though the calling statement supplies a *String* variable and the argument declaration requires an *Integer* variable. This works because behind the scenes, Visual Basic .NET creates an *Integer* copy of the *String* value and then makes the *aintArg* argument point to the copy. When the subroutine ends, however, Visual Basic .NET discards the *Integer* copy without converting it back into a *String* and storing it in the *strOne* variable.

Sidestepping Arguments

Normally, the calling statement must supply the same number of arguments that the declaration of a function or subroutine specifies. If, however, you want the calling statement to work even if it doesn't specify a full set of arguments, you can make one or more arguments optional. This requires special coding on the *Function* or *Sub* statement and there are two ways to do it. To use the first approach, follow this procedure:

1 Begin the declaration of each optional argument with the word *Optional*.

2 Specify a default value for each optional argument. To do this, add an equal sign and a constant expression to the end of the argument declaration.

3 Declare all the mandatory arguments first, and then all optional arguments.

In the following subroutine declaration, the arguments *astrFireman* and *astrConductor* are optional. If the calling statement doesn't specify values for them, they'll take on the values (none) and (nobody), respectively:

```
Sub SetCrew (ByVal astrEngineer As String, _
    Optional ByVal astrFireman As String = "(none)", _
    Optional ByVal astrConductor As String = "(nobody)")
```

To call this subroutine and specify only the *astrEngineer* and *astrConductor* arguments, you would code:

```
SetCrew("Wally", , "Doris")
```

There's no way that code inside a function or subroutine can tell whether the calling statement omitted an argument or just happened to supply the default value. The following calling statement, for example, would be indistinguishable from the preceding one:

```
SetCrew("Wally", "(none)", "Doris")
```

If this distinction is important to you, make sure the default value is a very unlikely one.

The second way to make arguments optional is to specify the *ParamArray* keyword when you declare the argument. Here's an example that's similar to the preceding one:

```
Sub SetCrew (astrEngineer As String, _
    ByVal ParamArray astrMember() As String)
```

When you call a subroutine coded this way, you must of course specify any mandatory arguments (one, in this case), but then you can specify as many arguments as you like: none, one, or many. Visual Basic .NET constructs an array just large enough to contain all the arguments and then provide access through the *ParamArray* variable. Suppose, for example that the calling statement were

```
SetCrew("Celia", "Florence", "Holly", "Wendy")
```

the *astrEngineer* argument would contain Celia. The *astrMember* array would contain three elements: Florence, Holly, and Wendy, with subscripts of 0, 1, and 2, respectively. The expression *UBound(astrMember)* would return 2, the largest permissible subscript. If the calling statement were

```
SetCrew("Casey")
```

then the *astrMember* array would be empty. *UBound(astrMember)* would therefore return –1.

Specifying Return Values

There are two different ways to set the return value of a function. The choice is entirely up to you. To use the first method, you assign a value to the function name as if it were a variable. Here's an example.

```
Function Proper(ByVal astrText As String) As String
    Dim strOut As String = ""
    Dim intPos As Integer
    If astrText = "" Then
        strOut = ""
```

```
    Else
        strOut = UCase(Mid(astrText, 1, 1))
        For intPos = 2 To Len(astrText)
            If Mid(astrText, intPos - 1, 1) = " " Then
                strOut &= UCase(Mid(astrText, intPos, 1))
            Else
                strOut &= LCase(Mid(astrText, intPos, 1))
            End If
        Next
    End If
    Proper = strOut
End Function
```

You're right, this example is a little more complicated than the ones you've seen so far, but you're supposed to be progressing. This function transforms text so that the first letter in each word is uppercase and all the other letters are lowercase.

■ If the argument value is an empty string, the function stores an empty string in a variable named *strOut*.

> **Note** *UCase* is a built-in function that converts an argument string to uppercase.

■ Otherwise, the function converts the first character of the argument value to uppercase and stores it in *strOut*.

> **Note** *Mid* is a built-in function that returns selected characters of an argument string. *Mid* takes three arguments: a string, a starting position, and a length. Mid("Margaret", 2, 3) equals *arg*.

Next, a *For…Next* loop varies an *Integer* variable named *intPos* from 2 to the length of the argument string.

> **Note** *Len* is a built-in function that returns the length of a string.

Within the *For…Next* loop, an *If* statement determines if the character at *intPos* − 1 is a space. If so, the function converts the character at *intPos* to uppercase and appends it to *strOut*. If not, the function converts the character to lowercase and appends it.

■ Finally, the next-to-last statement copies the value of the *strOut* variable to the function name *Proper*. This is what sets the return value.

Once you've added this function to your program, this statement

```
MsgBox(Proper("press button in case of emergency."))
```

would display

```
Press Button In Case Of Emergency.
```

The second way of setting a return code is to use a *Return* statement. This statement consists of the word *Return* followed by the return value you want to specify. Here's an example.

```
Return -1
```

The *Return* statement, however, also exits the function. The next topic has more to say about exiting functions and subroutines, but as an example, here's the *Proper* function again, this time illustrating the *Return* statement:

```
Function Proper(ByVal astrText As String) As String
    Dim strOut As String = ""
    Dim intPos As Integer
    If astrText = "" Then
        Return ""
    End If
    strOut = UCase(Mid(astrText, 1, 1))
    For intPos = 2 To Len(astrText)
        If Mid(astrText, intPos - 1, 1) = " " Then
            strOut &= UCase(Mid(astrText, intPos, 1))
        Else
            strOut &= LCase(Mid(astrText, intPos, 1))
        End If
    Next
    Return strOut
End Function
```

If the calling statement supplies an empty argument, this version of the *Proper* function executes a *Return* statement that specifies an empty return value and then exits the function. None of the other code in the function executes.

If the argument contains at least one character, the function uses the same code as before to convert the first letter of each word to uppercase and all other letters to lowercase. Then, it executes a *Return* statement that gets the return value from the *strOut* variable.

Regardless of how you set the return value, it must conform to the data type you declared on the *Function* statement. The *Proper* function declares itself to be of type *string*, for example, so the value you specify must either be a *string* or something Visual Basic .NET can convert to a *string*.

If you forget to specify a return value, Visual Basic .NET supplies the default value for the data type: zero for numeric types, empty strings for strings, and so forth.

If you invoke a function without using the return value in an expression, Visual Basic .NET discards it. The following statement, for example, simply runs and then discards the return value:

```
Proper("going nowhere fast")
```

Exiting Functions and Subroutines

The previous section described the *Return* statement, which provides one way to exit a function. The *Exit Function* statement provides another. The second and third statements shown here are equivalent to the first one:

```
Return strOut
```

```
Proper = strOut ' (Assuming Proper is the function's name.)
Exit Function
```

As you might suspect, there's also an *Exit Sub* statement that immediately exits a subroutine. Both kinds of *Exit* statements are useful for avoiding long *If* statements and therefore simplifying your code, but don't go crazy with them. A function or subroutine with dozens of exit points is hardly simple.

The most common—and often the best—way of exiting a function is simply to reach the *End Function* statement. Likewise, the best way of exiting a subroutine is to reach the *End Sub* statement. This achieves the worthy goal of each routine having a single entry point and a single exit point.

Lingo   Programmers often call reaching an *End Function* or *End Sub* statement "falling through the bottom."

Functions, Subroutines, Variables, and Scope

No, this section isn't an exercise in "Which of these objects doesn't belong?" *Scope*, in terms of programming, means the range of execution during which a variable exists. To realize the importance of this, consider these facts:

- When you call a function or subroutine, your program asks Windows for whatever memory the function or subroutine needs. This includes memory for *ByVal* copies of arguments, variables, and so forth.

- When your function or subroutine ends, it gives the memory for these items back to Windows.

Do you see the implications of this? Any variables you declare inside a function subroutine have no existence unless that function subroutine is running! You certainly can't access these variables with code located outside the function or subroutine because when outside code is running, inside code isn't.

Lingo *Accessibility* is another term for scope.

Now suppose two copies of a function or subroutine are running at the same time. To see how this could happen, consider this code:

```
NestMe (1)

Sub NestMe(ByVal aintLevel As Integer)
    Select Case aintLevel
        Case Is < 5
            NestMe(aintLevel + 1)
        Case 5
            MsgBox("Reached level 5.")
    End Select
End Sub
```

Did you realize that this subroutine calls itself? The argument *aintLevel* is 1 during the first execution, but because this is less than 5, the *Select Case* statement adds 1 to the *aintLevel* value and calls the *NestMe* subroutine again. This continues until *aintLevel* is 5, when the *Select* statement displays a message box.

When the message box appears, five copies of the *NestMe* subroutine are in memory at the same time. Each copy of the subroutine has its own data in memory and none of the subroutines get confused about which copy of the *aintLevel* argument to use. They each use their own, and they each relinquish it when they end.

Note A function or subroutine doesn't relinquish its memory when it calls another subroutine or function.

If you need a variable to *persist*—that is, remain in existence—for longer than the life of a given function or subroutine, define it outside either of them. Here's an example.

```
Dim intTally As Integer

Function LaunchGizmo ()
    intTally += 1
End Function

Sub StartDoodad ()
    intTally += 1
End Sub
```

The *intTally* variable remains in existence regardless of whether the *LaunchGizmo* function or the *StartDoodad* subroutine is running at the time. Furthermore, they're accessible both within and without those two routines.

The reserved words *Public*, *Private*, *Protected*, *Friend*, and *Protected Friend* all have to do with matters of scope. Chapter 7, "Creating Classes and Objects," explains classes and objects and has much more to say about these terms.

Designing Functions and Subroutines Effectively

Used properly, functions and subroutines not only make it easier to write programs, but easier to keep them running and to add features as well. Here are some guidelines that help make these benefits a reality:

- As you write code, watch for blocks of code that occur repeatedly. Instead of duplicating this code several times in your program, code it as a single function or subroutine and then call that function or subroutine as needed. That way, you only have to write and debug the code once. Similarly, if you ever need to change the code, you only need to change one occurrence of it.

- Try to design functions and subroutines so they only have one exit. If you need multiple exit points, make them obvious. Don't bury them inside nested *If* statements or loops.

- Write functions and subroutines that satisfy a single task. In other words, if you have two or three tasks to do, write two or three functions or subroutines. This makes life much easier when, inevitably, another part of the program needs only one of the tasks.

- Use *ByVal* (that is, read-only) arguments for input values and return values for output values. A function or subroutine's effect on *ByRef* arguments and shared memory variables is much less obvious when someone works with the code later.

Example: Writing a Four-Function Calculator

When you wrote the tape calculator example in Chapter 3, "Using Elementary Statements," you probably wondered why it didn't also multiply and divide. Perhaps, if you like to tinker, you tried adding those functions. Recall, though, that the *btnAdd_Click* and *btnSubtract_Click* subroutines contained a lot of duplicate code. The instructions even told you to cut and paste it. This example explains how to implement all four functions without duplicating any code. Follow this procedure:

1 In Visual Studio, create a new Windows Forms project named Calc3.

2 Either quit Visual Studio or make sure none of the files in the Calc3 project are open. (That is, make sure the main document window is empty.)

3 In Windows Explorer, copy the Form1.vb file from the Calc2 folder to the Calc3 folder. By default, these folders will be in C:\Documents and Settings*user*\My Documents\Visual Studio Projects, where *user* is the name of your Windows logon account.

4 With the Calc3 project open in VisualStudio, double-click the Form1.vb entry in the Solution Explorer window. This opens the form in Visual Studio.

5 Click anywhere in the background of the form. This should position the drop-down list at the top of the Properties window to Form1 System.Windows.Forms.Form. (If not, just select this entry from the drop-down list.) Then, change the *Text* property to Four Function Calculator.

6 Select either Add or Subtract, copy it (by pressing Ctrl+C, for example), and then paste it twice (by pressing Ctrl+V twice). Drag the new buttons into place under the Subtract button and name them as follows:

	First New Button	**Second New Button**
(Name)	*btnMultiply*	*btnDivide*
Text	Multiply	Divide

7 Fine-tune the placement of all the form elements so they resemble Figure 5-2.

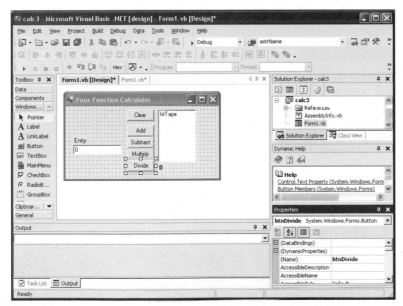

Figure 5-2 You can arrange the form elements for the Calc3 project like this.

8 Double-click Add to display the *btnAdd_Click* subroutine.

9 Just above the *btnAdd_Click* subroutine (that is, just above its *Sub* statement) add this subroutine declaration:

```
Sub Calculate(ByVal astrOper As String)
End Sub
```

This subroutine does all the calculating for all four buttons. The *astrOper* argument receives the operation the calculator should perform: +, -, *, or /.

10 Cut all the code out of the *btnAdd_Click* subroutine and paste it inside the *Calculate* subroutine. Don't copy the *Sub* and *End Sub* statements.

11 Add the following statement inside the now-empty *btnAdd_Click* subroutine:

```
Calculate("+")
```

12 Delete all the code inside the *btnSubtract_Click* subroutine and replace it with this statement:

```
Calculate("-")
```

13 Click the Form1.vb [Design] tab and then double-click Multiply. This creates and displays a *btnMultiply_Click* subroutine. Enter the following statement inside this subroutine:

```
Calculate("*")
```

14 Repeat step 13, this time double-clicking Divide. Enter the following statement inside this subroutine:

```
Calculate("/")
```

15 The only remaining work is to fix the *Calculate* subroutine so it handles all four operators correctly. To begin, locate this statement:

```
lstTape.Items.Add(dblEntry & " +")
```

and replace it with this:

```
lstTape.Items.Add(dblEntry & " " & astrOper)
```

This displays the proper operator in the tape display.

16 Locate this statement:

```
dblTotal = dblTotal + dblEntry
```

and replace it with this *Select Case* statement:

```
Select Case astrOper
    Case "+"
        dblTotal += dblEntry
```

```
        Case "-"
            dblTotal -= dblEntry
        Case "*"
            dblTotal *= dblEntry
        Case "/"
            dblTotal /= dblEntry
        Case Else
            MsgBox("Invalid Operator")
    End Select
```

This code simply performs the arithmetic operation that corresponds to the *astrtOper* argument. The *Case Else* condition should never occur, but it's good to know if it does. Fixing a program is much easier if you know what went wrong.

17 Choose Save All from the File menu, then press F5 to run the program.

You should find that all four buttons—Add, Subtract, Multiply, and Divide—now work properly. If they don't, verify the various *Click* subroutines containing the statements shown in steps 11 through 14. The complete code listing for the *Calculate* subroutine is shown here:

```
Sub Calculate(ByVal astrOper As String)
    Dim dblEntry As Double              ' Current entry
    If IsNumeric(txtEntry.Text) Then    ' Is entry valid?
        dblEntry = CDbl(txtEntry.Text)  ' Convert entry
        lstTape.Items.Add(dblEntry & " " & astrOper) ' Tape
        Select Case astrOper            ' Calc new total
            Case "+"
                dblTotal += dblEntry
            Case "-"
                dblTotal -= dblEntry
            Case "*"
                dblTotal *= dblEntry
            Case "/"
                dblTotal /= dblEntry
            Case Else
                MsgBox("Invalid Operator")
        End Select
        lblTotal.Text = dblTotal        ' Display total
        txtEntry.Text = ""              ' Clear entry box
    Else
        MsgBox("You must enter a number.", _
                MsgBoxStyle.Critical, _
                "Invalid Entry")        ' Error message
    End If
End Sub
```

Key Points

- Functions and subroutines provide a way of breaking your code into manageable, reusable units.

- Functions and subroutines differ mainly in that functions produce a return value and subroutines don't.

- Functional and subroutine arguments are positional. It doesn't matter what you name the arguments in the calling statement and what you name them in the function or subroutine declaration; it only matters that you get them in the correct order.

- By default, Visual Basic .NET passes arguments by value. This means that the function or subroutine gets a copy of the data item the calling statement specifies.

- If your function or subroutine needs direct access to the argument variable that the calling statement specifies (for example, to update that variable) then you should code *ByRef* as the first keyword when you declare the argument.

- To specify the return value for a function, either assign it to the function name or specify it on a *Return* statement.

- To exit a function, you can fall through the bottom, execute an *Exit Function* statement, or execute a *Return* statement.

- To exit a subroutine, either fall through the bottom or execute an *Exit Sub* statement.

Chapter 6

Using Built-In Functions

Microsoft Visual Basic .NET provides hundreds of built-in functions that make programming easier. To appreciate the importance of this, imagine Microsoft Excel without the formulas. The result would greatly resemble the classic definition of nothing: a balloon without the skin!

Fortunately, Excel has formulas and Visual Basic .NET has built-in functions. In fact, there are so many built-in functions that this chapter can't hope to explain them all or to describe individual functions in detail. It does, however, show you how to search for functions and provides introductions to the ones you'll probably use most often. Finally, it shows you how to write a program that shuffles cards. (You've probably had it with calculators, right?)

Don't make the mistake of thinking that built-in functions are for wimps. After all, if Microsoft has already written a function that does what you need to do, why should you reinvent the wheel?

Finding Built-In Functions

Using built-in functions presents only two difficulties: finding the function you need and then learning how to use it. Fortunately, the Help files that come with Visual Basic .NET provide several ways to look for built-in functions and excellent instructions on how to use them. To search for a built-in function, choose Contents from the Visual Studio .NET Help menu and then expand the following topics:

Visual Studio .NET
        Visual Basic and Visual C#
           Reference
              Visual Basic Language
                  Visual Basic Language and Run-Time Reference
                  Visual Basic Run-Time Library Members

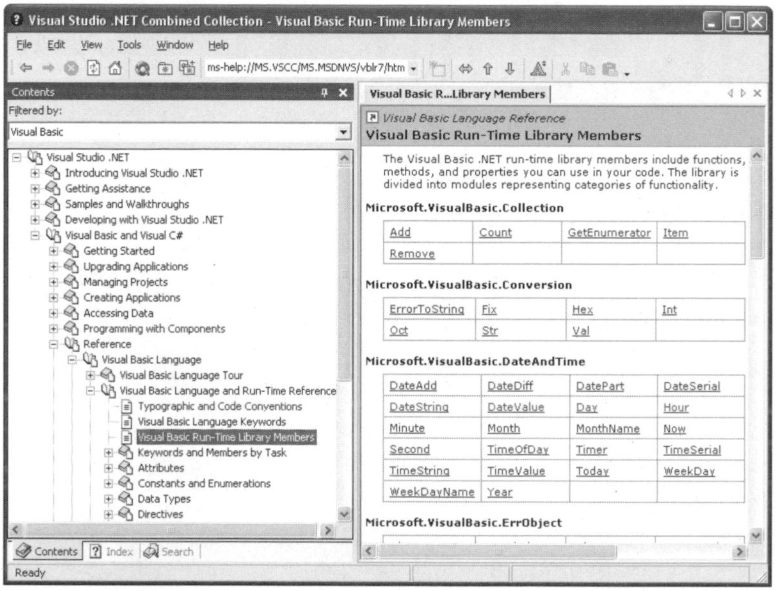

Figure 6-1 Expand the topics in the left pane to display the listing of built-in functions shown here in the right pane.

At this point, the Help window should display the page shown in Figure 6-1. This page lists not only the built in functions, but also built-in properties and methods grouped into the following categories:

■ **Collection functions** These functions manipulate groups of objects. Each choice in a drop-down menu, for example, is one object in a collection.

■ **Conversion functions** These functions convert data items from one type to another.

■ **DateAndTime functions** These functions modify and manipulate *Date* values. For example, these functions can determine the difference between two dates in any unit of measure you want, add and subtract intervals to and from dates, and return parts of a date such as the month, day, year, hour, minute, second, and day of the week.

- ***ErrObject* functions**   These functions work with a special object that Visual Basic .NET uses to communicate information about exceptions.

- ***FileSystem* functions**   These functions open, close, read, and update files and folders on your disk or on a network file server.

- ***Financial* functions**   These functions perform accounting calculations, such as loan payments and compound interest.

- ***Globals* properties**   These properties provide information about the version of Visual Basic .NET you're running.

- ***Interaction* functions**   These functions provide a way to request certain kinds of assistance from Microsoft Windows. For example, you can make the PC speaker beep, display a message box, or make a given form the active window on the Windows desktop.

- ***Strings* functions**   These functions manipulate *String* values. For example, you can search for occurrences of one string within another, extract portions of a string, replace all occurrences of one string with another, convert case, and convert characters to and from numeric identifiers.

- ***VbMath* functions**   These functions generate random numbers. (Yes, this is what they're supposed to do, and no, this isn't like that trigonometry class you had so much trouble with.)

An Incredibly Brief Introduction to Properties and Methods

Each different type of object (that is, each class) has its own uniquely suited properties and methods.

A *property* is a Data value that you access by coding a period and a name after the name of an object. All *Array* objects, for example, have a *Length* property. If you have an array named *intScores*, then the expression *intScores.Length* returns the total number of elements in all the dimensions of the array.

A *method* is a function or subroutine value that you access by coding a period and a name after the name of an object. All *String* objects have a method called *EndsWith* that determines whether the last few characters of a string match a given value. The expression *strBeans.EndsWith("Kidney")* returns *True* if the last six characters of the string equal Kidney and *False* in any other case.

In all cases, the exact properties and methods available for an object depend on the object's type.

If you look up the sequence of topics already shown in Figure 6-1 and click Keywords And Members By Task in the left pane, the Help page shown in Figure 6-2 appears. This provides a second index to the same functions as those that appeared previously.

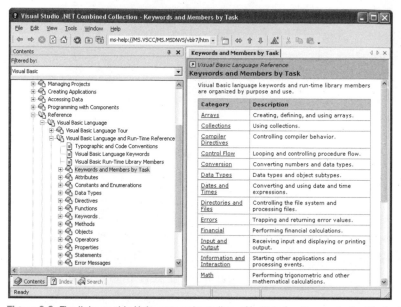

Figure 6-2 The links on this Help page point to lists of built-in functions organized by task.

To look up built-in functions alphabetically, click the Functions topic heading that appears under the Visual Basic Language And Run-Time Reference heading. If you know the name of the function you want, display the Help system's Index window and type the function name.

When you find the Help page for the function you want, you might be surprised to find a function declaration like the following (a picture of the corresponding Help page appears in Figure 6-3).

```
Public Function Choose( _
   ByVal Index As Double, _
   ByVal ParamArray Choice() As Object _
) As Object
```

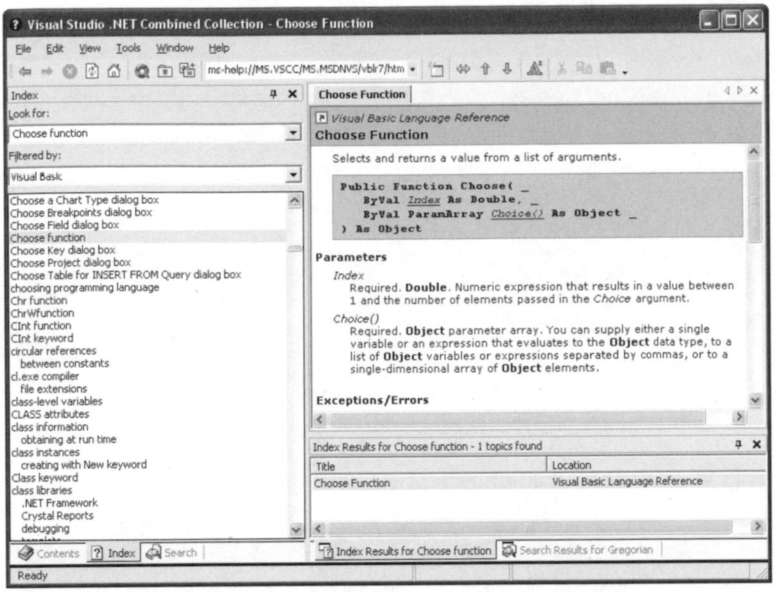

Figure 6-3 The documentation for built-in functions usually shows how you would declare the function if you were writing it.

This is the declaration you would use if you were going to write the built-in function yourself. Of course, Microsoft knows you wouldn't do that. Imagine, however, that you wanted to know how to call a custom function that you wrote yourself. How would you look this up? You'd look at the function declaration, right? That's how programmers think and that's why Help pages show you the declarations for built-in functions.

You should know that the full name of each Visual Basic .NET built-in function begins with the qualifier *Microsoft.VisualBasic*. Normally this isn't a concern and you can just code the short name of the function. Occasionally, however, the name of a built-in function might conflict with a property or method name. This happens, for example, when you try to use the *Left* function inside a form module, because all forms have a property named *Left*. If you try to use the *Left* function in this situation without specifying *Microsoft.VisualBasic.Left*, the compiler generates an error message claiming abuse of the form's *Left* property. Your options in this case are the following:

- Use the fully qualified function name (that is, *Microsoft.VisualBasic.Left*).

- Use a different function that still accomplishes what you want.

The next few sections briefly introduce some of the most useful built-in functions. For more detail, consult the Help pages.

Using Type Conversion Functions

Table 6-1 lists functions built into Visual Basic .NET for converting one data type to another. These functions accept arguments of almost any data type and convert them to the types listed. If the conversion isn't possible, the function raises an exception.

Table 6-1   Visual Basic .NET Type Conversion Functions

Result Data Type	Function	Description
Integer	Asc	Converts the first letter in a string to a number between -32,768 and 32,767 or, if the operating system doesn't support double-byte characters, between 0 and 255. Asc("A") returns 65, the ASCII (and Unicode) value for A.
Integer	AscW	Converts the first letter in a string to a number between 0 and 65535.
Boolean	CBool	Returns False if the argument is zero and True otherwise.
Char	CChar	Returns the character corresponding to argument values 0–65,535. For example, CChar(65) returns A.
String	Chr	Returns the character corresponding to argument values 0–255 or, if the operating system supports double-byte characters, between –32,768 and 65,535. Using Windows 2000 and Windows XP, CChar and Chr are synonymous.
String Byte Short Integer Long Date Single Double Decimal Object	CStr CByte CShort CInt CLng CDate CSng CDbl CDec CObj	Each of these functions converts an expression to the data type in the first column. If the value of the expression makes this impossible, an exception occurs. Attempting to evaluate the following expression, for example, raises an exception: CDate("glamour model")

Logical Functions

Visual Basic .NET supports all the logical functions listed in Table 6-2. The *Choose*, *Iif*, *Partition*, and *Switch* functions provide alternatives to the *If* and *Select Case* statements. The others test for special conditions you can't detect using normal comparison operators.

Table 6-2   Visual Basic .NET Logical Functions

Result Type	Function	Description
Object	Choose	Selects and returns a value from a list of arguments.
Object	IIf	Returns one of two objects, depending on the evaluation of an expression.
Boolean	IsDbNull	Returns a Boolean value indicating whether an expression evaluates to the System.DBNull class.
Boolean	IsError	Returns a Boolean value indicating whether an expression is an Error value.
Boolean	IsNothing	Returns a Boolean value indicating whether an expression has no object assigned to it.
Boolean	IsNumeric	Returns a Boolean value indicating whether Visual Basic .NET can convert an expression to a number.
Boolean	IsReference	Returns a Boolean value of True if the expression represents an Object variable that currently has no object assigned to it; otherwise, it returns False.
String	Partition	Returns a string indicating where a number occurs within a calculated series of ranges.
Object	Switch	Evaluates a list of expressions and returns a Variant value or an expression associated with the first expression in the list that's True.

The *Choose* function expects to receive an *Index* value followed by a series of expressions. If the *Index* value is 1, *Choose* evaluates and returns the first expression. If the *Index* value is 2, *Choose* evaluates the second expression, and so forth. Here's an example where the index is an integer variable named *intNum*:

```
strHobby = Choose(intNum, "Cycling", "Hiking", "Running")
```

The *IIf* function evaluates one of two expressions depending on whether an expression is *True* or *False*. Here's a case in point:

```
strStatus = IIf(dteArrival < #9:00 AM#, "Early", "Late")
```

The *Partition* function is a strange one. Here are its syntax and a typical statement:

```
Partition(Number, Start, Stop, Interval)
Partition(lngAge, 0, 74, 25)
```

When Visual Basic .NET evaluates this statement, it sets up a series of numeric ranges such as the following:

Range Name	Low Value	High Value
"0: 24"	0	24
"25: 49"	25	49
"50: 74"	50	74

The ranges start at the *Start* value and increase by *Interval* until they reach the *Stop* value. Visual Basic .NET then determines which range the given *Number* falls within and returns the name of that range as a string. For example, after Visual Basic .NET executes the following expression, *strBracket* will contain "25: 49":

```
strBracket = Partition(37, 0, 74, 25)
```

The *Switch* function interprets a list of paired expressions and values. If the first argument you pass to *Switch* is *True*, *Switch* evaluates and returns the second argument. If the third argument is *True*, *Switch* returns the fourth argument, and so on. Here's an example.

```
strHelper = Switch(strColor = "Cyan", "Cathy", _
                   strSize = "Small", "Stan", _
                   strToss = "Tails", "Talia", _
                   strGain = "Great", "Gary")
```

If *strColor* is Blue, *strSize* is Large, and *strToss* is Tails, this statement assigns Talia as *strHelper*, regardless of the value of *strGain*.

If none of the odd-numbered arguments are *True*, *Switch* returns the special value Nothing, indicating that a variable contains no value at all, not even zero or an empty string. If you want the *Switch* function to return a default value, code *True* and the value you want as the last two arguments.

Manipulating Dates

Like all other .NET languages and components, Visual Basic .NET stores times and dates as 64-bit integers that count the number of 100-nanosecond "ticks" since midnight, Coordinated Universal Time, January 1 of the year 1 in the Gregorian calendar. The Time value for one second after midnight on 1-Jan-0001 is 10,000,000.

Note   Coordinated Universal Time (UTC) is what you probably know as Greenwich Mean Time (GMT). UTC is the newer term that Microsoft uses in all its documentation.

One good thing about this date format is that comparisons involving dates and times are very easy. Equality comparisons are easy, too, provided that both values are accurate within 100 nanoseconds. Other kinds of date operations, however, would be difficult without the built-in functions described in Table 6-3.

Table 6-3   Visual Basic .NET *Date* Functions

Result Type	Name	Description	Argument Type
Boolean	IsDate	Indicates whether Visual Basic .NET can convert an expression to a date.	String
Date	DateAdd	Adds a specified interval.	Date
Date	DateSerial	Returns the *Date* value for a given year, month, and day.	Integers
Date	TimeSerial	Returns the *Date* value for a given hour, minute, and second.	Integers
Date	TimeValue	Returns the *Date* value for a given time.	String
Date	DateValue	Returns the *Date* value for a given date.	String
Integer	DatePart	Returns the specified part of a given date.	Date
Integer	Year	Returns the year.	Date
Integer	Month	Returns the month of the year.	Date
Integer	Day	Returns the day of the month.	Date
Integer	Hour	Returns the hour of the day.	Date
Integer	Minute	Returns the minute of the hour.	Date
Integer	Second	Returns the second of the minute.	Date
Integer	Weekday	Returns the day of the week.	Date
Long	DateDiff	Returns the number of intervals between two dates. You can specify intervals of minutes, days, years, and so on.	Strings, Dates
String	MonthName	Returns the name of a given month.	Integer
String	WeekdayName	Returns the name of a given day of the week.	Integer

---

Note   The *Date* type in Visual Basic .NET corresponds directly to the *DateTime* class in the Microsoft .NET Framework. As a result, all the properties and methods that the .NET *DateTime* class provides are available Visual Basic .NET *Date* variables.

The *IsDate* function is most useful for validating data that enters your program. Suppose, for example, that you have a text box named *txtDate* where the user is supposed to enter a date. To process this date, you'd probably start out by converting the text box value (a string) to a *Date* value. Here's the code:

```
Dim dteUserDate As Date
dteUserDate = CDate(txtDate.Text)
```

Unfortunately, a problem occurs if the user enters an invalid date such as 13/13/13. When the *CDate* function tries to process this value, it throws an exception. This is where the *IsDate* function comes to the rescue. The following code would avoid the exception:

```
Dim dteUserDate As Date

If IsDate(txtDate.Text) Then
    dteUserDate = CDate(txtDate.Text)
Else
    MsgBox(txtDate.Text & " isn't a valid date.")
End If
```

The *DateAdd* function takes three arguments: an interval code, an amount, and a date. The *DateInterval* call in the following statement adds one day to 2/28/2003. The statement therefore displays 3/1/2003. To subtract an interval, specify a negative number:

```
MsgBox(DateAdd(DateInterval.Day, 1, #2/28/2003#))
```

Tip The interval codes that the *DateAdd* function uses would be a nuisance to remember except that Microsoft Visual Studio remembers them for you. As soon as you type **DateAdd**, Visual Studio displays a selection list of available choices. Just highlight the interval you want and then press Tab.

The *DateDiff* function returns the difference between two dates. In the following code, for example, the message box displays 72 (which is 3 days). This function uses the same interval codes as *DateAdd*, and you can enter them just as easily:

```
Dim dteStart As Date = #5/30/2003#
Dim dteEnd As Date = #6/2/2003#
MsgBox(DateDiff(DateInterval.Hour, dteStart, dteEnd))
```

The *DateSerial* function returns the *Date* value for an Integer month, day, and year. The following expression, for example, returns the *Date* value for March 15, 2010. The *TimeSerial* function similarly returns a *Date* value based on a given hour, minute, and second:

```
DateSerial(2010, 3, 15)
```

One nice feature of the *DateSerial* and *TimeSerial* functions is that their argument values can exceed the normal range. To create a *Date* value 20 months from March 15, 2010 you could code the following expression, which returns November 15, 2011:

```
DateSerial(2010, 20 + 3, 15)
```

The *DateValue* and *TimeValue* functions both convert *String* values to *Date* values. The *DateValue* function ignores any *Time* values the string might contain, and the *TimeValue* function ignores any *Date* values. To convert dates, times, or both together, use the *CDate* function.

The remaining functions return selected parts of a *Data* value. The *Day* function, for example, returns the day of the month. The *Month* function returns the month of the year, and so forth. In the following code, the message box displays 6:

```
Dim dteTree As Date = #6/1/2003#
MsgBox(Month(dteTree))
```

To get the current date, the current time, or both, simply code one of these special property names:

Now	The current date and time
Today	The current date
Time Of Day	The current time4

The following expression, for example, always returns tomorrow's date:

```
DateAdd(DateInterval.Day, 1, Today)
```

When it comes to formatting dates and times for display, Visual Basic .NET provides overwhelming flexibility. For starters, there's a *FormatDateTime* function that converts dates to any of several predefined formats. Here's an example.

```
FormatDateTime(myDate, DateFormat.LongDate)
```

Note   Windows Control Panel settings on the local computer determine the exact results that predefined formats like *LongDate* and *ShortTime* produce.

For more flexibility, try the *Format* function, which uses custom formats as well as predefined ones. If you run the following code, for example, the message box displays 04-Jul-2004:

```
Dim dteStart As Date = #7/4/2004#
MsgBox(Format(dteStart, "dd-MMM-yyyy"))
```

For more information about the *FormatDateTime* and *Format* functions, choose Index from the Visual Studio Help menu and search for those function names.

Manipulating Strings

String-handling functions split, join, transform, and otherwise modify *String* data. Table 6-4 lists the *String* functions that Visual Basic .NET provides.

Table 6-4   Visual Basic .NET *String* Handling Functions

Result Type	Function	Description
Integer	*StrComp*	Compares two strings and returns the result.
Long	*Len*	Returns the number of characters in a string or the number of bytes required to store a variable.
Long	*InStr*	Returns the first position of one string within another, searching from left to right.
Long	*InStrRev*	Returns the first position of one string within another, searching from right to left.
Char	*GetChar*	Returns the character from the specified index in a given string.
String	*Mid*	Returns a specified number of characters from a specified position within a given string.
String	*Left*	Returns a specified number of characters from the left side of a string.
String	*Right*	Returns a specified number of characters from the right side of a string.
String	*Ltrim*	Returns the argument string with leading spaces removed.
String	*Rtrim*	Returns the argument string with trailing spaces removed.
String	*Trim*	Returns the argument string with leading and trailing spaces removed.
String	*LCase*	Converts the argument string to lowercase.
String	*UCase*	Converts the argument string to uppercase.
String	*StrConv*	Converts the argument string to a different case or character width.
String	*StrReverse*	Reverses the order of the characters in the argument string.
String	*RSet*	Returns the argument string with spaces added at the beginning, so that the string is a specified length and will be right-aligned with other strings of the same length.
String	*LSet*	Returns the argument string with spaces added at the end, so that the string is a specified length and will be left-aligned with other strings of the same length.
String	*Replace*	Replaces one substring with another a specified number of times.
String	*Space*	Returns a specified number of spaces.
String	*StrDup*	Returns the argument character repeated a specific number of times.

The *LTrim* function removes all spaces from the left side of a string. *RTrim* removes all spaces from the right and *Trim* removes all spaces from both ends.

The *Left*, *Right*, *Mid*, and *GetChar* functions all retrieve portions of a string. The expression *Left(strName, 3)*, for example, retrieves the leftmost three characters from the *String* value in the *strName* variable. *Right(strName, 4)* retrieves the rightmost four characters.

The *Mid* function retrieves a specified number of characters starting at some point within the string. *Mid(strName, 3, 4)* returns the third, fourth, fifth, and sixth characters in *strName*. If you omit the third argument, *Mid* returns all the characters from the starting position to the end of the string. *GetChar* works a lot like *Mid* except that it always returns a single character. As such, you don't code a length. *GetChar("Hamlet", 3)* returns *m*.

UCase converts a string to uppercase and *LCase* converts one to lowercase. *StrConv* converts a string to any case you want. The following statement displays This Is The String. As usual, Visual Studio displays a selection list of options for the second parameter:

```
MsgBox(StrConv("THIS is THE string.", VbStrConv.ProperCase))
```

The *InStr* function searches from left to right for one string within another, The expression *InStr("Walla Walla", "all")* returns 2 because the first occurrence of *all* begins at the second character. To begin the search at the second or later character, supply a number as the first argument. To override the default string comparison method, code *CompareMethod.Binary* or *CompareMethod.Text* as an additional argument at the right. The following expression, for example, returns 8:

```
MsgBox(InStr(3, "Walla Walla", "ALL", CompareMethod.Text))
```

The *InStrRev* function is similar to *InStr* but searches from right to left. *InStrRev("Walla Walla", "all")* returns 8. Even though the search begins from the right, the return value measures characters from the left. Another difference is that the starting position, if you specify one, has to be the third argument rather than the first one. You measure the start position from the left, by the way, even though the search is from the right. The following expression returns 2:

```
InStrRev("Walla Walla", "ALL", 7, CompareMethod.Text))
```

Both *InStr* and *InStrRev* return 0 if they fail to find a match. If you search for an empty string, both return the starting position.

The *Replace* function replaces occurrences of one string within another. The expression *Replace("looking good", "oo", "a")* would return *lacking gad*. A fourth parameter can specify a starting position, a fifth can specify a maximum number of replacements, and a sixth can specify the compare mode.

Space and *StrDup* both return strings with a repeating value. *Space* returns as many spaces as you specify: *Space(10)* returns a string of 10 spaces, for example. *StrDup(5, "x")* returns five xs.

Using Array Functions

Visual Basic .NET provides the array-related functions listed in Table 6-5.

Table 6-5 Visual Basic .NET Array Functions

Result Type	Function	Description
Array	Filter	Returns a subset of a *String* array containing only those elements that contain (or don't contain) a specified string.
Array	Split	Converts a delimited string into a one-dimensional array, based on the specified delimiter.
Boolean	IsArray	Indicates whether a variable is an array.
Long	Lbound	Returns the smallest available subscript for the indicated dimension of an array. In Visual Basic .NET, this is always zero.
Long	Ubound	Returns the largest available subscript for the indicated dimension of an array.
String	Join	Converts an array into a delimited string, inserting the specified delimiter between the values of each former array element.

The *Ubound* function in particular is worth noting, because it always returns an up-to-date value for the maximum subscript of a table. This is important because the size of an array tends to change over time. Suppose, for example, that you declared the table, the variables, and the loop in this code:

```
Dim strSports() As String = {"Baseball", "Football", "Hockey"}
Dim booIsASport As Boolean
Dim intPos As Integer
Dim strActivity As String = "Cycling"
booIsASport = False
For intPos = 0 to 2
    If strActivity = strSports(intPos) Then
        booIsASport = True
    End If
Next intPos
```

The *For* loop compares the *strActivity* variable to each element of the *strSports* table and sets *booIsASport* to *True* if it finds a match. Now, suppose you decide that cycling is a sport and add it to the *strSports* array. Are you absolutely sure you'll remember to change the maximum value in the *For* loop? What if you enlarge or shrink the array using a *ReDim* statement? For these reasons, it's much better to code the loop as shown here:

```
For intPos = 0 to UBound(strSports)
```

The *LBound* statement returns the minimum permissible subscript for an array. This makes it tempting to code the *For* statement:

```
For intPos = LBound(strSports) to UBound(strSports)
```

Resist that temptation if you're using Visual Basic .NET, however, because in Visual Basic .NET, *LBound* values other than zero are impossible. The presence of the *LBound* statement is a carryover from earlier versions of Visual Basic.

The *Join* function forms a *String* value that contains the first value from an array, then a delimiter (such as a comma), then the second value from the array, then another delimiter, and so forth. After executing the following statements, the *strStateList* variable would contain Gas,Liquid,Solid:

```
Dim strStates() As String = {"Gas", "Liquid", "Solid"}
Dim strStateList As String
strStateList = Join(strStates, ",")
```

The *Split* function does the reverse—it breaks apart a string based on some delimiter and puts the results in an array. The second statement here, for example, would set the size of the array to five elements. The elements themselves would contain Elm, Maple, Oak, Pine, and Sumac:

```
Dim strTrees() As String
strTrees = Split("Elm,Maple,Oak,Pine,Sumac", ",")
```

The *Filter* function forms one array from another. However, the destination array contains only those elements from the source array that contain a specified string. Here's an example.

```
Dim strElms() As String = {"earth", "air", "fire", "water"}
Dim strIrs() As String
strIrs = Filter(strElms, "ir")
```

After the last statement executes, the *strIrs* array would contain two elements: one containing air and one containing fire. That's because air and fire both contain the string *ir*, whereas earth and water don't.

Generating Random Numbers

Visual Basic .NET provides exactly one random number generator, a function named *Rnd()* that returns a pseudo-random Double between 0 and 1. After the following statements execute, the *dblWhoKnows* variable contains a random number between 0 and 1:

```
Dim dblWhoKnows As Double
dblWhoKnows = Rnd()
```

If you need random numbers in a different range, such as 25 to 75, just multiply the *Rnd()* result by the difference and add the starting value. In the following expression, *(Rnd() * 50)* returns a random number between 0 and 50. Adding an offset of 25 makes the complete expression return a value in the desired range:

```
25 + (Rnd() * 50)
```

The *Rnd()* function never returns a result of exactly 0 or exactly 1. As a result, the expression

```
Int(Rnd() * 10)
```

will never return 10. If you want random integral numbers between 0 and 10 inclusive, you need to code one of the following expressions:

```
Int(Rnd() * 11)
Int((Rnd() * 10) + 0.5)
```

Note, however, that the second expression will only return zero 5 percent of the time; that is, when the *Rnd()* function returns a number between 0 and 0.05. The first expression is therefore superior.

Note   The *Int* function returns the integral portion of a fractional number. For example, *Int(35.9)* equals 35. If you want a rounded result, add 0.5 to the argument expression.

Clearly, the generation of random numbers is too important to be left to chance. In this spirit, *Rnd()* actually generates *pseudo-random* numbers. This means that behind the scenes, the *Rnd()* function uses a mathematical formula to produce predictable results that only *look* random. If you use the *Rnd()* function in one of your programs, you'll find that it generates the same series of random numbers every time the program runs. To avoid this, you should call the *Randomize()* function at least once before calling *Rnd()*. Each time you call *Randomize()*, it initializes the random number generator to a different *Seed value*. This ensures that *Rnd()* produces a different set of random numbers each time your program runs.

If you want, you can specify your own seed value when you call *Randomize()*. If you don't specify a seed value, *Randomize()* uses the value of the system timer as a seed. This default is usually a good choice.

Example: Shuffling Cards

To illustrate a number of built-in functions, this example initializes, shuffles, and displays the playing cards in a standard deck.

Initialize the Deck

There are many ways to represent a deck of cards but this program uses an array of 52 Integers. The values 2 through 10 indicate deuce through 10. The values 11 through 14 represent jack, queen, king, and ace. If the suit is clubs, add 100. The three of clubs is therefore 103. For diamonds, hearts, and spades, add 200, 300, and 400, respectively. Are you ready to start? Follow these steps:

1 Launch Visual Studio .NET and create a new Windows Application project named Shuffle.

2 Set the *Text* property of the default form to Shuffle Cards.

3 Add three buttons and a list box to the default form. Assign the following names and *Text* values to each control and arrange them as shown in Figure 6-4:

Control	(Name) Property	Text Property
First Button	*btnNewDeck*	New Deck
Second Button	*btnShuffle*	Shuffle
Third Button	*btnExit*	Exit
List Box	*lstDeck*	n/a

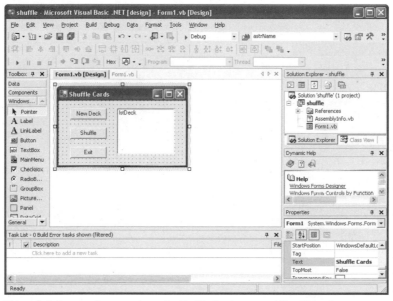

Figure 6-4 Arrange the controls on the Shuffle Cards program like this.

4 Double-click the form background. This should display a subroutine named *Form1_Load*. This subroutine automatically runs the first time your program loads the form into memory, which, in this case, means every time the program starts.

5 Add the following statements between the *Sub Form1_Load* statement and the *End Sub* statement. These call subroutines that the next few steps instruct you to write:

```
InitializeDeck()
DisplayDeck()
```

6 Scroll to the top of the code window and locate the first two statements shown next. Then add the third statement, which for clarity appears here in boldface. This declares the array that represents the deck of cards.

```
Public Class Form1
    Inherits System.Windows.Forms.Form
Dim intDeck(51) As Integer
```

7 Scroll back down to the *Form1_Load* subroutine and add the following statements after its *End Sub* statement:

```
Sub InitializeDeck()
End Sub
Sub DisplayDeck()
End Sub
```

8 The *InitializeDeck* subroutine populates the *intDeck* array with the proper code for each card in the deck. To start creating it, add the following declarations immediately after the *Sub InitializeDeck* statement you entered in the previous step:

```
Dim intSuit As Integer = 100
Dim intRank As Integer = 2
Dim intCard As Integer
```

The *intSuit* and *intRank* variables contain the current card's suit and rank. The *intCard* variable contains the card's position in the deck.

9 Add the following code after the declarations you entered in step 8:

```
For intCard = 0 To UBound(intDeck)
    intDeck(intCard) = intSuit + intRank
    If intRank < 14 Then
        intRank += 1
    Else
        intSuit += 100
        intRank = 2
    End If
Next intCard
```

The first statement starts a *For* loop that varies the *intCard* variable from zero to the maximum valid subscript for the *intDeck* array. This ensures that the loop processes all 52 cards. The second statement adds the current suit and rank (initially 100 and 2) and stores the result as the value of the current card.

The next six statements increment the *intRank* and *intSuit* variables. If *intRank* is less than 14, the code simply adds one to *intRank*. This advances from, say, the deuce of clubs to the three of clubs. However, if *intRank* is 14 (signifying ace), it's time to start a new suit. The code therefore adds 100 to *intSuit* and resets *intRank* to 2 (signifying the deuce).

The last two statements simply terminate the *If* statement and the *For* statement. This completes the code for the *InitializeDeck* subroutine.

10 The *DisplayDeck* subroutine displays the contents of the deck in the *listDeck* list box. To begin creating it, add the following declarations immediately after the *Sub DisplayDeck* statement you entered in step 7:

```
Dim intSuit As Integer
Dim intRank As Integer
Dim intCard As Integer
Dim strDeck As String = ""
```

The first three variables serve the same purpose as those in the *InitializeDeck* subroutine. The *strDeck* variable contains the character representation of a card, such as "7 S" for the seven of spades.

11 Add the following statement after the declarations you entered in step 10. This statement erases the current contents of the *lstDeck* list box.

```
lstDeck.Items.Clear()
```

12 Immediately after the statement you coded in step 11, add the *For* loop shown next. This sets the *intCard* variable to each valid subscript of the *intDeck* array.

```
For intCard = 0 To UBound(intDeck)
Next
```

13 Add the statements shown here in boldface to the loop you created in step 12:

```
For intCard = 0 To UBound(intDeck)
    intSuit = intDeck(intCard) \ 100
    intRank = intDeck(intCard) Mod 100
Next intCard
```

The first new statement divides the current card value by 100 to get the suit value. For all club cards—102 (the deuce of clubs), 111 (the jack of clubs), and so forth—dividing by 100 returns 1. For all diamonds the same division returns 2, and so forth.

The second new statement gets the remainder of dividing the current card value by 100. For example, the remainder from dividing the five of hearts—305—by 100 is 5.

14 To represent the card rank as a character, enter the following statement after those you added in step 13:

```
If intRank < 11 Then
    strDeck = CStr(intRank)
Else
    strDeck = Choose(intRank - 10, "J", "Q", "K", "A")
End If
```

If the rank is less than 11 (that is, 2–10) you can simply convert it to a *String* value and be done. Otherwise, the code subtracts 10 (so that 11, the jack, equals 1; 12, the queen, equals 2; and so forth) and feeds this into a *Choose* function that returns J, Q, K, or A.

15 Next, append a space and a suit abbreviation to the *strDeck* value you derived in step 14. Because step 13 set the *intSuit* value to 1 through 4 for clubs through spades, this is an easy job for the *Choose* function. Add this statement after the code from step 14.

```
strDeck &= " " & Choose(intSuit, "C", "D", "H", "S")
```

16 Finally, add the card to the list box. This requires entering the statement shown here in boldface. The entire *DisplayDeck* subroutine appears here for reference:

```
Sub DisplayDeck()
    Dim intSuit As Integer
    Dim intRank As Integer
    Dim intCard As Integer
    Dim strDeck As String = ""
    lstDeck.Items.Clear()
    For intCard = 0 To UBound(intDeck)
        intSuit = intDeck(intCard) \ 100
        intRank = intDeck(intCard) Mod 100
        If intRank < 11 Then
            strDeck = CStr(intRank)
        Else
            strDeck = Choose(intRank - 10, "J", "Q", "K", "A")
        End If
        strDeck &= " " & Choose(intSuit, "C", "D", "H", "S")
        lstDeck.Items.Add(strDeck)
    Next intCard
End Sub
```

17 Save your work by choosing Save All from the File menu. Then, press F5 to run the program. The names of the 52 cards should appear in the List box but none of the buttons will work. To end the program, click the Close box in the top right corner of the window.

Shuffle the Cards

This procedure explains how to add code that shuffles the deck of cards you created in the shuffle program. With the project still open in Visual Studio, proceed as follows.

1 To begin writing the subroutine that shuffles the cards, add the following statements after the *End Sub* statement that marks the end of the *DisplayDeck* subroutine:

```
Sub ShuffleDeck()
End Sub
```

2 The strategy for shuffling the cards will be to pick a random number between 0 and 51, then exchange the card at that position with the first card in the deck. (Note that there should be a 1 in 52 chance of the first card remaining in place.) Next, the program will pick a random number between 1 and 51 and exchange that card with the second card in the deck. Then it picks a number between 2 and 51 and exchanges the third card. This continues until no cards remain. To start this process, add the following declarations between the statements you entered in step 1:

```
Dim intCard As Integer
Dim intSwap As Integer
Dim intTemp As Integer
```

The *intCard* variable, as before, will point to a specific card in the *intDeck* array. The *intSwap* variable will identify the second card in each exchange. The *intTemp* variable will hold one of the card values during an exchange.

3 Code a *Randomize()* statement immediately after the variables you declared in the previous step. This ensures that the program doesn't shuffle the cards the same way every time it runs.

```
Randomize()
```

4 Next, add a loop that varies the *intCard* value from zero to one less than the number of cards in the deck. (The reason for not processing all 52 cards is the futility of exchanging the last card with itself.) Here's the code:

```
For intCard = 0 To UBound(intDeck) - 1
Next
```

5 Within this loop, choose a card to exchange with the current card. In other words, add this statement:

```
intSwap = intCard + _
    Fix(Rnd() * (UBound(intDeck) + 1 - intCard))
```

To appreciate this statement, imagine that *intCard* is 20. The program needs to exchange this card with one in a random position between 20 and 51.

● The expression *UBound(intDeck) + 1 – intCard* equals 32 because 51 + 1 – 20 = 32. This is the number of cards between the twentieth card and the end of the deck.

- Multiplying this expression by *Rnd()* produces a random floating-point number between 0.0 and 32.0 (but never exactly 0 and never exactly 32).

- The *Fix* function converts the floating-point number to a random integer between 0 and 31.

- Adding the *intCard* value 20 produces a random integer between 20 and 51.

6   Next, verify that the location of the current card and the location of the random card are different. Unless they are, there's no point in swapping them. Add this code next in sequence.

```
If intSwap <> intCard Then
End If
```

7   Within the *If* statement you just coded, swap the card at *intCard* and the one at *intSwap*. This requires the statements that appear next in boldface:

Tip   Whenever you swap two values, you must temporarily store one of them in a holding area. Otherwise, when you copy the first value to the second one, you lose track of the second value.

```
Sub ShuffleDeck()
    Dim intCard As Integer
    Dim intSwap As Integer
    Dim intTemp As Integer
    Randomize()
    For intCard = 0 To UBound(intDeck) - 1
        intSwap = intCard + _
            Fix(Rnd() * (UBound(intDeck) + 1 - intCard))
        If intSwap <> intCard Then
            intTemp = intDeck(intSwap)
            intDeck(intSwap) = intDeck(intCard)
            intDeck(intCard) = intTemp
        End If
    Next intCard
End Sub
```

This completes the *ShuffleDeck* subroutine. The entire subroutine appears here for reference.

8   All that remains now is adding the code that clicking the buttons executes. To begin, click the Form1.vb [Design] tab in Visual Studio and then double-click New Deck. This displays the first and last statements shown here. Between them, add the statements shown in boldface.

These are the same two statements that you added to the *Form1_Load* subroutine.

```
Private Sub btnNewDeck_Click( _
            ByVal sender As System.Object, _
            ByVal e As System.EventArgs) _
            Handles btnNewDeck.Click
    InitializeDeck()
    DisplayDeck()
End Sub
```

The first statement just shown, by the way, will actually appear on one long line rather than continued across four lines.

9 Click the Form1.vb [Design] tab again and then double-click Shuffle. This displays the *btnShuffle_Click* subroutine shown here. Add the statements shown in boldface:

```
Private Sub btnShuffle_Click( _
            ByVal sender As System.Object, _
            ByVal e As System.EventArgs) _
            Handles btnShuffle.Click
    ShuffleDeck()
    DisplayDeck()
End Sub
```

These statements shuffle and then redisplay the deck.

10 Click the Form1.vb [Design] tab a third time and then double-click Exit. Within the resulting *btnExit_Click* subroutine, enter this statement:

```
Me.Close()
```

The reserved word *Me* always refers to the object that contains it. In this case, that object is the program's one and only form. The *Close* method closes this form and that, in turn, quits the program.

11 Choose Save All from the File menu to save your work, then press F5 to run the program. The deck should still come up sorted when the program starts, but clicking Shuffle should rearrange it. (The screen shots here show the deck before and after shuffling.) Clicking New Deck should display a new, perfectly sorted deck. Clicking Exit should terminate the program.

Try This!   If you have any questions about what the *Randomize( )* statement does, try commenting it out. (To do this, simply type an apostrophe in front of it.) Start the program, shuffle the deck, and take note of the first few cards. Then quit the program, restart it, and shuffle. The same sequence of cards appears. Uncommenting the *Randomize* statement should ensure that you get a different result each time.

Key Points

■   The MSDN Library (which Visual Studio .NET provides through Help) provides the best way to look for built-in functions and find out how to use them.

■   Type Conversion functions convert values from one data type to another. If a conversion is possible, there's probably a built-in function that does it.

■   Logical functions are useful for making comparisons that operators can't. Also, in some situations, a logical function can do in one line what *If* and *Select Case* statements would take many lines to do.

■   Visual Basic .NET provides an abundance of functions for working with *Date* values. These make it easy to perform date arithmetic and extract portions of dates.

■   Built-in functions strongly support string handling. These functions make it easy to change case, trim leading and trailing spaces, search and replace *String* data, and extract portions of a string.

■   Array functions are useful for getting information about an array, converting arrays to delimited strings, converting delimited strings to arrays, and extracting matching values from an array.

■   The *Rnd( )* function generates an infinite supply of pseudo-random numbers. However, you should call *Randomize( )* at least once before calling *Rnd( )*. Otherwise, you'll get the same series of random numbers every time your program runs.

Chapter 7

Creating Classes and Objects

In the previous chapter you learned how to group statements that performed a specific job into functions and subroutines (at least, that was the plan). This broke the code into small pieces that were easy to understand, and it freed you from duplicating the same code everywhere your program needed the corresponding action to occur. Because functions and subroutines are reasonably self-contained units, it's easy to copy them out of one program and paste them into another.

Or is it? If you wrote another program that used a deck of cards, which functions, subroutines, and data items from the shuffle program would you need to copy? The answer might be obvious now, when you've just finished writing the program, but will it be so obvious a few months from now? What if the program were much larger, with dozens or hundreds of functions, subroutines, and common data items? What if you copied a function into dozens of programs and then found a bug in it? Finding all those programs and applying the same fix would be tedious and prone to error—at best.

To solve these problems, the masterminds of programming invented *objects*. Just as a function or subroutine packages a group of statements together, an object packages a group of related data items, functions, and subroutines together. The result is object-oriented programming, which, you'll soon discover, isn't nearly as difficult as some people claim. The whole point of object-oriented programming is to make life easier, and how could it do that if it were difficult?

The Deal with Objects

To dispel a common misconception, object-oriented programming doesn't necessarily involve graphical user interfaces. Although it's true that forms, buttons, drop-down lists, and text boxes can be objects, so can all sorts of things that have no visual aspect at all. Dates, arrays, orders, databases, tables, records, fields, and even decks of cards can be objects. The Microsoft .NET Framework includes more than 16,000 kinds of prewritten objects, and with this many available, it's a cinch that sooner or later you'll find some of them useful. Of course, you can also write your own objects.

As with functions and subroutines, this book addresses the subject of objects by first explaining how to write them. This makes it easier to understand what's going on inside (and therefore how to use) prewritten objects.

A Touch of Class

Now, here comes the first surprise: to write your own object, you don't write an object. Instead, you write a class. A *class*, in this sense, simply means a type of object. You program a type of object—a class—rather than individual objects.

To understand the reason for this, consider how inefficient it would be to program the behavior of, say, one specific deck of cards. If you ever wanted to manipulate another deck of cards, you'd have to redo all the programming (or copy and paste the code, with all the problems that entails). You get much greater benefit from programming the behavior of *any* deck of cards.

If a class is a type of object, why use the term class at all? Why not just call it a type of object? One reason is that the word *type* is already taken—it means a data type. Another reason is to keep the statement that defines a class simple. Here it is; the name of the class replaces *name*.

```
Class name
' Statements go here.
End Class
```

Scrupulous Methods

To make a function or subroutine part of a class, you simply put its code between the *Class* and *End Class* statements. Here's an example. The *InitializeDeck* subroutine comes straight from the *shuffle* program in the previous chapter. The name of this class is *Deck*.

```
Class Deck
    Sub InitializeDeck()
        Dim intSuit As Integer = 100
        Dim intRank As Integer = 2
        Dim intCard As Integer
        For intCard = 0 To UBound(intDeck)
            intDeck(intCard) = intSuit + intRank
            If intRank < 14 Then
                intRank += 1
            Else
                intSuit += 100
                intRank = 2
            End If
        Next
    End Sub
End Class
```

Putting the *InitializeDeck* subroutine inside the *Deck* class makes *Initialize-Deck* a *method* of that class. The same is true of functions; you just put the code that defines them between the *Class* and *End Class* statements and the function becomes a method as well.

Lingo   A *method* is a function or subroutine declared within a class.

Desirable Properties

If you tried to compile the code in the previous section, you'd get an error complaining that you forgot to declare the variable *intDeck*. To remedy this omission, you'd need to declare this variable somewhere between the *Class* and *End Class* statements, but not within any method declaration. Here's an example (the new statement appears in boldface).

```
Class Deck
    Dim intDeck(51) As Integer
    Public Sub InitializeDeck()
'        Statements for InitializeDeck method go here.
    End Sub
End Class
```

Declaring the *intDeck* variable inside the *Deck* class (but not inside any property or method) makes *intDeck* a *property* of that class. It's customary to put such data declarations at the top of the class.

Lingo   A *property* is variable declared within a class but not within any method.

Matters of Scope

When you declare a method or property, you can control how much access the rest of your program has to it. Table 7-1 lists the most common options.

Note   *Public, Friend,* and *Private* aren't the only access attributes, they're simply the most common.

Table 7-1   Common Access Attributes for Class Members

Attribute	Range of Access		
	Within the Same Class	**Within the Same Program**	**Within Other Programs**
Public	Yes	Yes	Yes
Friend	Yes	Yes	No
Private	Yes	No	No

The default access for methods is *Public*. To override this or not rely on the default, you code *Public, Friend,* or *Private* in front of the *Function* or *Sub* statement. Here's an example.

```
Public Sub InitializeDeck()
```

The default access for properties is *Private*. To specify this explicitly or to override it, you code *Public, Friend,* or *Private* instead of *Dim*.

```
Public Cards(51) As Integer
```

Virtually all classes have *Public* or *Friend* properties, *Public* or *Friend* methods, or both. This is how the calling program uses the class.

The need for *Private* properties and methods might be less clear. Many classes, however, have variables and methods designed strictly for use within that class. If code outside the class called these methods or updated these variables, the class could easily malfunction.

In the *Deck* class, for example, making the *intDeck* array *Public* would allow code elsewhere to swap cards, hide aces at the bottom of the deck, manufacture an entire deck of deuces, or practice any other mischief human frailty can conceive. To prevent such misadventures, an experienced programmer would make the *intDeck* array *Private* and then provide methods that manipulate the array in whatever ways the rest of the program requires.

The following points bear repeating, just in case you missed something along the way:

■   A class bundles together any number of data declarations, functions, and subroutines.

- The data declarations are properties.

- The functions and subroutines are methods.

- Properties and methods coded *Private* are only accessible to code inside the class.

- Properties and methods coded *Public* or *Friend* are accessible to code both inside and outside the class.

Creating Objects from Classes

Now that you understand how to write a class, you're probably wondering how to use it. In most cases, this requires creating an object of that class. To use the *Deck* class, for example, you must create a *Deck* object. Here are three ways to do this. The first pair of statements, the third statement, and the fourth statement each declare a *Deck* variable that points to a new *Deck* object. The end result in each case is the same.

```
Dim dckCards As Deck
dckCards = New Deck()

Dim dckCards As New Deck

Dim Emp As Deck = New Deck
```

Are you surprised to see the name of your class—*Deck*—used as if it were a data type? In fact, this is perfectly rational. It simply means the *dckCards* variable will contain a reference to a *Deck* object.

For most purposes, you can think of the *New* keyword as loading a class into memory and giving it a name. This is an important concept. If your program needed two decks of cards, it could load two *Deck* objects like this:

```
Dim dckBlueCards As New Deck
Dim dckRedCards As New Deck
```

Shuffling both of these decks would, in general, produce a different sequence of cards in each deck. This is perfectly acceptable because each instance of an object has its own memory. To initialize and shuffle the first deck you would code:

```
dckBlueCards.InitializeDeck()
dckBlueCards.ShuffleDeck()
```

and for the second deck you would code

```
dckRedCards.InitializeDeck()
dckRedCards.ShuffleDeck()
```

This assumes, of course, that the *Deck* class contains a *Public* or *Friend* subroutine named *InitializeDeck* and a *Public* or *Friend* subroutine named *ShuffleDeck*.

Notice that you call these methods through the object variable (such as *dckBlueCards*), and not using the class name (that is, *Deck*). This is because you might have more than one *Deck* object in memory. Specifying the object variable identifies which object to work on; specifying the class name *Deck* wouldn't.

The rules for accessing properties are pretty much the same as those for methods. You code the name of the object variable, then a period, then the name of the property. If the *Deck* class contains this property declaration:

```
Public Cards(51) as Integer
```

then the following expressions would return the value of the first card in the *dckBlueCards* deck and the first card in the *dckRedCards* deck:

```
dckBlueCards.Cards(0)
dckRedCards.Cards(0)
```

Example 1: Shuffling with Class

To cement your understanding of classes and objects, this exercise converts the deck of cards in the shuffle program from the previous chapter into a class. You'll be surprised how easy and obvious this can be. Just follow these steps:

1   Launch Microsoft Visual Studio .NET and create a new project named shuffleclass.

2   Close any open windows that pertain to Form1.vb. For example, if the main code window displays a tab titled Form1.vb or Form1.vb [Design], click the tab and then its Close box.

3   In Windows Explorer, open the folder where you created the example from the previous chapter. By default, this will be C:\Documents and Settings*user*\My Documents\Visual Studio Projects\Shuffle, where *user* is the name of your Windows logon account.

4   Copy the Form1.vb file from the shuffle folder you located in step 3 to the shuffleclass folder where your new project resides. When Windows displays the Confirm File Replace dialog box, click Yes.

5   With the shuffleclass project still open in Visual Studio .NET, locate the Form1.vb file in the Solution Explorer window and double-click it. The form design and code you created for the shuffle program should appear.

6   In the Solution Explorer window, right-click the shuffleclass project, select Add, then select Add Class.

7 When the Add New Item - Shuffleclass dialog box appears, select Class in the Templates window at the right and specify Deck.vb in the Name box at the bottom. Click Open to create the class. Figure 7-1 shows this operation in progress.

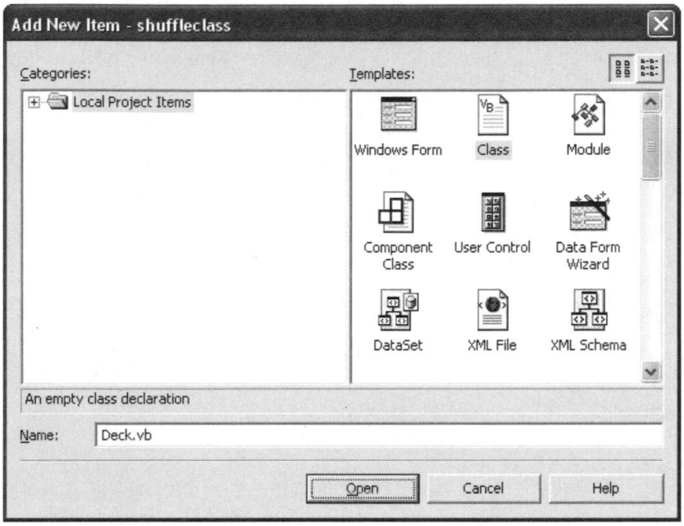

Figure 7-1 This dialog box adds a new class to your project.

8 The Solution Explorer window should now display the file name Deck.vb as a member of the shuffleclass project. The main code window should also have a tab titled Deck.vb. Clicking this tab should display the following code:

```
Public Class Deck
End Class
```

9 Open the code window for Form1.vb. Then, cut the following items out of the Form1.vb window and paste them between the *Class* and *End Class* statements in the Deck.vb window:

● The statement that declares the *intDeck* array:

```
Dim intDeck(51) As Integer.
```

● The entire *InitializeDeck* subroutine (from *Sub* through *End Sub*).

● The entire *ShuffleDeck* subroutine (from *Sub* through *End Sub*). *Don't* cut and paste the *DisplayDeck* subroutine.

10 In the *Dim* statement for the *intDeck* array, replace the keyword *Dim* with *Public*. The statement should then read:

```
Public intDeck(51) As Integer.
```

11 Add the word *Public* in front of each *Sub* statement you copied in
step 9. For example, the declaration for the *InitializeDeck* subroutine
should be:

```
Public Sub InitializeDeck()
```

12 In the code window for Form1.vb, scroll to the top and locate the first
two statements shown next. Then, add the third statement, which for
clarity appears here in boldface. This loads an instance of the *Deck*
class and assigns it to the variable *dckCards*.

```
Public Class Form1
    Inherits System.Windows.Forms.Form
Dim dckCards As New Deck()
```

13 The *DisplayDeck* subroutine, which is still in the Form1.vb file,
contains three references to *intDeck*. Change these references to
dckCards.intDeck. Here's an example.

```
Before: For intCard = 0 To UBound(intDeck)
```

```
After:  For intCard = 0 To UBound(dckCards.intDeck)
```

14 The *Form1_Load* and *btnNewDeck_Click* subroutines each contain a
reference to the *InitializeDeck* method. Change these:

```
From:  InitializeDeck()
To:    dckCards.InitializeDeck()
```

15 The *btnShuffle_Click* subroutine contains a reference to the *Shuffle-
Deck* method. Change this to *dckCards.shuffleDeck*.

16 This completes the changes to the shuffleclass project. To save your
work, select Save All from the File menu.

At this point, if you press F5, you should find that the program runs exactly
as it did before. However, despite the lack of outward change, this is a much
better program than the one in the previous chapter, all because it uses the *Deck*
class. Using a class provides these benefits:

■   The code is grouped into more logical units. The deck of cards is really
a separate entity from the form that displays it, and the code is cleaner
as two separate entities as well.

■   If you ever decide to write another program that involves a deck of
cards, you can just add the Deck.vb file to that project and have a large
part of the work already done.

There are, however, two troubling aspects to the shuffleclass program. First, it was your job to call the *InitializeDeck* method when the program started up. (This was the reason for the *dckCards.InitializeDeck()* statement in the *Form1_Load* subroutine.) It would preferable for the *Deck* class to initialize the deck automatically whenever it creates a *Deck* object. The next section, "Construction and Destruction," explains how to do just that.

Second, any program that uses the *Deck* class can do whatever it wants to the *intDeck* array. *Deck* objects would behave far more predictably if this array was *Private* and programs could only manipulate the deck in specifically permitted ways. A subsequent section, "Using Property Procedures," explains how this is possible.

Construction and Destruction

Many types of objects require some code to run every time the object comes into existence. This code typically sets properties to default values, initializes tables, gets information about the current operating environment, and so forth. To make this code run automatically, you can provide a *constructor method*.

Constructor methods are optional but no class can ever have more than one of them. In Microsoft Visual Basic .NET, a constructor method is always a subroutine named *New*. The following code shows a typical constructor method:

```
Public Class Deck
    Public Sub New()
        InitializeDeck()
    End Sub
    Public Sub InitializeDeck()
'       Contents of InitializeDeck procedure
    End Sub
'       Other properties and methods
End Class
```

The constructor method must be *Public*, but even so, you can't call it directly. If you want to let the calling program repeat all or part of the initialization process, place the required code in another method and call that method from the constructor. The preceding code does this.

Constructor methods can receive arguments. To prepare for this, you declare each argument on the *Sub New* statement just as you would any other function or subroutine argument. This also requires, of course, that you specify correct argument values when you create the object. Suppose, for example, that the *InitializeDeck()* method accepted a numeric argument that specified the size of the deck: 48 for a pinochle deck, 52 for a standard deck, 104 for a double deck, and so forth. The class declaration, in that case, might look like this (the argument declarations appear in boldface):

```
Public Class Deck
    Public Sub New(Optional aintSize As Integer = 52)
        InitializeDeck(aintSize)
    End Sub
    Public Sub InitializeDeck( _
            Optional aintSize As Integer = 52)
'       Contents of InitializeDeck procedure
    End Sub
'       Other properties and methods
End Class
```

Having done this (and, of course, added some code to the *InitializeDeck* method), you would code the following to create a deck of 104 cards:

```
Dim dckCards As New Deck(104)
```

The opposite of a constructor method is, of course, a *destructor method.* This is a method that runs automatically whenever the object is about to disappear from memory. In Visual Basic .NET, the destructor, if any, is a subroutine named either *Finalize* or *Dispose*. Here's an example:

```
Public Class Deck
    Public Sub Finalize()
'       Shutdown / cleanup statements go here
    End Sub
End Class
```

Tip   The use of constructor and destructor methods is completely optional. If they solve a problem for you, use them. If they don't, don't.

A destructor method is the best place to release any resources the object might have acquired during its life. For example, if you opened a file in the constructor method, the destructor method would be a good place to close it. However, there's no way to predict exactly when a destructor method will run. Consider, for example, the following code:

```
Dim dckCards As New Deck()
Dim dckCards As New Deck()
```

The first statement creates a new *Deck* object and stores its address in the *dckCards* variable. The second statement creates *another* new *Deck* object and stores *its* address in the *dckCards* variable, overwriting the address of the first *Deck* object. This leaves the first *Deck* object more or less dangling in memory, inaccessible because there's no variable to remember its address. Eventually, a background process called *garbage collection* notices that this object is dangling in memory and deletes it. This is when the first *Deck*'s object destructor method, if any, will run.

The point here is that the timing of destructor methods is unpredictable. You should never make any assumptions that the destructor method for one object will run before or after the destructor method for any other object or, for that matter, before or after any other point in time.

Tip   You can safely assume that a given object's constructor method will run before its destructor method.

Finalize destructors run automatically, but *Dispose* destructors run only when a programmer calls them. The reason for coding a *Dispose* destructor is usually so that calling programs can free resources immediately rather than waiting for garbage collection to call *Finalize*. Two cautions pertain to *Dispose* destructors.

- Writing a *Dispose* method doesn't free you from writing a *Finalize* method as well. The *Finalize* method will free up resources even if a programmer forgets to call *Dispose*.

- Programs can call the *Dispose* destructor even when other references to the object are alive. You should therefore provide code in each method that handles the case where one reference calls a method after another object has disposed it.

Using Property Procedures

Exposing variables by declaring them *Public* can be a dangerous practice. As more and more programs (and programmers!) use a given class, the likelihood increases that one of them will misinterpret or incorrectly modify a *Public* variable and cause your class to fail.

The best way to avoid this is to make variable declarations *Private*. If code outside your class can't access the variable at all, it can't access it improperly! This solution, of course, presents a second problem: with no access to *Public* variables, how can the calling program supply and retrieve data values? *Property procedures* provide the answer. To visualize how property procedure works, first consider the following code:

```
Public Class OrderData
    Private intOrdQty As Integer = 0

    Sub SetOrdQty(ByVal aintQty)
        If aintQty < 1 Then
            Throw New System.Exception( _
                "Order quantity must be at least one.")
```

```
        Else
            intOrdQty = aintQty
        End If
    End Sub

    Function GetOrdQty() As Integer
        Return intOrdQty
    End Function
End Class
```

The *intOrdQty* variable in this code is *Private*, but programs can update it by calling the *SetOrdQty* method. Here's an example.

```
Dim ordInfo As New OrderData()
ordInfo.SetOrdQty(5)
```

The *SetOrdQty* method also verifies that any value the calling statement provides is at least 1. If it isn't, the code throws an exception (that is, blows up the program). This provides you or whoever uses your class with a subtle hint to check the order quantity value before attempting to store it using the *SetOrdQty* method.

Note   The *Throw* statement deliberately causes an exception.

Similarly, programs can read the *intOrdQty* value by calling the *GetOrdQty* method. Here's an example.

```
Dim intOrderQuantity As Integer
intOrderQuantity = ordInfo.GetOrdQty()
```

If you want to write two methods of this type for each property value your class needs to expose, go for it. This is what programmers did for many years and the technique served them well. The following syntax, however, accomplishes the same result, requires less code, and provides more clarity:

```
Property OrdQty() As Integer
    Get
        Return intOrdQty
    End Get

    Set(ByVal Value As Integer)
        If Value < 1 Then
            Throw New System.Exception( _
                "Order quantity must be at least one.")
        Else
            intOrdQty = Value
        End If
    End Set
End Property
```

A normal property procedure actually contains two methods: *Get* and *Set*.
The *Get* method runs when the calling program tries to retrieve the named property (*OrdQty*, in this case) and the *Set* method runs when the calling program
tries to modify the named property. This approach has two primary advantages:

■   Visual Studio .NET automates most of the typing for you. When you type
    Property OrdQty( ) As Integer and press Enter, Visual Studio types the
    Get, *End Get*, *Set*, *End Set*, and *End Property* statements for you.

■   The calling program can access your properties using the same syntax
    that it uses for ordinary variables. Here's some sample code:

```
Dim ordInfo As New OrderData()
Dim intOrderQuantity As Integer
ordInfo.OrdQty = 5
intOrderQuantity = ordInfo.OrdQty
```

This is exactly the same syntax the calling program would use if
you had simply declared a *Public* variable named *OrdQty* inside your
class. This is more intuitive than either of the earlier forms repeated here:

```
ordInfo.SetOrdQty(5)
intOrderQuantity = ordInfo.GetOrdQty()
```

If accessing the property requires additional arguments (such as subscripts)
declare them on the *Property* statement. In this example, the argument *aint-
Team* provides a subscript value:

```
Class TeamResults
    Dim intScore(50) As Integer
    Property Score(ByVal aintTeam As Integer) As Integer
        Get
            Return intScore(aintTeam)
        End Get
        Set(ByVal Value As Integer)
            intScore(aintTeam) = Value
        End Set
    End Property
End Class
```

To read and write this property, the calling program would contain statements
such as those that follow. Both the *Get* and the *Set* property procedures would
find the given subscripts in the *aintTeam* argument.

```
Dim trsResults As New TeamResults
Dim intTeamScore As Integer

trsResults(10) = 85
intTeamScore = trsResults(25)
```

If you don't want the calling program to update a property, declare its property procedure as *ReadOnly* and omit the *Set* method. Here's an example.

```
ReadOnly Property OrdQty() As Integer
    Get
        Return intOrdQty
    End Get
End Property
```

You can declare *WriteOnly* property procedures in essentially the same way. Of course, with a *WriteOnly* property, you code the *Set* method and omit the *Get* method.

By default, property procedures have an access attribute of *Public*. You can override this by beginning the declaration with any of the standard attributes: *Private*, *Friend*, and so forth.

Using Structures

As you start to work with real-world data, you'll frequently encounter situations where you want to deal with a related group of data elements as if they were a single data element. Suppose, for example, that you need to store the following data elements in an array: employee ID, first name, middle initial, and last name.

You already know one way of doing this; you could declare a class named, say, *EmpInfo* that contained *EmpId*, *FirstName*, *MI*, and *LastName* properties, and then declare an array of *EmpInfo* objects. Here's how this would look in code.

```
Public Class EmpInfo
    Public EmpId As String
    Public FirstName As String
    Public MI As String
    Public LastName As String
End Class
Public Class Form1
    Dim empList(100) As EmpInfo
End Class
```

To access the first employee ID in the table, you would code *empList(0).EmpID*. To access the second middle initial you would code *empList(1).MI*, and so forth. This solution, however, has two drawbacks. First, it requires adding another class module to the project. Second, copying one array element to another is a nuisance. To appreciate this, compare the first four statements shown below to the last one.

```
empList(2).EmpId = empList(3).EmpId
empList(2).FirstName = empList(3).FirstName
empList(2).MI = empList(3).MI
empList(2).LastName = empList(3).LastName
empList(2) = empList(3)
```

The first four statements copy all the values from the fourth *empList* entry to the third. The last statement makes the third *empList* entry point to the same *EmpInfo* object as the fourth entry. Storing a new value into *empList(2).LastName* will then affect *empList(3).LastName* as well. This probably isn't what you want.

To avoid this kind of confusion, you could declare *EmpInfo* as a *structure* rather than a class. Like classes, structures can contain data declarations and property procedures. Unlike classes, however, structures are value types. This means that the statement

```
empList(2) = empList(3)
```

copies each property value in the fourth *empList* entry into each corresponding property value in the third *empList* entry. The following code repeats the previous example using a structure rather than a class.

```
Public Class Form1
    Structure EmpInfo
        Public EmpId As String
        Public FirstName As String
        Public MI As String
        Public LastName As String
    End Structure
    Dim empList(100) As EmpInfo
End Class
```

You can declare structures in a source file, module, interface, or class, but not inside a procedure. Once declared, you can access a structure anywhere within the same module or class. Structures can be *Public*, *Protected*, *Friend*, *Protected Friend*, or *Private*. The default is *Friend*.

You can declare structure members with *Dim*, *Friend*, *Private*, or *Public* statements. If you use *Dim*, the member will have *Public* access.

Trying Times and Exceptional Results

A great many things can go wrong when any program runs. In many cases, such problems result in exceptions, which are the sort of events that terminate your program with an error. Bombs away!

In many cases, fatal exceptions are a subtle hint that you need to fix your program code. Other times, however, they occur because of something you suspected might happen and wish to handle yourself. Lots of things can go wrong when you try to open a file, for example. Another program might have the file open and locked; the user may have deleted it; the user may lack security, and so forth. To intercept such events and handle them your own way, surround the risky statement with a *Try...Catch...End Try* block. Here's an example.

```
Try
'   Code that might raise an exception goes here.
Catch variable As exception-type-1
'   Code that deals with exception 1 goes here.
Catch variable As exception-type-2
'   Code that deals with exception 2 goes here.
Finally
'   Code that runs no matter what goes here.
End Try
```

If any statement you code between the *Try* and *Catch* keywords raises an exception, Visual Basic .NET will start looking for a *Catch* clause that matches it. For example, one exception that can occur while opening a file is *System.IO.FileNotFoundException*. If this exception occurs and the following clause follows the statement that caused it.

```
Catch ex as System.IO.FileNotFoundException
```

then the exception wouldn't bomb the program. Instead, any code between the *Catch* clause and the next *Catch, Finally*, or *End Try* would execute. If you code more than one *Catch* keyword, Visual Basic .NET compares the actual exception to the exception on each *Catch* clause until it finds a match. If there's no *Catch* clause that matches the exception, the system exception handler will take charge and terminate the program.

Tip   To find out what exceptions a given statement or method might raise, look up the statement or method in MSDN Library.

To catch all exceptions, catch the generic exception named *Exception*. An example appears below. If the *Try* statement contains several *Catch* clauses, be sure to code this one last.

```
Catch ex As Exception
```

Regardless of the type of exception you're catching, you can name the exception variable anything you want. The name *ex*, however is customary. Regardless of its name, the exception variable will contain the properties listed in Table 7-2. The *Message* property is probably the most useful.

Table 7-2   **Exception Object Properties**

Property	Description
HelpLink	Gets or sets a link to the help file that describes this exception.
InnerException	Gets the Exception object from the next deeper exception.
Message	Gets a message that describes the current exception.
Source	Gets or sets the name of the application or object that caused the error.

Table 7-2 **Exception Object Properties** *(continued)*

Property	Description
StackTrace	Gets a string representation of the frames on the call stack at the time the current exception occurred.
TargetSite	Gets the method that throws the current exception.

Catching an exception effectively defuses it. The exception will no longer blow up your program or set off any higher-level *Try...Catch...End Try* blocks. If you catch an exception and then decide to let it occur, you must raise it anew. To do this, code a *Throw* statement as shown below.

```
Throw Exception
```

Exception, in this case, points to a new or existing exception object. The first example below refers to an existing object named *ex* and the second one refers to a new one.

```
Throw ex
Throw New Exception("Goodbye cruel world.")
```

The *Finally* clause of a *Try...Catch...End Try* block is optional. If you code it, any statements it contains will execute no matter what else happens. Here's an example.

```
Dim srdFile As StreamReader
Dim booNeedToCreateFile as Boolean = False
Try
    srdFile = File.OpenText("c:\temp\whatever.txt")
Catch ex As System.IO.FileNotFoundException
    booNeedToCreateFile = True
Catch ex As System.Security.SecurityException
    MsgBox("Sorry, you donÕt have permission.")
    Exit Sub
Finally
    MsgBox("Attempted to open file.")
End Try
```

The code that follows the *Finally* keyword will execute in all of the following cases. In short, it executes no matter what.

- The statement after the *Try* keyword executes normally.

- The statement after the *Try* keyword throws a *System.IO.FileNotFound-Exception*.

- The statement after the *Try* keyword throws a *System.Security.Security-Exception*. Even though the code in this *Catch* block contains an *Exit Sub* statement, the *Finally* code will execute before the exit takes place.

■ The statement after the *Try* keyword throws some other exception, thereby blowing up the program. In this case, the code in the *Finally* block will execute after .NET displays the system error message and before Windows rips the program out of memory.

Example 2: Shuffling with Property Procedures

This example modifies the shuffle program once again, this time adding the following features:

■ A constructor method will initialize the deck of cards. That way, the class will work correctly even if the calling program forgets to call the *InitializeDeck* method.

■ A property procedure will replace the *Public* array *intDeck*. This ensures that the calling program doesn't accidentally (or mischievously) modify the deck.

To make these changes, start Visual Studio .NET and then follow these directions:

1 Create a new Windows Application project named shuffleclass2.

2 Make sure all code and design windows are closed and then, in Windows Explorer, copy the Form1.vb and Deck.vb files from the shuffleclass folder to the shuffleclass2 folder. By default, these folders will be at C:\Documents and Settings*user*\My Documents\Visual Studio Projects\, where *user* is the name of your Windows logon account.

3 Back in Visual Studio, locate the Solution Explorer window and right-click the entry for the shuffleclass2 project. (It should be the second line.) When the shortcut menu appears, click Add and then Add Existing Item.

4 When the Add Existing Item - Shuffleclass2 dialog box appears, locate the Deck.vb file you just copied into the Shuffleclass2 folder, select it, and click Open.

5 Double-click the Form1.vb file and the Deck.vb file in the Solution Explorer window. Verify that these files contain the changes you made in the earlier example.

6 Locate the statement in Deck.vb that declares the *intDeck* array and change its access attribute to *Private*. The statement should then look like this:

```
Private intDeck(51) As Integer
```

7 Add the following procedure to the *Deck* class (Deck.vb). Technically, this can go just before or after any existing procedure, but in this case, make it the first procedure in the class:

```
Public Sub New()
    InitializeDeck()
End Sub
```

8 Remove the following statement from the *Form1_Load* subroutine in the Form1.vb file. The constructor method you defined in step 6 will run the *InitializeDeck* method automatically.

```
dckCards.InitializeDeck()
```

9 Immediately after the code you entered in step 7, add a *ReadOnly* property procedure named *Size*. This procedure should return an *Integer* equal to the maximum subscript of the *intDeck* array. Here's the code:

```
ReadOnly Property Size() As Integer
    Get
        Size = UBound(intDeck)
    End Get
End Property
```

10 Next, add a second *ReadOnly* property procedure, this time named *Suit*. This procedure should return *C*, *D*, *H*, or *S*, depending on whether the card at a given position is clubs, diamonds, hearts, or spades. (Recall that card values in the range 100–199 are clubs, 200–299 are diamonds, and so forth.) Here's the code:

```
ReadOnly Property Suit(ByVal aintCard) As String
    Get
        Dim intSuit As Integer
        intSuit = intDeck(aintCard) \ 100
        Suit = Choose(intSuit, "C", "D", "H", "S")
    End Get
End Property
```

11 Add a third property procedure, this time named *Rank*. This procedure should return the rank of a specified card as a string. Recall that within the range assigned to each suit, values 2 through 10 indicate themselves and values 11 through 14 indicate jack, queen, king, and ace. The following code will do this:

```
ReadOnly Property Rank(ByVal aintCard) As String
    Get
        Dim intRank As Integer
        intRank = intDeck(aintCard) Mod 100
        If intRank < 11 Then
            Rank = CStr(intRank)
```

```
        Else
            Rank = Choose(intRank - 10, "J", "Q", "K", "A")
        End If
    End Get
End Property
```

12 In the Form1.vb file, replace the *DisplayDeck* subroutine with this code. The new code is shorter because it takes advantage of code in the *Size*, *Rank*, and *Suit* property procedures:

```
Sub DisplayDeck()

    Dim intCard As Integer
    lstDeck.Items.Clear()
    For intCard = 0 To dckCards.Size
        lstDeck.Items.Add(dckCards.Rank(intCard) & " " & _
                            dckCards.Suit(intCard))
    Next
End Sub
```

13 This completes the changes for this exercise. To save your work, select Save All from the File menu. To test your work, press F5. The program should run exactly as it did before.

At this point, you might be wondering why none of the exercises moved the *DisplayDeck* subroutine into the *Deck* class. The reason is that the *Display-Deck* subroutine deals directly with the elements on the display form, and these will likely vary from program to program. Notice, however, that the current exercise did move all the logic of decoding card values such as 311 into codes such as *H* for hearts and *J* for jack. There's no reason for each program that uses the *Deck* class to perform these transformations itself. If there are many such programs, at least a few of them are likely to get it wrong.

Notice also how property procedures can isolate programs from the actual structure of data. The *Deck* class, for example, now exposes properties named *Suit* and *Rank* that don't actually exist in the data but require computation to derive.

The shuffle program, despite the fact that it doesn't do anything very interesting, is now reasonably up-to-date in terms of programming approach. This provides a basis for more interesting programs to come. Complete listings of the Form1.vb and Deck.vb files appear below for your reference. Don't be concerned if your code has fewer line continuations or if the functions and subroutines appear in a different order; these factors don't affect the way the program works.

Form1.vb

```vb
Public Class Form1
    Inherits System.Windows.Forms.Form
    Dim dckCards As New Deck()

+ Windows Form Designer generated code

    Private Sub Form1_Load( _
            ByVal sender As System.Object, _
            ByVal e As System.EventArgs) _
            Handles MyBase.Load
        DisplayDeck()
    End Sub

    Sub DisplayDeck()
        Dim intCard As Integer
        lstDeck.Items.Clear()
        For intCard = 0 To dckCards.Size
            lstDeck.Items.Add(dckCards.Rank(intCard) & " " & _
                            dckCards.Suit(intCard))
        Next
    End Sub

    Private Sub btnShuffle_Click( _
            ByVal sender As System.Object, _
            ByVal e As System.EventArgs) _
            Handles btnShuffle.Click
        dckCards.ShuffleDeck()
        DisplayDeck()
    End Sub

    Private Sub btnNewDeck_Click( _
            ByVal sender As System.Object, _
            ByVal e As System.EventArgs) _
            Handles btnNewDeck.Click
        dckCards.InitializeDeck()
        DisplayDeck()
    End Sub

    Private Sub btnExit_Click( _
            ByVal sender As System.Object, _
            ByVal e As System.EventArgs) _
            Handles btnExit.Click
        Me.Close()
    End Sub
End Class
```

Deck.vb

```vb
Public Class Deck
    Public intDeck(51) As Integer

    Public Sub New()
        InitializeDeck()
    End Sub

    ReadOnly Property Size() As Integer
        Get
            Size = UBound(intDeck)
        End Get
    End Property

    ReadOnly Property Suit(ByVal aintCard) As String
        Get
            Dim intSuit As Integer
            intSuit = intDeck(aintCard) \ 100
            Suit = Choose(intSuit, "C", "D", "H", "S")
        End Get
    End Property

    ReadOnly Property Rank(ByVal aintCard) As String
        Get
            Dim intRank As Integer
            intRank = intDeck(aintCard) Mod 100
            If intRank < 11 Then
                Rank = CStr(intRank)
            Else
                Rank = Choose(intRank - 10, _
                        "J", "Q", "K", "A")
            End If
        End Get
    End Property

    Public Sub InitializeDeck()
        Dim intSuit As Integer = 100
        Dim intRank As Integer = 2
        Dim intCard As Integer
        For intCard = 0 To UBound(intDeck)
            intDeck(intCard) = intSuit + intRank
            If intRank < 14 Then
                intRank += 1
            Else
                intSuit += 100
                intRank = 2
            End If
        Next
    End Sub
```

```
Public Sub ShuffleDeck()
    Dim intCard As Integer
    Dim intSwap As Integer
    Dim intTemp As Integer
    Randomize()
    For intCard = 0 To UBound(intDeck) - 1
        intSwap = intCard + _
            Fix(Rnd() * (UBound(intDeck) + 1 - intCard))
        If intSwap <> intCard Then
            intTemp = intDeck(intSwap)
            intDeck(intSwap) = intDeck(intCard)
            intDeck(intCard) = intTemp
        End If
    Next
End Sub

End Class
```

Key Points

■ Objects are software entities that bundle together groups of related properties and methods.

■ Properties are data values that describe the real object that the software object represents.

■ Methods are ways of making things happen to an object. They are, in essence, software commands.

■ You don't actually write objects; instead you write classes. A class provides the code and data declarations for all objects of a certain type.

■ Variables inside a class can be accessible or inaccessible to code outside the class. Attributes such as *Public*, *Friend*, and *Private* control this. Declaring a variable as *Public* or *Friend* makes it available to calling code as a property.

■ If you declare functions and subroutines inside a class as *Public* or *Friend*, they become accessible to calling code as methods.

■ To create an object, assign the word *New* followed by the class name to a suitable variable.

■ Creating an object automatically causes its constructor method, if any, to run. Constructor methods initialize the object in preparation for further work.

- Terminating an object automatically causes its destructor method, if any, to run. A destructor method typically releases any system resources the object still holds.

- Property procedures provide a valuable layer of isolation between data inside an object and the calling program.

- Structures are custom data types that province one or more properties.

- To catch exceptions and handle them yourself, surround the risky statement with a *Try...Catch...End Try* block.

- Coding programs in terms of objects makes the program more organized and increases the chance that code you wrote for one program will be useful in another.

Chapter 8

Using Classes, Modules, and Forms

Now that you understand the basics of creating and using classes, you're no doubt ready to learn even more. For starters, this chapter explains how to peruse and use the vast .NET Framework class library. No matter what you want your program to do, there are probably .NET classes that will do most of the work with a minimum of fuss and bother. All you have to do is find the right class and understand its documentation.

Next, this chapter explains three very important concepts, all related to classes. The first two have names that can make your eyes go bleary: inheritance and polymorphism. Think of inheritance as "Here comes another one just like the other one." As for polymorphism, it's "Show me two of anything and I'll figure out a way to add them." The third concept is that of events, which are signals to anyone who cares that something has happened.

Microsoft Windows forms are an excellent example of inheritance, which is why this chapter explains inheritance first. Forms are important, so don't miss this exciting installment.

The last section explains the concepts of modules, which in Microsoft Visual Basic .NET are specialized objects rather than a generic term that means any software component. Modules are probably the least glamorous topic in the chapter, but when you need them, you really need them.

Using .NET Framework Classes

The Microsoft .NET Framework provides more than 16,000 classes ready for use in any program you care to write. For starters, these classes put all of the resources of the Windows operating system at your disposal. In addition, they provide a wealth of methods specifically designed for common tasks. If there was ever a software treasure trove, this is it.

The difficulty, of course, lies in finding the exact property that contains the information you want or the method that does what you want to do. This is usually the hard part. Once you find the necessary property or method, however, you still have to figure out what class it's in, how to make that class accessible to your program. You also need to know how to access the property or method without generating an error. The next three sections explain these tasks.

Finding .NET Methods and Classes

If you're looking for a property or method that relates to an object already in your program, the IntelliSense feature in Microsoft Visual Studio can be a big help. In code view, just type the name of the object and a period; IntelliSense then displays a list of all the properties and methods available for that object. Figure 8-1 shows the IntelliSense list for the array *strElms*.

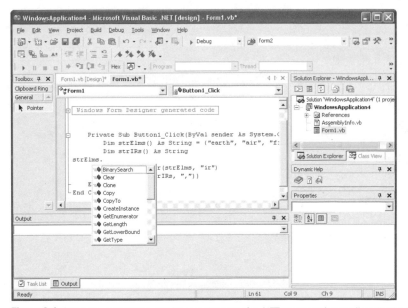

Figure 8-1 The code completion list for any element of a .NET program shows all available .NET properties and methods for that type of element.

You can also search for .NET classes, properties, and events in the MSDN (Microsoft Developer Network) Library, either by using the Help facility in Visual Studio or browsing the Web site at *http://msdn.microsoft.com/library*. Be as specific as possible with the search terms you enter and, especially on the Web, include the word *framework* in every search.

Microsoft has organized all the .NET classes into a hierarchical series of *namespaces*. The full name of the class for a Windows form, for example, is *System.Windows.Forms.Form*; as a result, you could locate this class by first looking up the *System* namespace, then the *System.Windows* namespace, then *System.Windows.Forms*, and so on. To display the top-level namespaces, open the following Help topics in order. Figure 8-2 shows the results.

Visual Studio .NET
   .NET Framework
      Reference
         Class Library

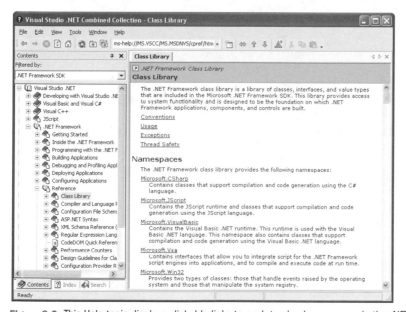

Figure 8-2 This Help topic displays clickable links to each top-level namespace in the .NET hierarchy.

Figure 8-3 shows the main Help page for the .NET *Array* object. The code in the gray boxes shows the declaration you would use to write the *Array* class from scratch in various languages. Of course, Microsoft doesn't expect you to actually rewrite the *Array* class; the declarations only appear for information.

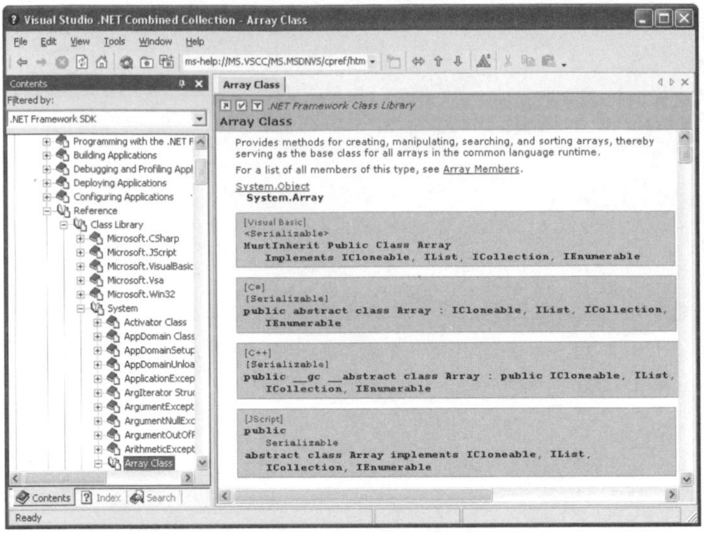

Figure 8-3 This is the top level of documentation for the *Array* class.

Interfaces   When you look at sample class declarations in the MSDN Library, you'll often see the word *Implements* followed by a series of strange-looking terms. In Figure 8-3, for example, the following code appears as part of the declaration for the *Array* class:

```
Implements ICloneable, IList, ICollection, IEnumerable
```

Any terms that follow the word *Implements* are the names of *interfaces* that the class supports. An interface, in this sense, is a collection of properties, methods, and events that meet certain specifications. The *System.Array* class, for example, claims to provide all the properties, methods, and events that the following interfaces require:

- **ICloneable**   This interface supports cloning, a process that creates a new object with the same values as an existing object.

- **IList**   This interface supports collections of objects that are individually accessible by means of an index.

- **ICollection**   This interface provides size, enumerators, and synchronization methods for collections of any kind.

- **IEnumerable**   This interface exposes an enumerator that iterates through a collection.

If you're writing a class and want it to support an interface, it's your job to provide all the properties, methods, and events that the interface requires. If you wanted the *For Next* statement to work with your class, you would need to implement all the properties, methods, and events in the *ICollection* and *IEnumerable* interfaces.

Below the sample declarations (and not visible in the screen shot) is a textual description of the class and a list of links to related topics. The most important link, however, is the one near the top (and visible in the screen shot) titled Array Members. Clicking this link displays a list of every property, method, and event for the class. This is usually the best place to look for the property or method you need. Figure 8-4 shows one of these pages. Clicking the property or method name displays yet another page that tells you how to use that member.

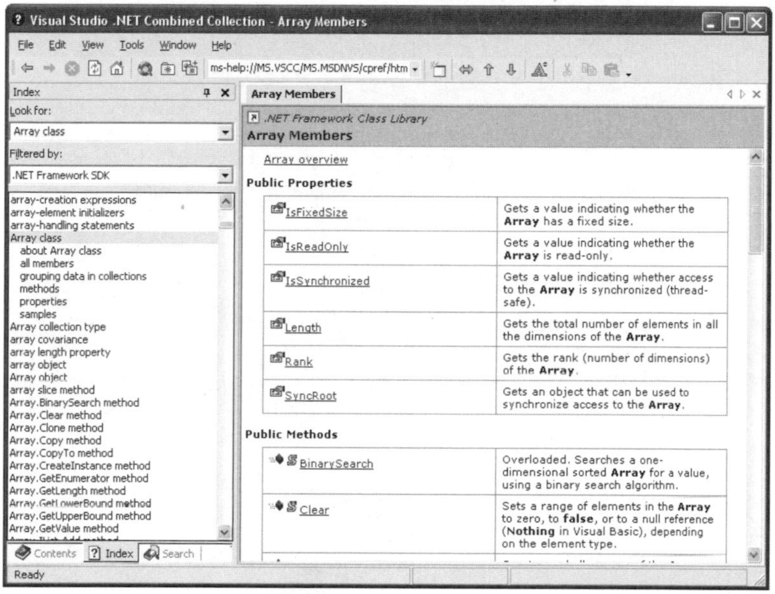

Figure 8-4 Pages like this list each property, method, and event for a given .NET class.

Notice that the small document icons identify properties in Figure 8-4 and that flying boxes identify methods. If an S icon also appears, it means that the method is *shared*. This means you can invoke the method straight from the class name as well as through a specific object you created from the class.

The *Clear* method of the *Array* class, for example, is shared. This method sets a range of array elements to their default value (usually an empty value or zero). It has three arguments: the array variable, a starting subscript, and a length. Because this method is shared, the usual way of coding it is this:

```
Dim strNames() As String = {"Amy", "Barry", "Cathy", "Dee"}
Array.Clear(strNames, 0, UBound(strNames) + 1)
```

If it suited your fancy, you could code the *Clear* method as a member of the *strNames* variable rather than directly as a member of the *Array* class. However, this wouldn't save you from having to specify the array name as the first argument.

Referencing Namespaces

When you create a new project, Visual Studio .NET configures the project with access to the most common .NET namespaces. This provides full access to all the classes you'll need for most of your programs.

In some cases, however, you might get an error message stating that a class doesn't exist even though the .NET documentation says that it does. To solve this problem, you must include a reference to the dynamic link library (DLL) that contains the namespace of the class you want to use.

The Solution Explorer window shows which references are already in effect. To view this information, expand the Project entry and then the References entry beneath it. If this proves you need to add a reference, proceed as follows:

> **Tip** Visual Studio doesn't identify project entries in Solution Explorer with the keyword *Project*; it identifies them with the name you assigned when you created the project. In Figure 8-1, for example, the project entry is the one titled *WindowsApplication4*.

1 Right-click the References entry and choose Add Reference from the shortcut menu.

2 When the Add Reference dialog box shown in Figure 8-5 appears, make sure the .NET tab is selected.

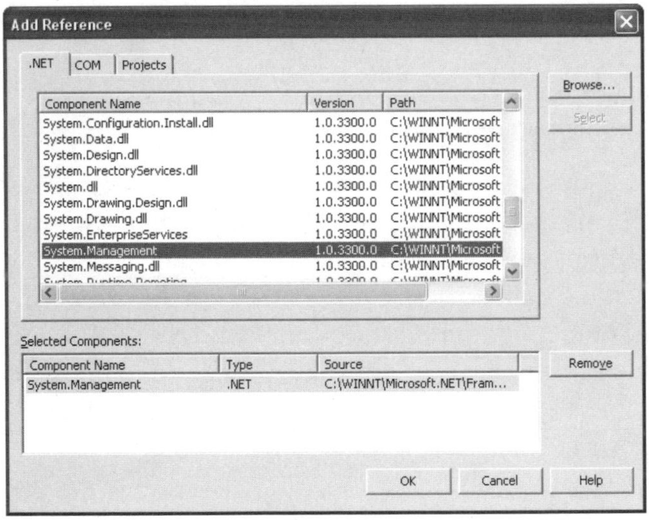

Figure 8-5 Use this dialog box to add references to DLLs that contain classes your project needs.

3 Select the references you want to add to your project, then click Select. This adds those references to the Selected Components list at the bottom of the dialog box.

4 Click OK to add the references.

Importing Namespaces

Once you have access to a class, you might find that you still can't use it unless you type its fully qualified name. For example, you might need to type *System.IO.Directory* rather than just *Directory*. To correct this, you need to *import* the namespace that contains the class you want to use.

Note *System.IO.Directory* is a class that reads, creates, and moves folders and subfolders.

There are two ways to import a class in Visual Basic .NET. If you want to import the class for use by a single source file, add an *Imports* statement to the top of the file. Here's a typical *Imports* statement:

```
Imports System.IO
```

To import more than one namespace, code a separate *Imports* statement for each one. However, all the *Imports* statements for a file must appear before any data declarations, *Module* statements, or *Class* statements. If an *Option* statement is present, all *Imports* statements must come after it.

You can also import namespaces at the project level. To take this approach, proceed as follows:

1 Right-click your project in Solution Explorer and choose Properties from the shortcut menu.

2 When the Property Pages dialog box shown in Figure 8-6 appears, select Common Properties and then Imports.

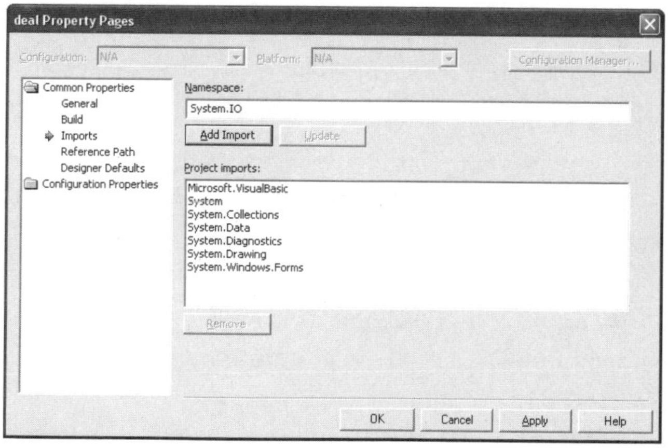

Figure 8-6 Importing a namespace through this dialog box makes it available throughout your project.

3 Type the namespace you want the entire project to import.

4 Click Add Import and then click OK.

Making the Most of Objects and Classes

This section describes three very important features of objects and classes: inheritance, overloading, and events. These concepts are a little more advanced than properties and methods but the payback from understanding them can be huge. If you need some coffee and a snack, now is the time to fetch them.

Inheritance (and Not from Uncle Otto)

If you're a sharp-eyed reader, you've noticed that the code for each form in the examples began with the same statement. Visual Basic .NET creates this statement automatically and the text didn't mention it. As a result, don't feel bad if you concerned yourself with more important matters. Here it is:

```
Public Class Form1
    Inherits System.Windows.Forms.Form
```

Note   An object is one specific instance of a class. Whenever you create a variable of some type, you're actually rating an object based on the corresponding class.

There are two important concepts here. The first is that every Windows form is an object. You might have intuitively grasped this already, but in any case, it's true. In each of the examples so far, Visual Basic .NET loaded an instance of the *System.Windows.Forms.Form* class into memory, named it *Form1*, and used it to display the form you saw on your screen. The form appeared automatically because, by default, *Form1* was the project's *startup object*.

Tip   To check or change the startup object for any project, right-click the project entry in Solution Explorer and choose Properties from the shortcut menu. The Startup Object setting appears under Common Properties, General.

The second statement, *Inherits System.Windows.Forms.Form*, is even more interesting; it tells Visual Basic .NET to base the *Form1* object on the *System.Windows.Forms.Form* class. At this point, whatever properties, methods, and events the *System.Windows.Forms.Form* class provides, the *Form1* object will automatically provide as well. This is what programming intellectuals mean when they talk about *inheritance*.

Almost every class in the .NET Framework inherits members of other classes. Possibly the only exception is the *Object* class, which provides generic methods that all other classes use. Some other classes inherit from the *Object* class, more classes inherit from those classes, and so forth up the proverbial food chain. This saves a great deal of programming effort.

None of the *Form1* objects in the examples needed any code to display the form on screen; to redraw the display when you moved or resized the form; to minimize, maximize, or normalize the form when you clicked the appropriate buttons; or to close the form when you clicked the Close box. All the *Form1* objects inherited these behaviors from the *System.Windows.Forms.Form* class.

.NET classes can only inherit one class. One class can't, for example, inherit all or some of the methods from two, three, or four other classes. If your class needs to provide members based on more than one class, you'll have to provide them some other way. Perhaps you can load instances of the additional classes and call them, for example.

As you might suspect, a lot of complexity can arise during inheritance. This is especially true if you want to override, overload, or extend any members of classes you inherit. These topics are largely beyond the scope of this book and the examples avoid them.

Overloading and Polymorphism

Consider the lowly *Plus* operator. If you give it two *Integers*, it performs Integer arithmetic. If you give it two *Doubles*, it performs double-precision floating-point arithmetic. If you give it two *Strings*, it concatenates them. Basically, the *Plus* operator runs a different method depending on the argument types you specify. This is an example of overloading.

Lingo *Overloading* means running a different method depending on the type and number of arguments.

You can also overload methods in the same class. To do this, code two or more functions with exactly the same name but either:

- A different number of arguments or
- A different combination of argument types

The following code, for example, overloads the *AddEm* method. A different version of the method will run depending on whether the calling statement specifies two *Integers*, two *Doubles*, or three *Integers*:

```
Public Class Class1
    Public Function AddEm(ByVal arg1 As Integer, _
                          ByVal arg2 As Integer) As Integer
        Return arg1 + arg2
    End Function
    Public Function AddEm(ByVal arg1 As Double, _
                          ByVal arg2 As Double) As Double
        Return arg1 + arg2
```

```
      End Function
      Public Function AddEm(ByVal arg1 As Integer, _
                            ByVal arg2 As Integer, _
                            ByVal arg3 As Integer) As Integer
          Return arg1 + arg2 + arg3
      End Function
End Class
```

The term *signature* refers to the number and types of arguments in a method call. The three declarations for the *AddEm* method have signatures of Integer-Integer, Double-Double, and Integer-Integer-Integer.

The calling statement, of course, also has a signature. Visual Basic .NET tries to match the signature of the calling statement to the closest available signature of the called method, applying normal type conversions if necessary. If the calling statement specifies an *Integer* and a *Double*, for example, Visual Basic .NET uses the method that accepts two *Doubles* (based on the fact that *Integer* to *Double* is a widening conversion).

Overloading occurs when one class contains or inherits several methods having the same name but different signatures.

Polymorphism, by contrast, occurs when two or more classes provide properties or methods having the same name, even if the various classes implement them in different ways. Many classes in the .NET Framework, for example, have a *ToString* method. For some classes—such as elementary data types—*ToString* returns the current value of an object expressed as a string. For other classes—especially those that that don't have simple, single values—*ToString* returns the fully qualified class name. The *ToString* method of the *Double* class returns strings that contain decimal points; the *ToString* method of a *DateTime* class returns values formatted with slashes and colons; the *ToString* method of an *Integer* object returns only numbers. In most cases, however, these differences don't concern you at all. If you want to display the value of any object in, say, an error message, you can simply call its *ToString* method and rest comfortably, knowing that a human-readable representation will result.

Sometimes polymorphism results because the programmers who wrote the classes cooperated in choosing like names for methods that performed like work. Other times, polymorphism results from two or more classes inheriting exactly the same property or method from some lower-level class.

When one class inherits another it's entirely possible that some properties and methods of the inherited class could be unsuitable for the higher-level class. When this occurs, the higher-level class can *override* the inherited property or method with one that makes more sense (given the nature of the higher-level class).

Polymorphism has nothing to do with tropical birds or unusual marital customs. The emperor of object-oriented programming just happened to run out of short words that day. Just don't try to say it when you're overloaded (polymorphism, that is).

Events (i.e., Getting a Raise)

In Windows programming, *events* are messages that one software component sends to another. The component that sends the message usually does so because something unpredictable has occurred. For example, the user of a Windows program might have clicked a button, a time-consuming process might have ended, or the response to a network query might have arrived. The possibilities are endless.

The official term for sending one of these messages is *raising an event*, and you could say it resembles a shout in the forest. The object that raises the event has no idea which, if any, other object will respond to it. If any other object has signed up to receive the event, that object will receive the message. If not, the message vanishes. It's the sender's job only to send.

Raising Events

Any class can raise an event, provided it satisfies two requirements. First, the class must declare the event. Here's a typical event declaration:

```
Event LapCompleted(ByVal intCarNum As Integer, _
                   ByVal dteEvTime As Date)
```

As you can see, this particular event accepts two arguments: a car number and the time at which it completed a lap. In fact, events can contain zero, one, or as many arguments as you like. An event declaration can appear anywhere inside the class, but not inside any method or other structure. It usually appears somewhere between the *Class* statement and the first *Function* or *Sub* statement.

To actually raise an event you must code (what else?) a *RaiseEvent* statement. Here's an example that would work with the *Event* statement you've already seen:

```
Dim intCar As Integer
Dim dteTime As Date
RaiseEvent LapCompleted(intCar, dteTime)
```

RaiseEvent statements must appear within a method that belongs to the class that declares the event. One class can't raise an event declared in another class, or even in a class it inherits. Here's the complete code for a class that declares and raises the *ReportLap* event:

```
Class LapCounter
    Event LapCompleted(ByVal CarNum As Integer, _
                       ByVal EvTime As Date)
```

```
    Function ReportLap(ByVal aintcar As Integer)
        Dim dteTime As Date
        dteTime = Now()
        RaiseEvent LapCompleted(aintcar, dteTime)
    End Function
End Class
```

That's it! The class that raises the event neither knows nor cares which other class receives it, if indeed any class receives it at all.

Handling Events

Any object that can raise events is an *event sender*. (The term *event source* is equivalent.) A method that receives events is an *event handler*. Event handler methods must be subroutines because there's no mechanism for returning values to the event source.

As the programmer, it's your job to specify which subroutines should act as event handlers for which events. (Microsoft sometimes calls this *wiring* the handler to the event.) You can specify this correlation either of two ways: declaratively or dynamically.

Wiring Event Handlers Declaratively

The first way of associating an event handler with an event is to tell the compiler. This is a two-step process:

1 Add the keyword *WithEvents* to the statement that creates the object that raises the event. Here's an example:

```
Dim WithEvents lapCtr As New LapCounter()
```

2 Append the following to the *Sub* statement for the subroutine you want to act as the event handler:

- The keyword *Handles*.

- The name of the object that raises the event. This will be the variable you declared in step 1.

- A period.

- The name of the event.

In addition, you must ensure that the handler subroutine has the same signature as the event. (That is, both must have the same number and types or arguments.) Here's an example, with the *Handles* clause in boldface for clarity:

```
Sub TallyLap(ByVal CarNum As Integer, _
          ByVal EvTime As Date) _
          Handles lapCtr.LapCompleted
```

```
      MsgBox("Car " & CarNum & vbCrLf & "Time " & EvTime)
   End Sub
```

Specifying *WithEvents* when you instantiate an object and *Handles* on the event handler is often the best choice for coding an event handler because the declarative syntax is easy to code, read, and debug. However, this technique has three significant limitations:

- You can't specify *WithEvents* on a variable declared as *Object*. You must code the specific class name when you declare the variable.

- You can't use *WithEvents* to handle shared events. Because shared events aren't tied to a specific object, there's no object name to specify after the *Handles* keyword.

- You can't create arrays of *WithEvents* variables.

If you want the same event handler to handle several different events, list all the events, separated by commas, after the *Handles* keyword, as shown in this example:

```
Sub DoItAll() Handles objOne.Event1, objTwo.Event2
```

Of course, all these events and the *Sub* statement itself must have the same signature.

No error occurs if you code the same *Handles* clause on two or more subroutines. Each event handler you specify for the same event gets a chance to see it. The order in which these event handlers run, however, is unpredictable.

In some cases, Visual Studio .NET declares events and creates empty event handlers for you automatically. When you double-click a form or control in the Form Designer, for example, Visual Studio .NET declares an event that looks like this:

```
Private Sub Button1_Click(ByVal sender As System.Object, _
   ByVal e As System.EventArgs) Handles Button1.Click
End Sub
```

These particular statements result from double-clicking a command button named Button1. To generate other kinds of event handlers, select the class name and event name you want in the two drop-down list boxes at the top of the code editor window.

The argument *sender As System.Object*, by the way, always refers to the object that raised the event. The argument *e As System.EventArgs* is a placeholder that doesn't contain any useful data. If a .NET event source wants to provide event data, it uses another class that inherits *System.EventArgs*.

Wiring Event Handlers Dynamically

If you require more flexibility than the *WithEvents* and *Handles* keywords provide, the *AddHandler* and *RemoveHandler* statements will likely provide a solution. The following statement, for example, eliminates the need to code the *WithEvents* keyword and the *Handles* keyword as the previous section described:

```
AddHandler lapCtr.LapCompleted, AddressOf TallyLap
```

The big difference between this method and the last is that *AddHandler* is an executable statement. The *TallyLap* subroutine—or whatever subroutine you specify—doesn't receive any events until your program executes the *AddHandler* statement. This is useful if you don't want the event handler to receive events the whole time your program is running.

Another big advantage is that when you use *AddHandler*, you don't have to code *WithEvents* when you instantiate the event source. This, in turn, avoids the three restrictions described in the previous section.

Finally, there's a *RemoveHandler* statement that stops an event handler from receiving any more events. The syntax for the *RemoveHandler* statement is exactly the same as that for the *AddHandler*, as in:

```
RemoveHandler lapCtr.LapCompleted, AddressOf TallyLap
```

Using Forms

All of the previous examples have involved the use of one Windows form. This is the default for new projects you create using the Windows Application template. In fact, however, Windows applications can have any number of forms. Here's the procedure for adding a new Windows form to any project:

1   Open the project in Visual Studio .NET.

2   Right-click the project entry in Solution Explorer. When the shortcut menu appears, select Add and then Add New Item (or, if you prefer, select Add New Item from the File menu).

3   When the Add New Item dialog box shown in Figure 8-7 appears, click the Windows Form template, enter the name you want in the Name box, and then click Open. This name identifies both the source file and the class that defines the form.

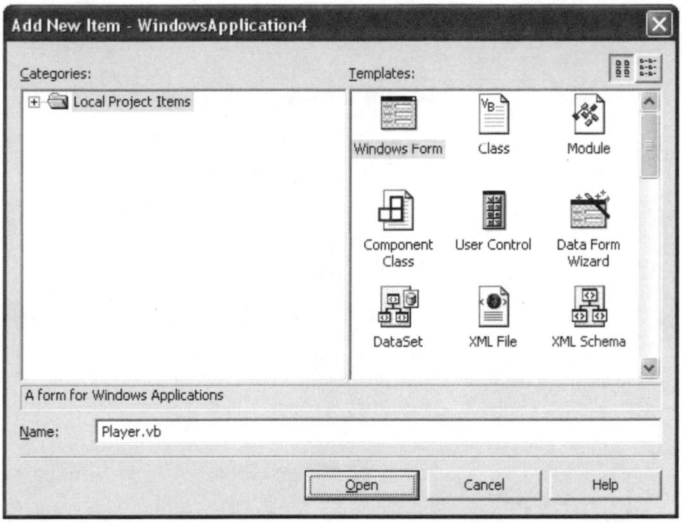

Figure 8-7 Among its many other capabilities, the Add New Item dialog box can add a new Windows form to your project.

Adding a new form this way doesn't make it appear when your project runs. In fact, it doesn't even load the form into memory. As you no doubt recall, Windows forms are instances of the *System.Windows.Forms.Form* class that comes with the .NET Framework. You can't use this class directly; instead, you must use it to create an object and then tell the object to show itself. Here's an example, assuming that you want to name the form Player:

```
Dim plyForm As Player
plyForm = New Player()
plyForm.Show()
```

> **Lingo**   *Instantiating* a class means creating one instance of that class. In even simpler language, it means creating an object based on that class.

The *Show* method comes with the *System.Windows.Forms.Form* class. All the properties, methods, and events of this class are available to your form because your form inherits it. For proof, open the code for any new form and you'll find the following statements:

```
Public Class formname
    Inherits System.Windows.Forms.Form
End Class
```

Windows forms come with a huge selection of properties and methods, most of which control the form's appearance. Table 8-1 lists a few examples.

Table 8-1 Some Properties as They Pertain to Forms

Property	Description
Text	Specifies the caption that appears in the window's title bar.
Top	Specifies the distance in pixels between the top of the computer screen and the top of the window.
Left	Specifies the distance in pixels between the left edge of the computer screen and the left edge of the window.
Width	Specifies the width of the window in pixels starting from the Left property.
Height	Specifies the height of the window in pixels starting from the Top property.
ControlBox	If true, specifies that the window should have a control box. This is the box that normally appears at the left side of the title bar with options of Restore, Move, Size, Minimize, Maximize, and Close. If this option is false, no control box appears.
ShowInTaskbar	If true, specifies that a button for this window will appear in the Windows taskbar. If this property is false, no such button will appear.
WindowState	Specifies the window's display state: Normal, Minimized , or Maximized.

Tip Hiding the control box also hides the Minimize, Maximize, and Close buttons that normally appear at the right of the title bar.

When a Windows form is open in the Windows Form Designer, you can initialize most of its properties by selecting the form and modifying entries in the Properties window. You can also inspect and modify these properties in code. While your program is running, for example, you can discover the form's screen position by inspecting its *Top* and *Left* properties. Your program can also move the form around by modifying those properties. Code within a *Form* class can center the form horizontally by executing the following line of code:

```
Me.Left = (Screen.PrimaryScreen.Bounds.Width - Me.Width) /2
```

Tip Within a *Function*, *Sub*, or *Property* method, the keyword *Me* always represents the current object.

Windows forms are an interesting application of inheritance. The *System.Windows.Forms.Form* class provides most of the properties, methods, and events your form needs to operate, and does so in a very reliable and standard way. To this, you add only the code that's unique to your program.

For a complete list of properties, methods, and events that Windows forms support, display the topic Form Class in the MSDN Library index.

Using Modules

Like classes, modules serve as containers for variables, functions, and subroutines. You can't, however, create an instance of a module the way you create an instance of a class. You just use the contents of a module "as is" and "in place." Everything you put in a module is, by default and not subject to change, Shared.

Modules are excellent places to put data or procedures that need to be available to your entire program, and that don't need the replication or protection features of classes. Just remember that the penalty for overusing shared data is code that you can't easily use in more than one program. Self-contained classes are much more portable.

To add a module to your project, select Add New Item from the File menu. When the Add New Item dialog box appears, select Module in the Templates box and then click Open.

Example: Dealing Cards

This example takes the playing card scenario three steps further; it creates four players, deals the cards, and gives each player a way to play a card. Figure 8-8 shows the application in action.

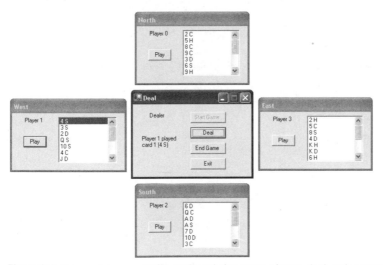

Figure 8-8 This program can shuffle cards and also create players, deal, and accept plays from each player.

Here's the procedure for creating this application, separated into sections. As fair warning, you'll be using the *Deck* class again.

Creating the Main Form

Follow these steps to create the main form for this example:

1   In Visual Studio .NET, create a new Windows Application project named *deal*.

2   In Windows Explorer, copy the Deck.vb file from the *suffleclass2* project you created in the previous chapter and add it to the deal folder you created in step 1.

3   In Visual Studio .NET, select Add Existing Item from the File menu and add the Deck.vb file you just copied. If you do this correctly, the Deck.vb file shows up in the Solution Explorer window.

4   Display Form1 form in Design view, select it, and set its *Text* property to *Deal*.

5   Add two Labels to the Form1 form and assign these properties:

Name	lblDealer	lblPlay
AutoSize	True	False
Text	Dealer	No Play

6   Add four Buttons to the Form1 form and assign these properties:

Name	btnStartGame	btnDeal	btnEndGame	btnExit
Enabled	True	False	False	True
Text	Start Game	Deal	End Game	Exit

7   Arrange the six controls on the Form1 form as shown in this graphic:

8   Double-click Exit. This displays an empty *btnExit_Click* subroutine in the code editor. To make the program end when the use clicks Exit, add the following statement to this subroutine:

```
Me.Close()
```

9 Click the Form1.vb [Design] tab to display the form in Windows Form Designer, then double-click any part of the form background. This displays an empty *Form1_Load* subroutine in the code editor. To center the form when the program starts, add these statements to the empty subroutine:

```
Me.Left = _
    (Screen.PrimaryScreen.Bounds.Width - Me.Width) / 2
Me.Top = _
    (Screen.PrimaryScreen.Bounds.Height - Me.Height) / 2
```

The first statement positions the left side of the current form to one half the width of the user's display minus the current width of the form. The second statement repeats this calculation for the vertical dimension.

10 To save your work, choose Save All from the File menu.

At this point, pressing F5 should start the program and display the Form1 form in the center of your screen. However, Exit will be the only button that works. The Deal and End Game buttons will appear dimmed. To make the program more functional, continue with the next series of steps.

Displaying the Player Forms

Follow these steps to add the capability of creating four windows for four players:

1 With the *deal* project open in Visual Studio .NET, select Add New Item from the File menu. When the Add New Item dialog box appears, select the Windows Form template, assign a name of Player.vb, and click Open.

2 Select the Player.vb form in the Form Designer window and then, in the Properties window, specify these settings.

Name	*Player*
Control Box	*False*
Show in Taskbar	*False*
Text	*Player*

3 Add a Label to the Player form. Name it *lblPlayer*, set its *Autosize* property to *True*, and set its *Text* property to *Player*.

4 Add a Button to the form. Name it *btnPlay* and set its *Text* property to *Play*.

5   Add a ListBox to the form. Name it *lstHand*, then arrange the controls and size the form as shown in this graphic:

6   Right-click the Player form and choose View Code from the shortcut menu.

7   Add the following declarations before the first *Function* or *Sub* statement, if any. If there are no *Function* or *Sub* statements, add these statements before the *End Class* statement:

```
Private intHand(12) As Integer
Private intCardsInHand As Integer = 0
Private intPlayerNum As Integer
```

The *intHand* array will contain one entry for each card in a player's hand. The *intCardsInHand* variable will count how many cards the hand currently contains. The *intPlayerNum* variable will contain a player number between 0 and 3.

8   Add the following property procedure immediately after the code you entered in step 7. Code outside the form will use this procedure to tell each instance of the form which player it's representing. Note that setting the property updates not only affects the *intPlayerNum* variable, but also the *Text* property of the *lblPlayer* label.

```
Public Property PlayerNum()
    Get
        Return intPlayerNum
    End Get
    Set(ByVal Value)
        intPlayerNum = Value
        lblPlayer.Text = "Player " & Value
    End Set
End Property
```

9   If the Form1.vb form isn't open, double-click its entry in the Solution Explorer window. If the form's code isn't visible, right-click the form and select View Code from the shortcut menu.

10 Add the following declaration after the *Windows Form Designer Generated Code* region and before the first subroutine that follows it. Make sure you're working on the *Form1* form and not on the *Player* form.

```
Dim plyForm(3) As Player
```

This array will contain a pointer to each instance of the *Player* form.

11 Display the *Form1* form in design mode and then double-click Start Game. The code editor will then display an empty *btnStartGame_Click* subroutine. To make the button display a form for each player, add this code to the empty subroutine:

```
Dim intPlayer As Integer
For intPlayer = 0 To UBound(plyForm)
    plyForm(intPlayer) = New Player()
    plyForm(intPlayer).PlayerNum = intPlayer
    plyForm(intPlayer).Text = Choose(intPlayer + 1, _
        "North, "West", "South""", "East")
    plyForm(intPlayer).Show()
    AlignPlayerForm(intPlayer)
Next
```

The *For* loop in this code varies the *intPlayer* variable from 0 to 3: one value for each player. The first statement inside the loop creates a new *Player* object—that is, a new form—and stores a reference to the new form object in the *plyForm* array. The next two statements store a player number and a player name in the new form object. The *Show* method makes the new form visible and the *AlignPlayerForm* method positions the new form on the user's display.

12 Add the following statements after the code you entered in step 11:

```
btnStartGame.Enabled = False
btnDeal.Enabled = True
btnEndGame.Enabled = True
```

These statements change the *Enabled* state of three buttons. The first statement dims the Start Game button because the game is already started. The next two statements enable the Deal and End Game buttons for the same reason.

13 Add the following subroutine after the *End Sub* statement that completes the *btnStartGame_Click* subroutine you just worked on:

```
Sub AlignPlayerForm(ByVal aintPlayer As Integer)
    If IsNothing(plyForm(aintPlayer)) Then
        Exit Sub
    End If
```

```
Select Case aintPlayer
    Case 0
        plyForm(0).Top = Me.Top _
                        - (plyForm(0).Height + 10)
        plyForm(0).Left = Me.Left + (Me.Width / 2) _
                        - (plyForm(0).Width / 2)
    Case 1
        plyForm(1).Top = Me.Top + (Me.Height / 2) _
                        - ((plyForm(1).Height) / 2)
        plyForm(1).Left = Me.Left + Me.Width + 10
    Case 2
        plyForm(2).Top = Me.Top + Me.Height + 10
        plyForm(2).Left = Me.Left + (Me.Width / 2) _
                        - (plyForm(2).Width / 2)
    Case 3
        plyForm(3).Top = Me.Top + (Me.Height / 2) _
                        - ((plyForm(3).Height) / 2)
        plyForm(3).Left = Me.Left _
                        - (plyForm(3).Width + 10)
End Select
End Sub
```

This code is a bit tedious, but basically, the *If* statement at the top
verifies that the *aintPlayer* argument points to an object. If it doesn't,
an *Exit Sub* statement terminates processing.

The *Select Case* statement computes a different position for each
possible player window. Player 1's form is supposed to be centered
above the main form, Player 2's form centered to its right, and so forth.
Each assignment statement sets a player form's *Top* or *Left* property relative to the main form's *Top* or *Left* property.

14 To save your work, select Save All from the File menu.

At this point, pressing F5 should start the program and display the Form1
form as before. Now, however, clicking Start Game should display four new
player forms, arranged as shown previously in Figure 8-8. The Deal and End
Game buttons still won't work, nor will the Play buttons on each Player form.

Note carefully, however, that you have four player forms for the effort of
coding one. This is the kind of productivity you get when you build your programs out of classes.

Moving the Player Forms

Even if you got the four player forms to appear in their proper positions, you
might have noticed that if you moved the main window around the screen, the
player forms didn't follow. To correct this, add the following subroutine before or
after any other subroutine in the Form1 form. (Just before the *AlignPlayerForm*
subroutine would be a good choice.)

```
Sub MoveMe(ByVal sender As Object, ByVal e As EventArgs) _
      Handles MyBase.Move
    Dim intPlayer As Integer
    For intPlayer = 0 To UBound(plyForm)
       AlignPlayerForm(intPlayer)
    Next
End Sub
```

The *Handles MyBase.Move* expression on the second line tells Visual Basic .NET that this subroutine wants to receive event notifications whenever the screen position of the main form changes. The *For* loop then calls the *AlignPlayerForm* subroutine once for each form. This is the subroutine you coded in step 13 of the preceding procedure.

The *System.Windows.Forms.Form* class raises a *Move* event whenever a form changes location on the screen. This is true even though another class, such as *Form1*, is inheriting *System.Windows.Forms.Form*. As a result, there's no such form event as *Me.Move*. The *MyBase* keyword points to the base class that *Me* inherits, and is therefore suitable for locating the *Move* event.

Select Save All from the File menu to save your work, then press F5 to run the program. After clicking Start Game, you should find that moving the main form causes the player forms to follow it around the screen.

Declaring a Deck of Cards

Deciding where to declare the object variable for the deck of cards presents a problem, because both the *Form1* form and the four *Player* forms will need access to it. One solution might be declaring it as a public property of the *Form1* form, but a cleaner solution is to declare the deck inside a module. To create a module that contains an object variable for the deck, proceed as follows:

1 Select Add New Item from the File menu.

2 When the Add New Item dialog box appears, select the Module template and then click Open. (The default module name Module1.vb is satisfactory for this project.)

3 With the Module1 module open in code view, add the statement shown here in boldface:

```
Module Module1
    Public dckCards As New Deck()
End Module
```

The *dckCards* variable will now be available to every piece of code in your project.

Dealing the Cards

This procedure makes the Deal button on the main form work. The button will shuffle the deck, then give the first card to player 1, the second card to player 2, and so forth. Finally, it will show each player's hand in the appropriate list box. Just follow these steps:

1 Display the *Form1* form in Windows Form Designer, then double-click Deal. The code editor will then display an empty *btnDeal_Click* subroutine. Enter the following code within this subroutine:

```
Dim intPlayer As Integer
Dim intCard As Integer
For intPlayer = 0 To UBound(plyForm)
    plyForm(intPlayer).ClearHand()

Next
dckCards.ShuffleDeck()
intPlayer = 0

For intCard = 0 To dckCards.Size
    plyForm(intPlayer).TakeCard(intCard)
    If intPlayer < UBound(plyForm) Then
        intPlayer += 1
    Else
        intPlayer = 0
    End If
Next
For intPlayer = 0 To UBound(plyForm)
    plyForm(intPlayer).DisplayHand()
Next
```

The first two statements declare variables to use for iterating through players and cards. The next three statements are a *For* loop that varies *intPlayer* from zero through all available forms, calling the *ClearHand* method of each player's form. Step 2 will develop the *ClearHand* method.

The next two statements shuffle the deck and initialize the *intPlayer* variable to zero. This will be the first player to receive a dealt card.

Next, a *For* loop varies *intCard* from zero through the maximum for the deck. The first statement within this loop calls the *TakeCard* method of the current player's form, passing the card number as an argument. Step 3 will develop the *TakeCard* method. Finally, the code inside the loop examines the *intPlayer* variable. If this is already at the maximum, the code sets its back to zero. Otherwise, the code adds one. This has the effect of giving cards 0, 4, 8, and so forth to player 0; cards 1, 5, 9, and so forth to player 1; and so on for players 2 and 3.

The last loop calls the *DisplayHand* method of each player's form. Step 4 will develop the *DisplayHand* method.

2 Display the code for the Player.vb form in the code editor. Then, enter the following subroutine immediately before any existing *Function* or *Sub* statement, or immediately after any *End Function* or *End Sub* statement:

```
Public Sub ClearHand()
    Array.Clear(intHand, 0, UBound(intHand) + 1)
    lstHand.Items.Clear()
    intCardsInHand = 0
End Sub
```

The first statement in this method calls the *Clear* method of a .NET array. The first argument specifies the array to clear, the second argument specifies the first subscript to clear, and the third argument specifies how many array elements to clear. This is easier than writing a loop that varies a subscript and moves zero to each array element.

The second statement calls the *Clear* method of the *lstHand* list box. This removes any existing entries from the box.

The third statement sets the count of currently held cards to 0. The *intCardsInHand* variable is one you declared previously, outside any *Function* or *Sub* statement.

3 Enter the following subroutine immediately after the one you entered in step 2. This is the method that receives cards from the *btnDeal_Click* subroutine in the Form1 form.

```
Public Sub TakeCard(ByVal aintCard As Integer)
    intCardsInHand += 1
    If intCardsInHand - 1 <= UBound(intHand) Then
        intHand(intCardsInHand - 1) = aintCard
    End If
End Sub
```

This method receives one argument: the current card's number within the deck. To store this card number in the current player's hand, the code first increments the number of cards in the hand by one. If this minus one is less than or equal to the maximum permissible subscript in the *intHand* array, the code saves the given card number in that position of the *intHand* array. (Note that the count varies from 1 to 13, but the subscript ranges from 0 to 12.)

4 Next, enter the following subroutine after the one you entered in step 3. It makes the cards in the current hand visible in the list box in the current Player form.

```
Public Sub DisplayHand()
    Dim intCardPos As Integer
    Dim intCurCard As Integer
    lstHand.Items.Clear()
    For intCardPos = 0 To intCardsInHand - 1
        intCurCard = intHand(intCardPos)
        lstHand.Items.Add(dckCards.Rank(intCurCard) & " " & _
                          dckCards.Suit(intCurCard))
    Next
End Sub
```

First, the subroutine declares a variable to use for iterating through the cards in the hand and another for temporarily holding a card. Then, it clears anything currently in the list box, using the *Clear* method just as the *ClearHand* method in step 2 did. Finally, a *For* loop varies the *intCardPos* value from 0 to the number of cards in the hand, again adjusting by –1. For each card in the hand, the loop retrieves the card's number in the deck, then calls the *Rank* and *Suit* methods of the *dckCards* object, then adds the results as a new item in the list box.

5 To save your work, select Save All from the File menu.

6 Press F5 to run the program.

Once the program is running, click Start Game. This should display the four player windows as before. Now, however, clicking Deal should distribute 13 cards to each player.

Ending the Game

At this point, the program is still missing two key features: playing a card and ending the game. Ending the game is easier, so that one comes first. Proceed as follows:

1 Display the *Form1* form in Windows Form Designer, then double-click End Game. This displays an empty subroutine named *btnEndGame_Click*.

2 Enter the following code inside the *btnEndGame_Click* subroutine:

```
Dim intPlayer As Integer
For intPlayer = 0 To UBound(plyForm)
    plyForm(intPlayer).Dispose()
```

```
Next
btnStartGame.Enabled = True
btnDeal.Enabled = False
btnEndGame.Enabled = False
```

The first statement declares a variable named *intPlayer* for use in iterating through each *Player* form. The next three statements constitute a *For* loop that varies the *intPlayer* variable from zero to the subscript of the last *Player* form, disposing of each *Player* form as it goes. The last three statements enable the Start Game button and dim the Deal and End Game buttons.

3 To save your work, select Save All from the File menu.

Now, when you press F5 to run the program, clicking Start Game displays four *Player* forms as before. However, clicking End Game now makes the *Player* forms disappear.

Playing a Card

When the user clicks Play in any *Player* form, the click handler for the Play button needs to send information about the played card to the Form1 form, which, as you've probably noticed, is the central control point for the program. The click handler could do this by calling a method designed for that purpose in the Form1 form, but this would mean ending the chapter with no example that uses events. That, of course, would be a pity.

To communicate information about a played card, then, each *Player* form will declare an event named *PlayCard*, and it will raise that event whenever the user clicks Play. An event handler in the *Form1* form will receive these events and display appropriate messages in the *Form1* form itself. To conjure up this magic, proceed as follows:

1 Open the *Player* form in code view and add the declaration shown here in boldface:

```
Private intHand(12) As Integer
Private intCardsInHand As Integer = 0
Private intPlayerNum As Integer
Event PlayCard(ByVal intPlayer As Integer, _
              ByVal intCard As Integer)
```

This declares an event named *PlayCard* that accepts two arguments: a player and a card.

2   Display the *Player* form in the Windows Form Designer, then double-click Play. This displays an empty subroutine named *btnPlay_Click*. Add the following code inside this subroutine:

```
If (lstHand.SelectedIndex < 0) _
Or (lstHand.SelectedIndex > UBound(intHand)) Then
    MsgBox("No card selected.", MsgBoxStyle.Critical, _
        "Error by player " & intPlayerNum & _
        " (" & Me.Text & ")")
Else
    RaiseEvent PlayCard(intPlayerNum, _
        intHand(lstHand.SelectedIndex))
End If
```

This code starts out by checking the *SelectedIndex* property of the *lstHand* list box. A value less than 0 indicates that no entry is currently selected. Values of 0 or more indicate the position of a selected item: 0 for the first item, 1 for the second, and so forth. Of course, the selected item should never have an index larger than the number of cards in the hand. So, if the *SelectedIndex* property is too low or too high, the code simply displays an error message and doesn't try to play a card.

If *lstHand.SelectedIndex* does contain an acceptable value, the code raises the *PlayCard* event, passing the current player number and the played card as arguments.

To get the played card, the code uses *lstHand.SelectedIndex* as a subscript to the *intHand* table. The *lstHand.SelectedIndex* property indicates whether the user played the first card in the hand, the second card in the hand, or another card. Using this value as a subscript to the *intHand* table translates the card's position in the hand to the card's position in the deck. The event handler in the Form1 form will use the card's position in the deck to look up its rank and suit.

Note   This example won't implement a complete card game, but if it did, code in this subroutine would also need to remove the played card from the *intHand* array and from the *lstHand* list box.

---

3   To save your work, select Save All from the File menu. Then, press F5 to run the program. After starting the game and dealing, you can select a card and click Play in any of the *Player* windows, but nothing will happen. Did you expect an error? Well, sending out an event when no corresponding event handler is active doesn't generate an error.

4 Click Exit to end the program, then display the Form1 form in code view. Then, just before or after any existing function or subroutine, add the following code:

```
Sub PlayerCard(ByVal intPlayer As Integer, _
            ByVal intCard As Integer)
    lblPlay.Text = "Player " & intPlayer & _
        " played card " & intCard & " (" & _
        dckCards.Rank(intCard) & " " & _
        dckCards.Suit(intCard) & ")"
End Sub
```

This code is going to be the event handler for any and all *PlayCard* events. It receives two *Integer* arguments, a signature that corresponds to the *PlayCard* event declaration.

> **Note**   If this example were implementing a complete card game, the *PlayerCard* subroutine would also determine whether the play was in turn or out of turn, determine whether all cards for the current trick had been played, and, if so, determine the outcome and keep score.

5 To designate the *PlayerCard* subroutine as a handler for the *PlayCard* event for each *Player* form, add the statement shown here in boldface to the *For* loop in the *btnStartGame_Click* subroutine:

```
For intPlayer = 0 To UBound(plyForm)
    plyForm(intPlayer) = New Player()
    plyForm(intPlayer).PlayerNum = intPlayer
    plyForm(intPlayer).Text = Choose(intPlayer + 1, _
        "North", "West", "South", "East")
    AddHandler plyForm(intPlayer).PlayCard, _
            AddressOf PlayerCard
    plyForm(intPlayer).Show()
    AlignPlayerForm(intPlayer)
Next
```

The *AddHandler* statement takes two arguments: the name of the event and the address of the event handler subroutine. The name of the event consists of a variable that points to the object that raises the event, a period, and the name of the event.

6 You should also remove the event handler when you discard the *Player* forms. To do this, add the statement shown here in boldface to the *For* loop in the *btnEndGame_Click* subroutine:

```
For intPlayer = 0 To UBound(plyForm)
    RemoveHandler plyForm(intPlayer).PlayCard, _
            AddressOf PlayerCard
    plyForm(intPlayer).Dispose()
Next
```

Notice the similarity between the *AddHandler* statement in the previous step and the *RemoveHandler* statement in this one. You must specify both the event name and the handler address when you remove a handler because the same event can have multiple handlers.

7 To save your work, select Save All from the File menu.

Now, after you press F5 to run the program, click Start Game, and then click Deal, you should be able to select any card in a Player list box, click that player's Play button, and see a corresponding message in the Form1 form.

Here are complete listings of the Form1.vb and Player.vb files for your reference. Don't be concerned if your code has fewer line continuations or if the functions and subroutines appear in a different order; these factors don't affect the way the program works.

Form1.vb

```
Public Class Form1
    Inherits System.Windows.Forms.Form

+ Windows Form Designer generated code
    Dim plyForm(3) As Player

    Private Sub Form1_Load( _
            ByVal sender As System.Object, _
            ByVal e As System.EventArgs) _
            Handles MyBase.Load
        Me.Left = _
            (Screen.PrimaryScreen.Bounds.Width - Me.Width) _
            / 2
        Me.Top = _
            (Screen.PrimaryScreen.Bounds.Height - Me.Height) _
            / 2
    End Sub

    Private Sub btnStartGame_Click( _
            ByVal sender As System.Object, _
            ByVal e As System.EventArgs) _
            Handles btnStartGame.Click
        Dim intPlayer As Integer
        For intPlayer = 0 To UBound(plyForm)
            plyForm(intPlayer) = New Player()
            plyForm(intPlayer).PlayerNum = intPlayer
            plyForm(intPlayer).Text = Choose(intPlayer + 1, _
                "North", "West", "South", "East")
            AddHandler plyForm(intPlayer).PlayCard, _
                    AddressOf PlayerCard
            plyForm(IntPlayer).Show()
            AlignPlayerForm(intPlayer)
```

```vbnet
        Next
        btnStartGame.Enabled = False
        btnDeal.Enabled = True
        btnEndGame.Enabled = True
    End Sub

    Private Sub btnDeal_Click( _
                ByVal sender As System.Object, _
                ByVal e As System.EventArgs) _
                Handles btnDeal.Click
        Dim intPlayer As Integer
        Dim intCard As Integer
        For intPlayer = 0 To UBound(plyForm)
            plyForm(intPlayer).ClearHand()
        Next
        dckCards.ShuffleDeck()
        intPlayer = 0
        For intCard = 0 To dckCards.Size
            plyForm(intPlayer).TakeCard(intCard)
            If intPlayer < UBound(plyForm) Then
                intPlayer += 1
            Else
                intPlayer = 0
            End If
        Next
        For intPlayer = 0 To UBound(plyForm)
            plyForm(intPlayer).DisplayHand()
        Next
    End Sub

    Private Sub btnEndGame_Click( _
                ByVal sender As System.Object, _
                ByVal e As System.EventArgs) _
                Handles btnEndGame.Click
        Dim intPlayer As Integer
        For intPlayer = 0 To UBound(plyForm)
            RemoveHandler plyForm(intPlayer).PlayCard, _
                        AddressOf PlayerCard
            plyForm(intPlayer).Dispose()
        Next
        btnStartGame.Enabled = True
        btnDeal.Enabled = False
        btnEndGame.Enabled = False
    End Sub

    Sub MoveMe(ByVal sender As Object, _
                ByVal e As EventArgs) _
                Handles MyBase.Move
        Dim intPlayer As Integer
```

```
        For intPlayer = 0 To UBound(plyForm)
            AlignPlayerForm(intPlayer)
        Next
    End Sub

    Sub AlignPlayerForm(ByVal aintPlayer As Integer)
        If IsNothing(plyForm(aintPlayer)) Then
            Exit Sub
        End If
        Select Case aintPlayer
            Case 0
                plyForm(0).Top = Me.Top _
                                - (plyForm(0).Height + 10)
                plyForm(0).Left = Me.Left + (Me.Width / 2) _
                                - (plyForm(0).Width / 2)
            Case 1
                plyForm(1).Top = Me.Top + (Me.Height / 2) _
                                - ((plyForm(1).Height) / 2)
                plyForm(1).Left = Me.Left + Me.Width + 10
            Case 2
                plyForm(2).Top = Me.Top + Me.Height + 10
                plyForm(2).Left = Me.Left + (Me.Width / 2) _
                                - (plyForm(2).Width / 2)
            Case 3
                plyForm(3).Top = Me.Top + (Me.Height / 2) _
                                - ((plyForm(3).Height) / 2)
                plyForm(3).Left = Me.Left _
                                - (plyForm(3).Width + 10)
        End Select
    End Sub

    Sub PlayerCard(ByVal intPlayer As Integer, _
                ByVal intCard As Integer)
        lblPLay.Text = "Player " & intPlayer & _
                    " played card " & intCard & " (" & _
                    dckCards.Rank(intCard) & " " & _
                    dckCards.Suit(intCard) & ")"
    End Sub

    Private Sub btnExit_Click( _
                ByVal sender As System.Object, _
                ByVal e As System.EventArgs) _
                Handles btnExit.Click
        Me.Close()
    End Sub

End Class
```

Player.vb

```vb
Public Class Player
    Inherits System.Windows.Forms.Form

+ Windows Form Designer generated code
    Private intHand(12) As Integer
    Private intCardsInHand As Integer = 0
    Private intPlayerNum As Integer
    Event PlayCard(ByVal intPlayer As Integer, _
                ByVal intCard As Integer)
    Public Property PlayerNum()
        Get
            Return intPlayerNum
        End Get
        Set(ByVal Value)
            intPlayerNum = Value
            lblPlayer.Text = "Player " & Value
        End Set
    End Property

    Sub ClearHand()
        Array.Clear(intHand, 0, UBound(intHand) + 1)
        lstHand.Items.Clear()
        intCardsInHand = 0
    End Sub

    Public Sub TakeCard(ByVal aintCard As Integer)
        intCardsInHand += 1
        If intCardsInHand - 1 <= UBound(intHand) Then
            intHand(intCardsInHand - 1) = aintCard
        End If
    End Sub

    Public Sub DisplayHand()
        Dim intCardPos As Integer
        Dim intCurCard As Integer
        lstHand.Items.Clear()
        For intCardPos = 0 To intCardsInHand - 1
            intCurCard = intHand(intCardPos)
            lstHand.Items.Add(dckCards.Rank(intCurCard) & _
                        " " & dckCards.Suit(intCurCard))
        Next
    End Sub

    Private Sub btnPlay_Click(_
                ByVal sender As System.Object, _
                ByVal e As System.EventArgs) _
                Handles btnPlay.Click
        If (lstHand.SelectedIndex < 0) _
        Or (lstHand.SelectedIndex > UBound(intHand)) Then
            MsgBox("No card selected.", _
```

```
                    MsgBoxStyle.Critical, _
                    "Error by player " & intPlayerNum & _
                    " (" & Me.Text & ")")
        Else
            RaiseEvent PlayCard(intPlayerNum,
                    intHand(lstHand.SelectedIndex))
        End If
    End Sub

End Class
```

Key Points

■ The .NET Framework provides more than 16,000 classes you can use in Visual Basic .NET programs. The number of properties and methods these classes offer is even larger. You can search for useful classes several different ways in the MSDN Library.

■ Microsoft organizes .NET classes into hierarchical categories called namespaces.

■ If your program contains an *Imports* statement for a given namespace, you don't need to specify fully qualified names for classes in that namespace.

■ Inheritance refers to the ability of one class to inherit the properties of another class. If one class does almost everything you want, you can write a new class that inherits it and then code only the additional features or exceptions. A derived class inherits from a base class.

■ Overloading involves creating two or more methods with the same name but different signatures. (The number and type of arguments determines a function or subroutine's signature.) When you call the method name, Visual Basic .NET runs the version that best matches the arguments you specify.

■ Polymorphism involves using the same method and property names in different classes, even though the effect on each class might be customized to that class.

■ Events are signals that indicate something has occurred. Visual Basic .NET provides special statements to declare events, raise events, designate subroutines as event handlers, and remove subroutines as event handlers.

■ All Windows forms are derived classes that inherit a base .NET class named *System.Windows.Forms.Form*. The base class provides all the standard form behaviors such as drawing the form on screen, resizing it, responding to clicks, and so forth.

■ Modules provide handy containers for declaring items that should be globally available to all parts of your programs.

Chapter 9

Designing and Using Windows Forms

For any Microsoft Windows program, forms are the essence of the user interface. A Windows desktop program that never displays a form has no way to directly interact with its user and therefore no way to find out what the user wants it to do. Even systems tasks that run in the background and never display a form themselves have configuration programs that display forms. Forms are everywhere.

Blank forms, of course, are about as informative as a blank sheet of paper and about as useful as an elevator with no buttons. That's why designers fill them with menu bars, toolbar buttons, text boxes, picture boxes, drop-down lists, and all the other paraphernalia of modern user interfaces.

This chapter deals a bit with form design and then discusses some issues having to do with form and control properties, message boxes, and icons. It concludes with a fairly detailed example that illustrates how to design and use menu bars and toolbars. The example also shows how to display pictures and interact with the clipboard.

Designing User Interfaces

Everyone wants user interfaces that are attractive, functional, and intuitively obvious. Microsoft Visual Basic .NET gives you all the components you need to achieve this goal in every program you write, but of course it's your job to use them properly. Even if you buy the best canvas, oils, and brushes, you can still paint an ugly picture.

In general, the best approach to designing user interfaces begins with consistency. Menu bars, for example, should appear at the top of the window and use the same conventions as all other Windows programs: File, Edit, and View at the left, Window and Help at the right, and everything else in between. Boring and humdrum as this might be, whoever uses your program will expect and appreciate it. (Of course, if your program doesn't require a File menu, you should omit it completely.)

Subcommands should also follow established patterns: New, Open, Close, Save, Print, and Exit usually appear in that order in the File menu, for example. When in doubt, open a few popular programs of the same general type as yours, see what they've done, and combine the best features of each of them.

Toolbars usually appear just below the menu bar, and status bars are at the bottom of the window. Toolbar icons are subject to more copyright restrictions than the names of menu items, but even so, you should avoid unnecessary cleverness. Icons such as these, for example, appear so commonly that they seem to be in the public domain.

These icons, by the way, usually mean New, Open, Save, Print, Spell Check, Cut, Copy, Paste, Undo, and Redo.

If you decide to use a status bar, it should usually appear at the bottom of the form. Keep the status bar updated with (what else?) messages that indicate the status of the program.

Lingo   In the context of a form, a *control* is one user interface element: one text box, one option box, or any element you add to the form one at a time.

The central area of a form displays the data your program works with, be that text, pictures, database fields, option settings, or anything else. It might contain a single large control, such as a word processing document or picture, or an assemblage of controls such as text boxes, check boxes, and option buttons.

Lingo   *Option buttons* are what some people call *radio buttons*.

It's important to lay out form controls in a logical sequence and to use the right control for the right job. Controls for the most important, most general information should usually appear at the top-left corner of the form. Controls for the least important, most specific information should, of course, appear at the lower right. However, it's also important to group controls for related information and to present them in a conventional order. For example, you should almost always lay out name, address, city, state, and zip code in that order, no matter which of these fields you consider the most important.

Figure 9-1 shows a simple but representative form open in Microsoft Visual Studio .NET. A menu bar and a toolbar appear at the top of the form and a status bar appears at the bottom. There are no surprises here. The developer added these elements in Windows Form Designer (and, in the next exercise, so will you) by double-clicking the MainMenu control type, the ToolBar control type, and the StatusBar control type on the Windows Forms tab of the Toolbox window. Of course, adding these controls to your form isn't the end of the job; you must also configure them.

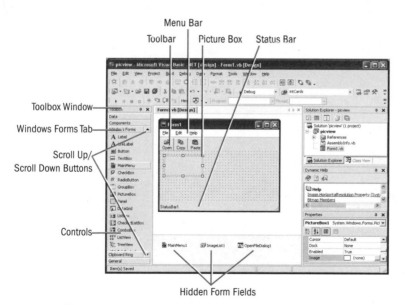

Figure 9-1 The Windows Form Designer in Visual Studio .NET displays forms much as the eventual user would see them.

The central part of the form contains one control, a so-called *PictureBox*. This will display any picture the user cares to open or paste.

The shaded area at the bottom of the Form Design window displays three *hidden* form controls. These controls have no physical appearance when the form is actually running, but they're nevertheless part of the form. The control named *MainMenu1* controls the menu bar. The control named *ImageList1* provides a collection of pictures that other controls can then use. In this program, for example, the toolbar gets its icons from the *ImageList1* control. The control named *OpenFileDialog1* displays a standard Windows File Open dialog box.

Setting Form and Control Properties

As you've seen in all the examples so far, both forms and form controls have a multitude of properties that control their behavior. You can initialize the value of many such properties in the Windows Form Designer, and you can change them from code as well. Figure 9-2, for example, shows the properties that Visual Studio .NET can initialize at design time.

Properties	廿 ✕
PictureBox1 System.Windows.Form ▼	
⊞ (DataBindings)	
⊞ (DynamicProperties)	
(Name)	**PictureBox1**
AccessibleDescription	
AccessibleName	
AccessibleRole	Default
Anchor	Top, Left
BackColor	☐ Control
BackgroundImage	☐ (none)
BorderStyle	None
ContextMenu	(none)
Cursor	Default
Dock	None
Enabled	True
Image	☐ (none) ...
⊞ Location	**16, 56**
Locked	False
Modifiers	**Friend**
⊞ Size	100, 50
SizeMode	**AutoSize**
Tag	
Visible	True

Figure 9-2 This version of the Properties window shows the settings Windows Form Designer can initialize for a *PictureBox* control.

Figure 9-3 shows what happens when you type the name of a *PictureBox* and a period in Visual Studio .NET's Code Editor. The IntelliSense feature lists all the properties, methods, and events available to a *PictureBox* when the program that contains it is running. Notice, however, that the Windows Form Designer and the IntelliSense lists differ. In Windows Form Designer, for example, you can change some properties (such as *Name*) that you can't change from code. In code you can change some properties (like *AllowDrop*) that the Form Designer can't touch.

```
Private Sub mnuFileOpen_Click(ByVal sender As System.Object, _
                             ByVal e As System.EventArgs) _
                    Handles mnuFileOpen.Click
    If OpenFileDialog1.ShowDialog() = DialogResult.OK Then
        Try
            PictureBox1.
            AdjustFor [icon] ■ AccessibleDescription   ▲ alog1.FileName)
        Catch ex As E [icon] ■ AccessibleName
            MsgBox("C  [icon] ■ AccessibleRole
                    C  [icon] ■ AllowDrop              me & _
                    v  [icon] ■ Anchor
                    M  [icon] ■ BackColor                 h, _
                    A  [icon] ■ BackgroundImage           e)
        End Try        [icon] ■ BorderStyle
    End If             [icon] ◆ BringToFront
End Sub               [icon] ■ CausesValidation       ▼
```

Figure 9-3 The IntelliSense feature offers this list of properties, methods, and events for a *PictureBox* control. Note the discrepancies between this list and the list in Figure 9-2.

There are usually good reasons for these disparities. Changing a control's name, for example would require recompiling the program, and you can't do that after the program is already running (not for the current run, anyway). Methods and events, of course, have no meaning in Windows Form Designer and for that reason don't appear there. Some properties, such as *AllowDrop*, are so tightly associated with code that the Form Designer simply doesn't bother listing them.

When searching for properties in Windows Form Designer, don't overlook the Plus and Minus icons that appear in front of some entries. The property you're looking for could be hidden and unexpanded behind a Plus icon!

If a property can accept hand-typed text or digits as its value, clicking the property name changes the box at its right into a text box. If the property can only accept certain values, the box at its right changes to a drop-down list. You can recognize a drop-down list by its button, which always contains a down-pointing arrow.

If setting the property requires a full-blown dialog box, the box at its right will display an ellipsis button containing three dots. For an example, refer to the *Image* property in Figure 9-2. If you come across one of these (and sooner or later, you will) just click the button and fill in whatever blanks the dialog box provides. Ellipsis buttons are especially common for properties that require file names and those that contain collections.

For a complete reference to all the properties, methods, and events of a particular form control, open the Help index and search for the control's name. Look for an article with the name of the control followed by *members*. For example, the article that describes all the properties, methods, and events for the *DropDownList* control is titled DropDownList Members.

Using Message Boxes

Most of the examples you've seen in this book have used the *MsgBox* function without ever explaining it. Well, the buck stops here. The *MsgBox* function displays a message in a simple dialog box, waits for the user to click a button, and then returns an integer that indicates which button the user clicked.

The *MsgBox* function accepts one, two, or three parameters. However, only the first is required. Here are the parameters:

- **Prompt**   This parameter provides the text that the dialog box will display. This must be a *String* value of at most 1024 characters, depending on the width of the characters used. To create line breaks in the displayed text, include carriage returns, line feeds, or both in the *String* value. The following expressions provide these values:

Carriage return	*Chr(13)*	*vbCr*
Line feed	*Chr(10)*	*vbLf*
Carriage return and line feed	*Chr(13) & Chr(10)*	*vbCrLf*

- **Buttons**   This parameter specifies which buttons the dialog box will display, which button is the default, how the dialog box presents itself, and certain formatting options. To do this all in one parameter, you add together the options you want. Table 9-1 lists the valid options.

  When you specify a *Buttons* value, you can add together at most one value from the Button category, one value from the Icons category, one value from the Default category, and as many values as you like from the Other category. The following expression, for example, displays a dialog box with three buttons titled Yes, No, and Cancel. The dialog box also displays a Question Mark icon and the second button (No) is the default.

  ```
  MsgBoxStyle.YesNoCancel + _
  MsgBoxStyle.Question + _
  MsgBoxStyle.DefaultButton2
  ```

  If you omit this parameter or specify 0, the *MsgBox* function displays an OK button and no icon.

- **Title**   The third and final parameter specifies a *String* value that should appear in the dialog box's title bar. If you omit this parameter, the title bar will display the program name (minus the .exe extension).

Table 9-1   Values for the *MsgBox* Buttons Property

Category	Property	Description
Button	MsgBoxStyle.OKOnly	Displays an OK button only. This is the default.
	MsgBoxStyle.OKCancel	Displays OK and Cancel buttons.
	MsgBoxStyle.AbortRetryIgnore	Displays Abort, Retry, and Ignore buttons.
	MsgBoxStyle.YesNoCancel	Displays Yes, No, and Cancel buttons.
	MsgBoxStyle.YesNo	Displays Yes and No buttons.
	MsgBoxStyle.RetryCancel	Displays Retry and Cancel buttons.
Icons	MsgBoxStyle.Critical	Displays a Critical Message icon.
	MsgBoxStyle.Question	Displays a Warning Query icon.
	MsgBoxStyle.Exclamation	Displays a Warning Message icon.
	MsgBoxStyle.Information	Displays an Information Message icon.
Default	MsgBoxStyle.DefaultButton1	Makes the first button the default.
	MsgBoxStyle.DefaultButton2	Makes the second button the default.
	MsgBoxStyle.DefaultButton3	Makes the third button the default.
Display Modes	MsgBoxStyle.ApplicationModal	The user must close the message box before continuing work in the current application.
	MsgBoxStyle.SystemModal	The user must close the message box before continuing work in any application.
	MsgBoxStyle.MsgBoxSetForeground	Displays the message box window as the foreground window.
	MsgBoxStyle.MsgBoxRight	Right-aligns text within the message box.
	MsgBoxStyle.MsgBoxRtlReading	Displays text for right-to-left reading on Hebrew and Arabic systems.

The *ApplicationModal* setting means that the user can't activate any other form in your program until he or she responds to the message box. *SystemModal* further restricts the user from activating any other desktop programs that happen to be running. The *MsgBoxSetForeground* setting means that when the dialog box appears, it will be the top window on the desktop. This ensures that the message box will be visible even if some other program has the foreground when your program calls the *MsgBox* function.

If you tell the *MsgBox* function to display more than one button, you'll no doubt what to know which button the user clicked. To capture this information, compare the function's return code to this list of property values:

MsgBoxResult.OK
MsgBoxResult.Cancel
MsgBoxResult.Abort
MsgBoxResult.Retry

MsgBoxResult.Ignore
MsgBoxResult.Yes
MsgBoxResult.No

Here's an example:

```
Select Case MsgBox("Are you sure?", MsgBoxStyle.YesNo)
    Case MsgBoxResult.Yes
'       Code to process Yes response would go here.
    Case MsgBoxResult.No
'       Code to process No response would go here.
End Select
```

The *MsgBox* function is usually trouble-free but it can throw exceptions. The usual cause is a *Prompt* or *Title* value that isn't a *String* or a *Buttons* value that isn't a valid combination of options.

Finding and Creating Icons

Creating artwork and creating program code seem to require opposite mindsets. When someone who's good at artwork watches someone write program code, the artist frequently ends up walking away, shaking his or her head, and muttering. Of course, watching an artist work usually afflicts programmers in the same way. Don't be depressed if you can't excel at both of these tasks.

Icons that appear on toolbars and other user interface elements are usually 16 pixels in both height and width, but can be almost any bitmapped file format. BMP, GIF, ICO, and JPEG formats are all acceptable. Unless your icon fills the entire 16 × 16 space, however, you should use a file format like GIF or ICO that supports transparent backgrounds. This will keep your icon's background from sticking out like a sore thumb. (Remember, you have little or no control over the colors Windows uses when it displays your forms. Each user can use the Windows Control Panel to configure these colors any way he or she wants.)

ICO is a specialized file format that Microsoft devised just for making icons and when it comes to the program and form icons, ICO is the only acceptable format. This can be a nuisance because very few picture-editing programs support the ICO format. Visual Studio .NET comes with its own editor for ICO files, but it probably doesn't have all the features your favorite GIF or JPEG editor has. The first example steps you through the process of creating an ICO file in Visual Studio .NET.

The ICO file format only supports specific resolutions such as 16 × 16, 32 × 32, 48 × 48, and it supports color pallets of 2, 16, or 256 colors only. ICO files do, however, have one feature that other file formats don't: they can store multiple versions of the same picture. So, for example, a single ICO file can contain a 16-color, 16 × 16 pixel version; a 16 color, 32 × 32 pixel version; and a 256-color, 32 × 32 pixel version of the same icon.

Example: Creating a Picture Viewer

In this exercise you'll create the Picture Viewer program shown in Figure 9-4. This program displays pictures in any of the standard bitmapped formats: BMP, GIF, JPEG, and so forth. However, its main purpose is to illustrate how to create and configure icons, menus, and toolbars, and how to control them once the program is running. You'll probably be surprised at the number of things that go on behind the scenes of a Windows user interface.

Figure 9-4 This program displays pictures you open from a file or paste from the clipboard.

Creating the Picture Viewer Form

To begin creating the Picture Viewer program, launch Visual Studio .NET and then perform each of these steps:

1 Create a new Windows application project named *picview*.

2 Make sure the *Form1* form is open in the Windows Form Designer, then locate the Toolbox window. If it isn't visible, select Toolbox from the View menu.

3 In the Toolbox window, click the Windows Forms tab and then double-click each of the following items once. To find all six items, you'll have to scroll up and down the Windows Forms tab a bit:

● MainMenu

● PictureBox

● ImageList

- ToolBar

- StatusBar

- OpenFileDialog

When you double-click MainMenu, a menu temporarily appears in the body of the form. Because this is a new menu and doesn't contain any items, it disappears when you start working on another control. This is normal.

4 To configure the main menu, click the *MainMenu1* item that appears at the bottom of the Windows Form Designer window. This displays the menu bar and one menu option titled Type Here. Replace this title with the text shown here and then press Enter:

&File

The ampersand indicates which key the user would press to activate this menu. Entering *&File* (but underscore the *F*) means that when the program runs, the menu title will appear as File (again, with the *F* underscored) and pressing Alt+F will select it.

5 Reselect the File menu item and then, in the Properties window, change the Name property from *MenuItem1* (or whatever it is) to *mnuFile*.

Tip   When designing a main menu, don't forget to press Enter after you type each menu item. Otherwise, when you start working on something else, your changes to the menu will be lost. Think of Enter as the *save* key in this instance.

---

6 The menu bar should now resemble this graphic:

You can enter a new menu item either below or to the right of File. Type **&Open...** in the Type Here space below File.

Be sure to press Enter after you type the three periods, then reselect the option and change its name to *mnuFileOpen* in the Properties window.

This time, the ampersand makes O the shortcut key. The three periods (which constitute an ellipsis) alert the user that this menu choice opens a new window.

7 Spaces for additional menu choices now appear below and to the right of Open. Type the following choice in the space below Open:

`&Exit`

> Be sure to press Enter after you type **t**, and to change the name of this menu item to *mnuFileExit*.
>
> This time, the ampersand makes x the shortcut key. This is the practice in nearly every Windows program you'll see.

8 In the Type Here space to the right of File, type **&Edit**. Then, add &Copy and &Paste choices to the Edit menu just as you added Open and Exit choices to the File menu. None of these choices requires ellipses, but don't forget to press Enter after typing each one. Name them *mnuEdit, mnuEditCopy*, and *mnuEditPaste*.

9 In the Type Here space to the right of Edit, add a &Help menu with one choice: &About. . . . Don't forget to press Enter. Name these items *mnuHelp* and *mnuHelpAbout*.

10 To save your work, select Save All from the File menu.

At this point you can press F5 to run the program. The options on the main menu will be visible, but of course they won't do anything. Also, the toolbar will be blank. The next section explains how to get icons for the toolbar, the *Form1* form, and the entire program.

Creating the Picture Viewer Icons

The toolbar in the Picture Viewer program needs to display three icons: Open, Copy, and Paste. Fortunately, one of the sample applications you installed with Visual Studio .NET has icon files you can use for this purpose. Their names are Open.bmp, Copy.bmp, and Paste.bmp. By default, you can find these files at C:\Program Files\Microsoft Visual Studio .NET\FrameworkSDK\Samples\ QuickStart\Winforms\Samples\Controlreference\Tooltipctl\Vb. To use these files "as is," copy them into the Picview folder you created in step 1 of the previous procedure. By default, this will be C:\Documents and Settings*user*\ My Documents\Visual Studio Projects\Picview where *user* is your Windows logon ID. However, your form will be more attractive if you open each of the BMP files in your favorite picture editor, assign a transparent background color, and save the file into the Picview folder in GIF format.

To create an ICO file suitable for use as a program or folder icon, proceed as follows:

1   With the *picview* project open in Visual Studio .NET, follow these steps:

- Select Add New Item from the File menu.

- When the Add New Item dialog box appears, choose the Icon File template. This template appears near the bottom of the Templates list. To find it, you'll probably need to scroll down.

2   In the Name box, specify Picture.ico.

3   Click Open. Visual Studio .NET opens a picture-editing window for the new icon. This should resemble Figure 9-5. A palette of colors appears at the far left, then a normal sized view of the icon, then an enlarged view you can edit. The default resolution will be 32 × 32, 16 colors.

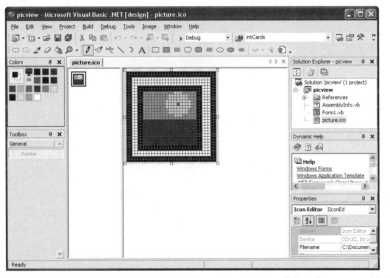

Figure 9-5 You can design and save icon files using the Image Editor that comes with Visual Studio .NET.

4   Draw any icon you like. To do this, you'll probably need the tools that appear on the Image Editor toolbar, which is the bottom toolbar in Figure 9-5. This provides tools for selecting parts of an image, painting individual pixels, and drawing lines, rectangles, curves, and so forth. Notice that an Image menu also appears on the main menu bar (between Tools & Window) whenever Image Editor is open.

If you like, you can copy images from other programs and paste them into the Visual Studio Icon Editor. If you decide to do this, you'll get better results by resizing the images and adjusting their palettes before you cut and paste them, rather than after.

5 When you're done drawing the 32 × 32 pixel icon, select New Image Type from the Image menu. Then, when the New Icon Image Type dialog box appears, choose 16 × 16, 16 Colors, and then click OK.

> If the choice 16 × 16, 16 Colors doesn't appear, it's probably because your file already contains an icon of that type. To check this possibility, click Cancel in the New Icon Image Type dialog box and then select Current Icon Image Types from the Image menu. Here you can select a 16 × 16, 16-Color icon if one exists.

6 Again, draw any icon you like. By convention this should be a reduced-size version of the of the 32 × 32 pixel icon, but in fact you can draw whatever you like.

7 When you're done drawing or just want to save your work, make sure that the Icon Editor is the active window and then select Save Picture.ico from the File menu.

Configuring the Form and Toolbar Icons

To configure the application, form, and toolbar to use the icons you just created, proceed as follows:

1 The application icon represents your program in Windows Explorer, on the Windows Start menu, on the Windows desktop, and so forth. To configure this icon, follow these steps:

- Right-click the picview project in the Solution Explorer window, then click Properties.

- When the Picview Property Pages dialog box appears, open the Common Properties heading and select Build.

- Select Picture.ico from the Application Icon drop-down list and click OK. Figure 9-6 shows this operation in progress.

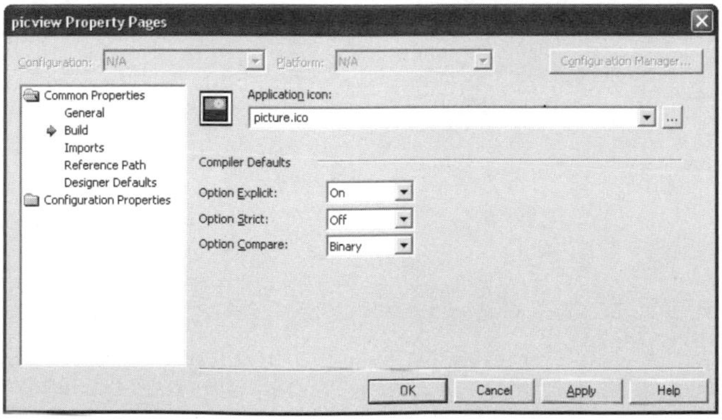

Figure 9-6 Use this dialog box to specify the icon for an entire application.

If Picture.ico doesn't appear in the drop-down list, you've either forgotten to save it or you saved it somewhere other than the Picview folder where your project resides. Either save the icon, move it to the right place, or look for it by clicking the ellipsis button at the right of the drop-down list.

2   The icon for the *Form1* form is the one that appears in its top-left corner and on the Windows taskbar. To specify this icon, follow these steps:

● Display the form in Windows Form Designer.

● Select the entire form by clicking its title bar or background.

● In the Properties window, scroll to the *Icon* property, select it, and click the ellipsis button (the one with the three periods).

● When the Open dialog box appears, select the icon file you want (Picture.ico, in this case) and then click OK.

The icon should now appear in the top left corner of the *Form1* form.

3   To configure the toolbar icons, you must first add all the pictures for the same toolbar to the same *ImageList*. To do this, follow these steps:

● Display the *Form1* form in Windows Form Designer.

● Select the *ImageList1* control you added in the first procedure.

● In the Properties window, locate and select the *Images* property, then click the ellipsis (…) button.

● When the Image Collection Editor dialog box appears, click Add.

● When the Open dialog box appears, locate the Open.bmp or Open.gif file you prepared in the previous section and then click OK.

● Repeat steps 4 and 5 for the copy and paste pictures. Your Image Collection Editor dialog box should now resemble the one shown in Figure 9-7. If it does, click OK.

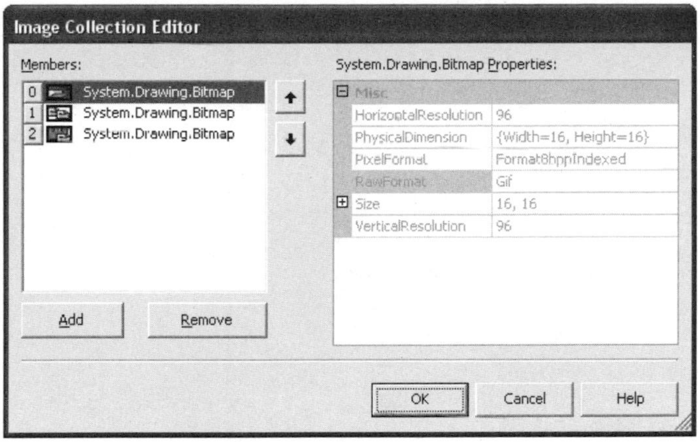

Figure 9-7 This dialog box adds and removes pictures from an *ImageList* control.

4 To configure the toolbar buttons, follow these steps:

- Select the toolbar in Windows Form Designer.

- In the Properties window, select the *ImageList* property and choose *ImageList1* from the drop-down list.

  This specifies that all the images for this toolbar will come from the *ImageList* you configured in step 3.

5 With the toolbar still selected, locate the *Buttons* property and click the ubiquitous ellipsis button. (Remember, dot-dot-dot in Morse code would be *S*.)

6 When the ToolBarButton Collection Editor dialog box appears, click Add and then specify the following properties:

Name	*tbbOpen*
ImageIndex:	*0*
Text	*Open*
ToolTipText	*Open*

7 Create two more toolbar buttons just as you did in the previous step. Assign these properties:

Name	*tbbCopy*	*tbbPaste*
ImageIndex	*1*	*2*
Text	*Copy*	*Paste*
ToolTipText	*Copy*	*Paste*

The ToolBarButton Collection Editor dialog box should now resemble Figure 9-8. If so, click OK.

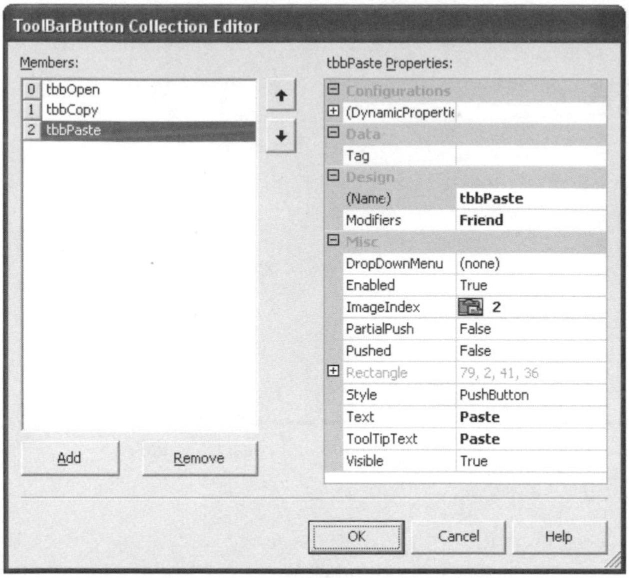

Figure 9-8 Add, change, and remove toolbar buttons using this dialog box. To display it, click the ellipsis button in the toolbar's Buttons property.

8 Your form should now resemble the one shown previously in Figure 9-1. To save your work, select Save All from the File menu.

If you press F5, the form, the menu, and the toolbar should all appear, but of course none of the menu options or buttons will work. Before writing that code, however, you need to set some additional project properties.

Specifying Assembly Information

During your Visual Studio .NET adventures thus far, you might have noticed a file named AssemblyInfo.vb in Solution Explorer. This file centrally records a number of useful and important facts about your program. To enter and start using this information, take these steps. They're not terribly drastic:

1 Double-click the AssemblyInfo.vb file in Solution Explorer and locate the following block of statements:

```
<Assembly: AssemblyTitle("")>
<Assembly: AssemblyDescription("")>
<Assembly: AssemblyCompany("")>
<Assembly: AssemblyProduct("")>
<Assembly: AssemblyCopyright("")>
<Assembly: AssemblyTrademark("")>
<Assembly: CLSCompliant(True)>
```

Enter the value *Picture Viewer* between the quotes that follow *AssemblyProduct*. In other words, change this line to:

```
<Assembly: AssemblyProduct("Picture Viewer")>
```

2   Feel free to fill in the other values as well. Among their many other uses, these values appear when you right-click the finished program in Windows Explorer and choose Properties. Figure 9-9 provides an example.

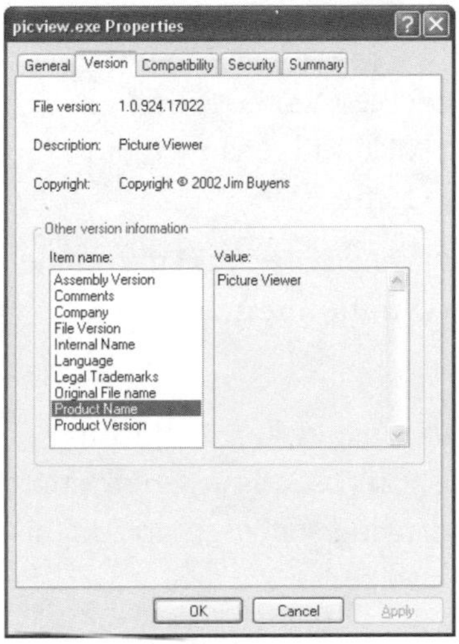

Figure 9-9 Property values you specify in the AssemblyInfo.vb file of a project appear as properties of the finished executable.

3   To make the product name appear as the title of the *Form1* form, display that form in Windows Form Designer and then double-click the form background. This displays a *Form1_Load* subroutine in the Code Editor. Add the line shown here in boldface to this subroutine:

```
Private Sub Form1_Load(ByVal sender As System.Object, _
                       ByVal e As System.EventArgs) _
                       Handles MyBase.Load
    Me.Text = Application.ProductName
End Sub
```

4   To save your work, select Save All from the file menu.

At this point, if you press F5 to run the program, you should find that Picture Viewer appears in the title bar of the main window. The cool thing about getting the program name this way, however, isn't just that the name appears once in the main title bar. It's not even that you can access this name from anywhere in your program. The best feature is that if you copy some code or even a complete class to another project, it'll pick up the name of that other project automatically.

Responding to File Exit and Help About Events

In this procedure you'll make the two simplest menu choices work. There's nothing wrong with starting out easy, right? With the *picview* project still open in Visual Studio .NET, proceed as follows:

1 Display the *Form1* form in the Windows Form Designer, then click the File menu and double-click Exit. This displays a *mnuFileExit_Click* subroutine in the Code Editor.

If a subroutine with some other name appears, such as *MenuItem3_Click*, it means you didn't rename the menu options correctly. Now would be a good time to go back and rename them *mnuFile*, *mnuFileOpen*, *mnuFileExit*, and so forth.

2 Enter the following statement inside the *mnuFileExit_Click* subroutine. Disposing of the startup form will shut down the program:

```
Me.Dispose()
```

3 Display the form in Windows Form Designer again, then select the Help menu and double-click About. This should display a subroutine named *mnuHelpAbout_Click*. Enter the following statement inside this subroutine:

```
MsgBox(Application.ProductName & vbCrLf & _
        Application.ProductVersion & vbCrLf & _
        Application.CompanyName, _
        MsgBoxStyle.Information, _
        "About " & Application.ProductName)
```

This, of course, simply displays an ordinary message box that contains the product name, the product version, and the company name for the current program. All this information comes from the Assembly-Info.vb file. The expression *vbCrLf* is a built-in constant that returns two characters: a carriage return and a line feed. In a message box, this begins a new line. (To review the parameters for displaying a *MsgBox*, refer to the section titled Using Message Boxes earlier in this chapter.)

4 To save your work, select Save All from the File menu.

At this point, after starting the program, selecting About from the Help menu should display a message box that looks like this. The URL *www.interlacken.com* comes from the <Assembly: AssemblyCompany("")> line in the AssemblyInfo.vb file. Your results, of course, will be different.

Selecting Exit from the File menu should, of course, shut the program down.

Displaying a Picture File

Here, finally, is where the program actually starts to do some work. This, however, is typical. Most Windows programs expend far more code managing the user interface than actually doing the work for which they exist. To actually display a picture file, follow these steps:

1 Display the *Form1* form in the Windows Form Designer, then click its File menu and double-click Open. This displays a subroutine named *mnuFileOpen_Click*. If a subroutine name like *MenuItem2_Click* appears, go back and rename the menu choice correctly.

2 Add the following code to the subroutine that appeared in step 1:

```
If OpenFileDialog1.ShowDialog() = DialogResult.OK Then
' More code will go here
End If
```

The first statement displays the File Open dialog box *OpenFileDialog1* you created in the first procedure in this chapter. If the *ShowDialog* method returns *DialogResult.OK*, the user successfully selected a file. If it returns any other value, the user clicked Cancel or otherwise failed to select a file.

Note   *DialogResult.OK* is a read-only property of the *System.Windows.Forms.Form* class. When you compare the result of the *ShowDialog* method to this value, you're guaranteed to be testing for the same value that the *ShowDialog* method sends.

---

3 Replace the comment in step 2 with the following code:

```
PictureBox1.Image = _
    Image.FromFile(OpenFileDialog1.FileName)
```

PictureBox1, as you no doubt recall, is the picture box you created in the first procedure in this chapter. The *OpenFileDialog1.FileName* property returns the complete path and file name that the user selected in the Open File dialog box. The *Image.FromFile* method creates a .NET *Image* object from a specified file.

All in all, then, this statement loads whatever file the user specified into memory as an image, and then makes the *Image* property of
the *PictureBox1* control refer to that image.

4   Unfortunately, the statement you entered in step 3 is highly prone to
failure. If the user selects a text file, a defective picture file, or anything
but a valid picture file, the *Image.FromFile* method will throw an
exception. To keep this from bombing the entire program, surround
the statement from step 3 in a *Try...Catch...End Try* block. The complete code listing for the *mnuFileOpen_Click* subroutine will then consist of this:

```
If OpenFileDialog1.ShowDialog() = DialogResult.OK Then
    Try
        PictureBox1.Image = _
            Image.FromFile(OpenFileDialog1.FileName)
'       Code to adjust the application window will go here.
    Catch ex As Exception
        MsgBox("Can't open file " & _
                OpenFileDialog1.FileName & _
                vbCrLf & ex.Message, _
                MsgBoxStyle.Exclamation, _
                Application.ProductName)
    End Try
End If
```

If the code between *Try* and *Catch* blows up, the code in the
Catch block will execute. Because the *Catch* clause simply states *As
Exception*, the clause will occur no matter what kind of exception
occurs. The code inside the *Catch* block displays a message box containing the file name and whatever message the exception provides.

5   At this point, if you press F5, select Open from the application's File
menu, select a picture file, and then click OK, the application should
display the picture, or maybe just the upper left corner, if the picture is
larger than the *PictureBox1* control. To correct this, quit the Picture
Viewer application, select the *PictureBox1* control, and then, in the
Properties window, set the *SizeMode* property to *AutoSize*.

6   Now that the *PictureBox1* control will expand to fit the picture, it
might grow larger than the application window. If this happens, the
user will expect scroll bars to appear. To activate this behavior, select
the entire form and then, in the Properties window, set the *AutoScroll*
property to *True*.

7   If you press F5 and open a picture now, the *PictureBox1* control
should display the whole picture. The problem now, however, is that
the Picture Viewer window, even though it provides scroll bars, might
still be too small. To begin correcting this and a few other flaws,
replace the comment in step 4 with this code:

```
AdjustFormToPicture(OpenFileDialog1.FileName)
```

and add the following declaration after the *End Sub* statement that terminates the *mnuFileOpen_Click* subroutine:

```
Sub AdjustFormToPicture(ByVal astrFilename As String)
End Sub
```

8   To automatically widen the Picture Viewer window so it displays the
entire picture, add the following code to the *AdjustFormToPicture* subroutine you just declared:

```
Dim intNewWidth As Integer
Dim intNewHeight As Integer

Me.AutoScroll = False
intNewWidth = (2 * PictureBox1.Left) _
            + PictureBox1.Image.Width _
            + Me.Width - Me.ClientSize.Width
If Me.Width < intNewWidth Then
    Me.Width = intNewWidth
End If
```

The first two statements declare variables that will store temporary
results. The next statement turns off the form's *AutoScroll* property so
that the width of the scroll bar, if visible, doesn't upset the subsequent
calculations.

The fourth statement calculates the new form width as twice the left
margin of the *PictureBox1* control, plus the width of the *PictureBox1*
image, plus the difference between the *Width* and the *ClientWidth*
properties of the current form.

The reason for including twice the left margin is that this margin
should be available on the right side as well as the left. The picture
width, of course, is the main factor in the calculation. Adding this to
the combined width of the margins gives the number of pixels that
should be available between, but not including, the window borders.

Windows forms have two width properties:

- The *Width* property gets or sets the distance from the outside of one border to the outside of the opposite border.

- The *ClientWidth* property gets the distance from the inside of one border to the other.

Note that computing twice the *PictureBox1* left margin plus the *PictureBox1* width yields an answer comparable to the *ClientWidth* property, which, unfortunately, is read-only. To get an answer comparable to the *Width* property, which is read/write, the program computes and adds the total width of the borders, which is

```
Me.Width - Me.ClientSize.Width.
```

The last three lines determine if the new width you computed and stored in *intNewWidth* is larger than the form's current width. If so, it widens the form accordingly.

9 The code for automatically heightening the Picture Viewer window to display the entire picture appears next. Enter this code after the code from the previous step:

```
intNewHeight = (2 * PictureBox1.Top) _
            + PictureBox1.Image.Height _
            + StatusBar1.Height _
            + Me.Height _
            - (Me.ClientSize.Height + ToolBar1.Height)
If Me.Height < intNewHeight Then
    Me.Height = intNewHeight
End If
Me.AutoScroll = True
```

This code is essentially the same as that for widening the form, except that it uses *Top* and *Height* measurements rather than *Left* and *Width* measurements. It also accounts for the height of the status bar and sets the form's *AutoScroll* property back to *True* after all calculations are finished.

10 To display the name of the picture file in the application's title bar and status bar, add the code shown here immediately after the code you entered in the previous step:

```
If astrFilename = "" Then
    Me.Text = Application.ProductName
    StatusBar1.Text = ""
Else
    Me.Text = Application.ProductName & " - " & _
        astrFilename
    StatusBar1.Text = astrFilename & " "
End If
```

Note that this code provides different results depending on whether the *astrFilename* argument is empty. This argument should never be empty if the current picture came from a file, but it will be empty when the picture comes from the clipboard.

Tip   If the calculations in steps 9 and 10 leave too much or too little margin around the picture, stop the program and move the *PictureBox1* control around the form as necessary.

---

11 To also show the current picture's pixel dimensions in the status bar, add the following code just before the end of the *AdjustFormToPicture* subroutine:

```
StatusBar1.Text &= PictureBox1.Image.Width() & "x" & _
                   PictureBox1.Image.Height()
```

12 If you try running the application again, you might notice two more fit and finish details that need cleaning up. First, when you start the program, the status bar displays the text *StatusBar1*. To get rid of this, select the status bar in Windows Form Designer and then, in the Properties window, set the *Text* property to an empty string.

13 The last nagging detail is that the File Open dialog box always displays files with all file name extensions. To provide the user with some filters, add the following code to the *Form1* forms's *Form1_Load* subroutine:

```
OpenFileDialog1.Filter = _
    "Picture Files(*.bmp;*.gif;*.jpg)|*.bmp;*.gif;*.jpg|" & _
    "BMP files (*.bmp)|*.bmp|" & _
    "GIF files (*.gif)|*.gif|" & _
    "JPEG files (*.jpg)|*.jpg|" & _
    "All files (*.*)|*.*"
```

The *Filter* property loads the Files Of Type drop-down list in the File Open dialog box with one or more choices that limit the files that the dialog box displays. The filter string consists of a human-readable title, a vertical bar, a wildcard specification, another vertical bar, another title, and so forth.

You could also enter this string in the Windows Form Designer; just select the *OpenFileDialog1* control and modify its *Filter* property. However, entering this long, complicated string into a tiny text box might be difficult.

14 To save your work, select Save All from the Visual Studio .NET File menu.

This completes all the work to make the File Open command work properly. In a very real sense, all the work you've done on this program had the single objective of executing one statement, namely this:

```
PictureBox1.Image = Image.FromFile(<file>)
```

Everything else you've done here supports interaction with the user. Don't be depressed: no user interaction, no picture, no program, no matter how fine the picture display code might be.

Copying a Picture to the Clipboard

This procedure explains how to make the Picture Viewer program copy the picture in *PictureBox1*, if any, to the clipboard. This one is short and sweet:

1   Display the *Form1* form in Windows Form Designer.

2   Click Picture Viewer's Edit menu, then double-click the Copy command. This should display a *mnuEditCopy_Click* subroutine.

3   Enter the following code inside the *mnuEditCopy_Click* subroutine:

```
If IsNothing(PictureBox1.Image) Then
    MsgBox("There's no picture to copy", _
        MsgBoxStyle.Exclamation, _
        Application.ProductName)
Else
    Clipboard.SetDataObject(PictureBox1.Image)
End If
```

The *If* statement first determines whether the *Image* property of the *PictureBox1* control actually points to an *Image* object. If not, a message box provides the user with an error message.

If the *PictureBox1.Image* property does point to an object, the code calls the *Clipboard.SetDataObject* method with this object as an argument. This method makes data available to other applications using the Windows clipboard.

4   To save your work, select Save All from the Visual Studio .NET File menu.

If you run the Picture Viewer program now, display a picture, and then select Copy from the Edit menu, you should find that choosing a Paste command in any other picture-capable program pastes the picture you opened in Picture Viewer. For example, you could paste the picture into Microsoft Word, Microsoft Paint, or Microsoft FrontPage.

Displaying a Picture from the Clipboard

The code for pasting a picture into Picture Viewer is only slightly more complicated. Here's the procedure for creating it:

1 Display the *Form1* form in the Windows Form Designer.

2 Click Picture Viewer's Edit menu, then double-click the Paste command. A *mnuEditPaste_Click* subroutine should appear.

3 Enter the following code inside the *mnuEditPaste_Click* subroutine:

```
Dim iData As IDataObject = Clipboard.GetDataObject()
If iData.GetDataPresent(DataFormats.Bitmap) Then
    PictureBox1.Image = iData.GetData(DataFormats.Bitmap)
    AdjustFormToPicture("")
Else
    MsgBox("The clipboard doesn't contain a picture.", _
        MsgBoxStyle.Exclamation, _
        Application.ProductName)
End If
```

The first statement declares and creates a so-called *IDataObject*, which provides information about what, if anything, is in the clipboard. The second statement queries that object's *GetDataPresent* method to determine if a bitmapped picture is available. (*DataFormats.Bitmap* is another of those read-only properties.) If a bitmapped picture is present, the third statement directs the *Image* property of the *PictureBox1* control to that object. The fourth statement then calls *AdjustFormToPicture* as before, except that in this case there's no file name.

If the clipboard doesn't contain a bitmapped picture, the *MsgBox* statement following the *Else* informs the user of this fact.

4 To save your work, select Save All from the Visual Studio .NET File menu.

Now if you open another picture-oriented program, open or create a picture, and copy it to the clipboard, you should find that choosing Paste from the Edit menu in Picture Viewer displays that picture.

Making the Toolbar Buttons Work

The toolbar is now the only remaining feature in Picture Viewer that doesn't work. You might think that toolbar buttons act like menu bar commands, where each command has its own event handler. This, however, is not the case. All the buttons on the same toolbar activate the same event handler, passing the address of the toolbar button as an argument. Here's how to make this work.

1 Display the *Form1* form in the Windows Form Designer.

2 Double-click the toolbar anywhere you like. A *ToolBar1_ButtonClick* subroutine should appear.

3 Enter the following code inside the *ToolBar1_ButtonClick* subroutine. Warning: it cheats!

```
Dim evtArgs As New System.EventArgs()
Select Case e.Button.Text
    Case "Open"
        mnuFileOpen_Click(sender, evtArgs)
    Case "Copy"
        mnuEditCopy_Click(sender, evtArgs)
    Case "Paste"
        mnuEditPaste_Click(sender, evtArgs)
End Select
```

If you look at the full declaration for the *ToolBar1_ButtonClick* subroutine, you'll see that it's second argument, *e*, is an object of type *System.Windows.Forms.ToolBarButtonClickEventArgs*. The *Button* property of this argument points to the toolbar button that raised the event, and the *Button.Text* property contains that button's text. This is all the information you need to call the subroutine that runs when you choose a menu command. If the user clicked the Open toolbar button, for example, then you can just call the *mnuFileOpen_Click* subroutine and be done.

The only catch (and isn't there always a catch?) is that each of the menu bar subroutines expects a *sender As Object* argument and an *e As EventArgs* argument. The sender object is easy because the *ToolBar1_ButtonClick* subroutine receives one that it can pass along. The *EventArgs* argument is a little tougher to come by; the first line of code has to create one of these objects so that the rest of the code can pass it along.

4 To save your work, select Save All from the Visual Studio .NET File menu.

That's it! If you run the Picture Viewer program now, you should find that the three toolbar buttons do exactly the same thing as the corresponding menu commands. This completes the Picture Viewer program.

For your reference, a complete listing of Picture Viewer's Form1.vb file appears here. Don't be concerned if your code has fewer line continuations or if the subroutines appear in a different order; these factors don't affect the way the program works.

Picture Viewer's Form1.vb

```vb
Public Class Form1
    Inherits System.Windows.Forms.Form
+ Windows Form Designer generated code
Private Sub Form1_Load(ByVal sender As System.Object, _
                        ByVal e As System.EventArgs) _
                        Handles MyBase.Load
    Me.Text = Application.ProductName
End Sub

Private Sub mnuFileOpen_Click(ByVal sender As System.Object, _
                            ByVal e As System.EventArgs) _
                            Handles mnuFileOpen.Click
    If OpenFileDialog1.ShowDialog() = DialogResult.OK Then
        Try
            PictureBox1.Image = _
                Image.FromFile(OpenFileDialog1.FileName)
            AdjustFormToPicture(OpenFileDialog1.FileName)
        Catch ex As Exception
            MsgBox("Can't open file " & _
                    OpenFileDialog1.FileName & _
                    vbCrLf & ex.Message, _
                    MsgBoxStyle.Exclamation, _
                    Application.ProductName)
        End Try
    End If
End Sub

Private Sub mnuFileExit_Click(ByVal sender As System.Object, _
                            ByVal e As System.EventArgs) _
                            Handles mnuFileExit.Click
    Me.Dispose()
End Sub

Private Sub mnuEditCopy_Click(ByVal sender As System.Object, _
                            ByVal e As System.EventArgs) _
                            Handles mnuEditCopy.Click
    If IsNothing(PictureBox1.Image) Then
        MsgBox("There's no picture to copy", _
            MsgBoxStyle.Exclamation, _
            Application.ProductName)
    Else
        Clipboard.SetDataObject(PictureBox1.Image)
    End If
End Sub
```

```
Private Sub mnuEditPaste_Click(ByVal sender As System.Object, _
                           ByVal e As System.EventArgs) _
                           Handles mnuEditPaste.Click
    Dim iData As IDataObject = Clipboard.GetDataObject()
    If iData.GetDataPresent(DataFormats.Bitmap) Then
        PictureBox1.Image = iData.GetData(DataFormats.Bitmap)
        AdjustFormToPicture("")
    Else
        MsgBox("The clipboard doesn't contain a picture.", _
            MsgBoxStyle.Exclamation, _
            Application.ProductName)
    End If
End Sub


Private Sub mnuHelpAbout_Click(ByVal sender As System.Object, _
                           ByVal e As System.EventArgs) _
                           Handles mnuHelpAbout.Click
    MsgBox(Application.ProductName & vbCrLf & _
            Application.ProductVersion & vbCrLf & _
            Application.CompanyName, _
            MsgBoxStyle.Information, _
            "About " & Application.ProductName)
End Sub


Private Sub ToolBar1_ButtonClick( _
    ByVal sender As System.Object, _
    ByVal e As _
        System.Windows.Forms.ToolBarButtonClickEventArgs) _
    Handles ToolBar1.ButtonClick
    Dim evtArgs As New System.EventArgs()
    Select Case e.Button.Text
        Case "Open"
            mnuFileOpen_Click(sender, evtArgs)
        Case "Copy"
            mnuEditCopy_Click(sender, evtArgs)
        Case "Paste"
            mnuEditPaste_Click(sender, evtArgs)
    End Select
End Sub

Sub AdjustFormToPicture(ByVal astrFilename As String)
    Dim intNewWidth As Integer
    Dim intNewHeight As Integer
    Me.AutoScroll = False
    intNewWidth = (2 * PictureBox1.Left) _
            + PictureBox1.Image.Width _
            + Me.Width - Me.ClientSize.Width
    If Me.Width < intNewWidth Then
        Me.Width = intNewWidth
    End If
```

```
        intNewHeight = (2 * PictureBox1.Top) _
                    + PictureBox1.Image.Height _
                    + StatusBar1.Height _
                    + Me.Height _
                    - (Me.ClientSize.Height + ToolBar1.Height)
        If Me.Height < intNewHeight Then
            Me.Height = intNewHeight
        End If
        Me.AutoScroll = True

        If astrFilename = "" Then
            Me.Text = Application.ProductName
            StatusBar1.Text = ""
        Else
            Me.Text = Application.ProductName & " - " & _
                astrFilename
            StatusBar1.Text = astrFilename & " "
        End If

        StatusBar1.Text &= PictureBox1.Image.Width() & "x" & _
                    PictureBox1.Image.Height()
        End Sub
End Class
```

Key Points

- Attractive and intuitive user interfaces are a key element of any successful Windows program.

- Unless your program provides an extremely unique type of processing, the most intuitive user interface is usually one that resembles that of other Windows programs.

- You can initialize most properties of forms and controls in Windows Form Designer, and modify most properties from code as your program runs. However, the two sets of properties aren't always the same.

- Message boxes provide an easy way to inform the user of unusual events and to prompt for simple responses.

- Visual Studio .NET contains a simple icon editor, but your best source might involve full-featured picture-editing programs, outside sources, or both.

- Creating and configuring menu bars and toolbars isn't difficult, but it can easily exceed the work of performing the program's main function. Then again, user interaction is a key function of any Windows program.

Chapter 10

Interacting with Windows Form Controls

At first glance, the user interface for most Microsoft Windows desktop programs appears to be a Windows form. In fact, however, a program that displayed only a blank Windows form wouldn't have much of a user interface at all. The form only becomes useful when you embellish it with text boxes, list boxes, check boxes, option boxes, buttons, labels, and all the other gizmos now so familiar to millions of people. Each such gizmo is a *Windows form control*.

The term *control* might seem a bit abstract but if steam valves, oven dials, and accelerator pedals can be controls, so can buttons and list boxes. The term *control* also has historical significance because at one time all these objects were ActiveX controls. Now, however, Windows form controls are simply classes in the Microsoft .NET Framework.

Every example so far in this book has used Windows form controls in one way or another. As a result, you should have some familiarity with the material in this chapter already. Rest assured, however, that there's plenty more to learn. The good news (and the bad news) is that no topic related to programming ever seems to run out of detail.

Form Control Categories

The *System.Windows.Forms* namespace provides a variety of controls that are highly suited to creating rich user interfaces. It's often useful to think of these controls as belonging to seven general categories.

- The *Form* class represents a window within an application. This includes dialog boxes, modeless windows, and Multiple Document Interface (MDI) client and parent windows.

- Data entry controls are those that the user can manipulate. Text boxes, list boxes, and buttons are all data entry controls.

- Informational controls display application data while your program is running, but the user doesn't interact with them. The *Label*, *ListView*, *NotifyIcon*, *StatusBar*, and *ProgressBar* controls are all in this category.

Note   The *NotifyIcon* control displays a clickable icon in the notification area of the Windows taskbar.

- Command controls display and invoke commands within the application. The *Button*, *Menu*, *MenuItem*, *ToolBar*, and *ContextMenu* controls are all in this category.

- Container controls group data entry and informational controls into a unit. This is useful for grouping controls visually, for making the entire group visible or invisible, and for assembling groups of *RadioButton* controls. The *GroupBox*, *Panel*, and *TabControl* controls belong to this category. The *Form* control is also a container.

- Component controls have no visible appearance in and of themselves; they're simply objects that your program can use. The *Timer*, *ImageList*, *ToolTip*, *ErrorProvider*, *Help*, and *HelpProvider* controls are in the category.

- Common dialog box controls display a number of common dialog boxes that give your application a consistent user interface for tasks such as opening and saving files, manipulating font or text color, or printing.

  - The *OpenFileDialog* and *SaveFileDialog* classes display dialog boxes for the user to locate, select, and enter the name of a file.

  - The *FontDialog* class displays a dialog box to change elements of the Font object your application uses.

  - The *PageSetupDialog*, *PrintPreviewDialog*, and *PrintDialog* classes display dialog boxes that control aspects of printing documents.

More Info   For more information on printing from a Windows-based application, see the *System.Drawing.Printing* namespace. (If you've forgotten what a namespace is, refer to the section of Chapter 8 entitled "Finding .NET Methods and Classes.")

In addition, the *System.Windows.Forms* namespace provides the *MessageBox* class for displaying a message box that can display and retrieve data from the user.

Finally, the *PropertyGrid* control provides a user interface for browsing the properties of an object. This is the control that normally occupies the Properties window in Microsoft Visual Studio .NET when the Windows Form Designer is active.

Try This!   The *PropertyGrid* control doesn't normally appear in the Toolbox window. If you want to use this control in one of your applications you must either create an instance completely in code or add it to the Toolbox. Here's the procedure for adding a control to the Toolbox:

1   Right-click the Toolbox window in Visual Studio .NET.

2   When the shortcut menu appears, choose Customize Toolbox.

3   When the Customize Toolbox dialog box appears, select either the COM Components tab or the .NET Framework Components tab, depending on the type of control. Figure 10-1 illustrates this step in progress.

4   Activate the check box in front of the control you want, then click OK.

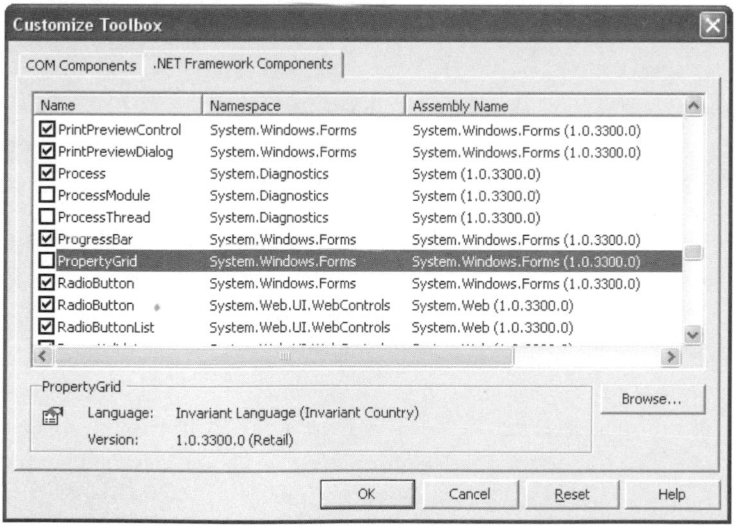

Figure 10-1 To add a control to the Visual Studio Toolbox, display this dialog box and activate the control's check box.

Adding and Arranging Form Controls

The part of Visual Studio .NET that adds controls to a Windows form is, of course, the Windows Form Designer. Whenever this occupies the main Visual Studio window, the Windows Forms portion of the Toolbox window lists the controls that are available on your system. By default, these are the controls that come with Visual Studio. Of course, if you download or purchase additional controls, those appear as well.

Tip   If the Toolbox window isn't visible, choose Toolbox from the View menu.

There are three basic procedures for adding controls to a form, at least two of which you've probably discovered already:

■   First, you can add any control to the current form by double-clicking the control's entry in the Toolbox window. In most cases, the new control will appear in the upper left corner of the form.

   If, however, the current selection in Windows Form Designer is a *GroupBox* control, a *Panel* control, or a page in a *TabControl* control, the new control appears in the upper left corner of that selection.

■   Alternatively, you can first select the control you want in the Toolbox window and then drag the mouse diagonally across any part of the open form. The new control then appears in the location and size of the area you dragged.

■   You can also add controls to a form by copying and pasting. To do this, select an existing control, press Ctrl+C to copy it, and then Ctrl+V to paste it. (Of course, any other keystrokes or menu commands that perform the copy and paste functions will work just as well.)

Once a control is on your form, you can move it around by dragging its center and, in most cases, resize it by dragging its edges. Of course, you can't resize invisible controls, controls that are fixed in size, or controls that size themselves automatically.

The moment after adding a control to a form is also a good time to rename it, especially if you'll be accessing the control from code. Suppose, for example, you create five text boxes for entering name, street address, city, state, and zip code. If you name them *txtName*, *txtStreet*, *txtCity*, *txtState*, and *txtZIP*, any code that deals with them will be easy to understand. If you retain default names like *TextBox1*, *TextBox2*, *TextBox3*, and so forth, coding the correct name initially will be difficult and reading the code later will be worse.

If the need arises, you can also create and display form controls directly from code. This is generally a four-step process:

1 Create the new form control just as you would any other object. To create a text box, for example, you would code:

```
Dim txtNewBox As New System.Windows.Forms.TextBox
```

2 Assign a value to the *Name* property and to any other properties you want. The following code, for example, gives the *TextBox* from step 1 a name, a location, and a size:

```
txtNewBox.Name = "txtNewBox"
txtNewBox.Location = New Point(100, 20)
txtNewBox.Size = New Size(100, 20)
```

3 Add the control to the form's *Controls* collection. Here's some typical code:

```
Me.Controls.Add(txtNewBox)
```

4 Dynamically add any event handlers the new control requires. Chapter 8, "Using Classes, Modules, and Forms," describes how to do this, but here's an example anyway:

```
AddHandler txtNewBox.TextChanged, _
    AddressOf(txtNewBox_TextChanged)
```

To remove a control, call the control collection's *Remove* method. This requires a statement such as the following:

```
Me.Controls.Remove(txtNewBox)
```

If you plan to do this, however, you should generally declare the control outside any function or subroutine. Otherwise, the original object reference will be inaccessible or lost and you'll have to search through the *Controls* collection for the control you no longer want. Here's some typical code that performs such a search:

```
Dim ctlControl As Control
For Each ctlControl In Me.Controls
    If ctlControl.Name = "txtNewBox" Then
        Me.Controls.Remove(ctlControl)
        Exit For
    End If
Next
```

Working with Control Properties

All the interactive, informational, and container controls inherit the properties, methods, and events of the *System.Windows.Forms.Control* class. This class has quite a few such members, all of which the Visual Studio Help files adequately describe. (Just look up the class name in the Help Index). A few, however, are so useful that it's worth mentioning them here.

Achieving Positions of Control

The *Position* property of any control specifies the coordinates of its upper left corner. This requires both X and Y coordinates, measured in pixels and relative to the upper left corner of the control's container. To modify the *Position* property in Windows Form Designer, either drag the control in the main window or modify the *Position* property in the Property window.

Modifying a control's *Position* property in code is a little tricky because the *Position* property isn't an elementary data type; it's a .NET object of type *System.Drawing.Point*. If you wanted to reposition a text box named *txtCity* 200 pixels from the left edge of its container and 300 pixels below the top of its container, you would code as follows:

```
txtCity.Position = New System.Drawing.Point(200, 300)
```

Alternatively, you could set the control's *Left* and *Top* properties directly, as shown next. This accomplishes exactly the same result as the preceding code:

```
txtCity.Left = 200
txtCity.Top = 300
```

In general, only controls that present a visual appearance have *Position* properties. This makes sense if you think about it for a moment; if the control never displays anything on screen, why would it need a *Position* property?

Oohs, Ahs, and Size

The *Size* property of any control specifies its height and width. Like the *Position* property, its value consists of an X coordinate and a Y coordinate, and it is therefore an object of type *System.Drawing.Point*.

In Windows Form Designer, you can change the size of a control by dragging its edge, by dragging its corner, or by modifying the *Size* property in the Property window. In code, you can resize a control by setting its *Size* property to a new *Point* object like this:

```
txtCity.Size = New System.Drawing.Point(100, 50)
```

or by setting its *Height* or *Width* properties like this:

```
txtCity.Width = 100
txtCity.Height = 50
```

Controls that present no visual appearance obviously have no need for *Size*, *Height*, or *Width* properties. In addition, controls that set their own height or width might ignore any changes to these properties that you try to make. A drop-down list box, for example, controls its own height and ignores any changes you make to its *Height* property.

Amazing Disappearing Form Control Tricks

If a form control can be visible at all, either of the following actions will make it invisible:

- Set the control's *Visible* property to *False*.
- Invoke the control's *Hide* property.

Normally, making a control invisible has no effect on surrounding controls. There are, however, two exceptions:

- If you make a menu item invisible, any menu items that follow it move up in the list. There won't be a blank space on the menu where the invisible item formerly appeared.
- If you make a container invisible (that being either a *Form*, *GroupBox*, *Panel*, or *TabControl*), any controls within that container vanish as well.

The process for making a control visible is just about what you'd expect. Again, there are two possible approaches:

- Set the control's *Visible* property to *True*.
- Invoke the control's *Show* property.

Remember that the *Visible* property, the *Hide* method, and the *Show* method only work on controls that can be directly visible in and of themselves. They don't work on the *OpenFileDialog* control, for example, because although that control displays a dialog box, the dialog box and the control are two different objects. The *OpenFileDialog* control itself remains hidden.

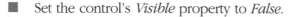

Tip   The common dialog box controls each have a *ShowDialog* method that tells them to display their dialog boxes.

To dim a control (that is, to prevent input and display the control in gray rather than black) set its *Enabled* property to *False*.

Tabs, Tab Orders, and TabIndex (But No Tab Dancing)

In any Windows form that has more than one date entry control, pressing the Tab key changes the focus from one control to another. When the form first appears, the focus is usually on the control closest to the upper left corner. Pressing the Tab key generally advances the focus in a logical top-to-bottom, left-to-right direction.

The order in which controls receive the focus (that is, the *tab order*) is neither random nor automatic. Instead, each control has a numeric *TabIndex* property that specifies its position in the tab order.

When Windows first displays the form, it sets focus on the enterable control that has the lowest *TabIndex* value on the form. When the user presses the Tab key, Windows gives focus to the enterable control with the next highest *TabIndex* property. If no enterable controls have higher *TabIndex* values than the control that has the focus, Windows reverts to the enterable control with the lowest *TabIndex*.

The Windows Form Designer in Visual Studio automatically increments the *TabIndex* value for every control you add to a form. Unfortunately, this hardly ever results in a logical tab order. For one thing, you'll probably add form controls in the order in which you think of them, and not in optimal tab order sequence. For another, you'll probably edit, reedit, and rearrange the form several times before deeming it well done, attractive, and complete. Such is art, but the resulting tab order will be abstract at best.

Fortunately, achieving a logical tab order needn't be complicated. Just follow these steps when your form design is complete:

1   Display the form in the Windows Form Designer.

2   Select the form control that should have the focus when the form first appears.

3   In the Property window, set that control's *TabIndex* property to 0.

4   Select the form control that should most logically receive the focus next.

5   In the Property window, set that control's *TabIndex* property to one more than the last *TabIndex* value you assigned.

6   If any enterable controls remain on the form, go to step 4.

Working With Text Boxes, Check Boxes, and Radio Buttons

The properties for getting data values in and out of Windows Form controls vary somewhat from one control to the next. This can be a nuisance, but it's a necessary one, driven by differences in the way each control operates.

Getting data in and out of a *TextBox* control is simplicity itself—just retrieve or set the value of its *Text* property. The same approach works for *Label* controls and most others where the data value consists of one and only one *String* value.

CheckBox and *RadioButton* controls, by contrast, have a *Checked* property that's either *True* or *False*. If the *Checked* property is *True*, the control is checked; otherwise, it's cleared. To check or clear a check box or radio button from code, set its *Checked* property to *True* or *False*.

If your form includes more than one group of *RadioButton* controls, be sure to enclose each group in its own container; that is, in its own *GroupBox*, *Panel*, or *TabControl*. Otherwise, clicking a radio button in one group deselects any radio buttons on the other group. In Figure 10-2, for example, you wouldn't want clicking one of the Type Of Dragon radio buttons to disturb the Type Of Peril selection. That's why each group of radio buttons appears in its own group box.

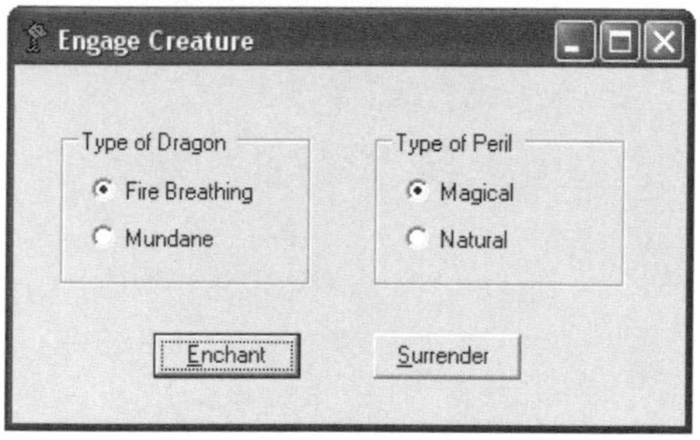

Figure 10-2 At any given time, only one *RadioButton* control in the same container can be selected. That's why these radio buttons appear in two different containers.

Working with List Boxes

For good reason, list boxes are among the most popular form controls. Text boxes are very flexible, but they demand typing from the user and stringent validity checking in the program. Check boxes are great for yes/no or true/false types of entries but life is often more complicated. Radio buttons are unwieldy for more than a few items.

List boxes provide a happy medium. They can present dozens of choices in a small space; they require little or no typing; they prompt the user to make correct choices; and, in most cases, they prevent the user from entering an illegal value.

List boxes are so wonderful that the .NET Framework actually provides five different kinds. Naturally, all of these are available in Microsoft Visual Basic .NET as well. Figure 10-3 provides examples of each.

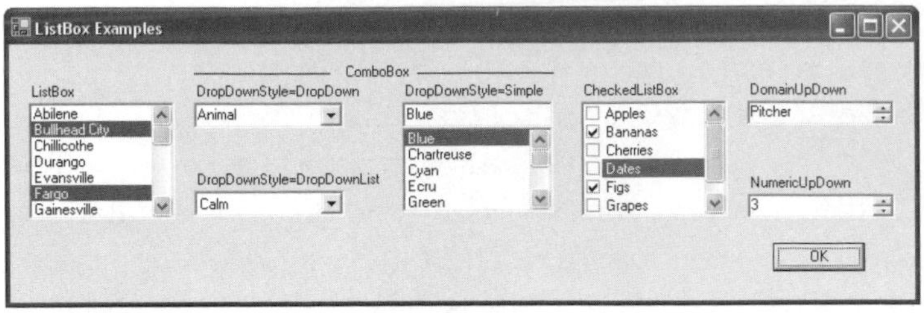

Figure 10-3 The .NET Framework provides these four kinds of list boxes.

Here are the names and descriptions of each type of list box the .NET Framework provides. Each gives the user a list of textual choices, but each in a different way.

- **ListBox**   This control provides a scrollable list of choices. There's no drop-down facility but there is a facility (turned off by default) for selecting multiple choices.

- **ComboBox**   This control displays both a *TextBox* control and a *List-Box* control. Selecting an item in the *ListBox* enters the corresponding text in the *TextBox*. A *ComboBox* has three major variations, depending on how you configure the *DropDownStyle* property. Here are the possible values:

  - *DropDown*   The *TextBox* is editable, which means the user can manually type an entry. The *ListBox* is normally invisible but appears when the user clicks an arrow button. This is the default style.

  - *DropDownList*   The user can't directly edit the *TextBox*. The user can only change it by clicking the arrow button to display the *List-Box* and then clicking one of the listed items.

  - *Simple*   The text portion is editable and the *ListBox* is always visible. The user can manually type an entry in the text box or select an item in the list box.

Tip   If you change the *DropDownStyle* property of a combo box to *Simple*, and the list box still isn't visible, it's probably because the combo box isn't tall enough. If you drag the top edge of the combo box up or drag the bottom edge down, the list box should appear.

- ■ ***CheckedListBox***   This control displays a *ListBox* that provides a check box in front of each item. A given item's check box can be selected or not, regardless of whether the item is selected or not.

- ■ ***DomainUpDown***   Strictly speaking, this control isn't a list box at all. However, in many respects it acts like one.

    Like a true *ListBox* control, a *DomainUpDown* control contains a list of possible values. Unlike a *ListBox*, however, a *DomainUpDown* always displays one item at a time. The user can traverse the *Items* list by clicking Up or Down buttons that are part of the control, or by entering text directly. However, entering text is only possible if the control's *ReadOnly* property is *False*.

- ■ ***NumericUpDown***   This control works much like the *DomainUpDown* control, except that it only accepts numeric values. Also, it has no *Items* collection; instead, you specify permissible values by means of *Minimum*, *Maximum*, and *Increment* properties.

Coping with Single-Selection List Boxes

ListBox controls are a bit more complicated than *TextBox* controls because they display an array of values instead of a single value. Furthermore, for most *ListBox* controls, multiple selection is possible. This depends on the value of the control's *SelectionMode* property, which can take on these values.

- ■ *SelectionMode.One* permits selection of only one item at a time. This is the default for all new ListBoxes.

- ■ *SelectionMode.MultiExtended* permits selection of multiple items. The user can use the Shift, Ctrl, and arrow keys to make selections.

- ■ *SelectionMode.MultiSimple* permits selection of multiple items, but only by clicking with the mouse.

- ■ *SelectionMode.None* blocks selection of any items.

To determine from code which item in a single-selection *ListBox* is currently selected, use any of these properties:

- ■ *SelectedIndex* sets or returns the zero-based index of one currently selected item in a *ListBox*. If, for example, the third item in a list named *lstState* is selected, the following expression would equal 2. If no item is selected, the same expression would equal –1:

```
lstState.SelectedIndex
```

■ *SelectedItem* works a lot like the *SelectedIndex* property, except that it returns the string value of the selected item rather than a zero-based index. If an item containing the text Happy is selected in a *ListBox* named *lstState*, the following expression would equal Happy:

```
lstState.SelectedItem
```

This property has the same limitation as *SelectedIndex*; if the *ListBox* permits multiple selections, there's no guarantee which of them will appear in the *SelectedItem* property.

■ *Text* is essentially the same as the *SelectedItem* property. Hard-core programmers prefer to use the specialized *SelectedItem* property but if you, as a beginner, specify *Text*, the code still works.

There are two ways to select a *ListBox* item from code. The choice is entirely yours:

■ Set the *ListBox*'s *SelectedIndex* property to the index of the item you want, or to −1 if you want no item selected.

■ Set the *ListBox*'s *SelectedItem* or *Text* property to the text of the item you want. Be careful with this approach, however. If you specify a text value that doesn't exist in the *ListBox*, no error occurs but neither does the selection change.

Coping with Multiple-Selection ListBoxes

If you set a *ListBox*'s *SelectionMode* property to *SelectionMode.MultiSimple* or *SelectionMode.MultiSelected*, the user can select any number of items at the same time. This presents a problem with respect to the *SelectedIndex*, *SelectedItem*, and *Text* properties that the previous section described. If several items are selected, those properties only refer to one of them, and there's no guarantee of which item that will be. To avoid such problems, use the following properties when working with a multiple-selection *ListBox*:

■ *SelectedIndices* returns a collection of zero-based indexes, one for each selected item. If the third, seventh, and ninth items were selected, the loop shown here would execute three times, with the *intIndex* variable equaling 2, 6, and 8.

```
Dim intIndex As Integer
For Each intIndex In lstState.SelectedIndices
'    Code to process each selected item goes here.
Next
```

■   *SelectedItems* works like *SelectedIndices* except that it returns the string value rather than the index of each selected item. If a *ListBox* named *lstState* had two selected items with text values of Warm and Fuzzy, the following loop would execute twice. The variable *strState* would equal Warm during the first iteration and Fuzzy during the second:

```
Dim strState As String
For Each strState In lstState.SelectedItems
'    Code to process each selected item goes here.
Next
```

To select an item in a multiple-selection *ListBox* from code, use the *List-Box*'s *SetSelected* method. This method takes two arguments: a zero-based index and a *True/False* value that means selected or not selected. Here are a couple of examples. The first one selects item 6 and the second one clears item 8.

```
lstState.SetSelected(5, True)
lstState.SetSelected(7, False)
```

CheckedListBox controls work very much like ordinary *ListBox* controls except that they display a check box in front of each item. The *CheckedIndices* collection of this control contains one entry for each checked item. Suppose, for example, that in a *CheckedListBox* with 10 items, item 4 and item 9 are checked. The *CheckedIndices* collection would then contain two entries. *CheckedIndices(0)* would equal 3 and *CheckedIndices(1)* would equal 8. Another collection named *CheckedItems* would also contain two entries: the text for item 4 and the text for item 9.

To set the value of a *CheckedListBox* check box from code, call the *SetItemCheckState* method as shown here:

```
clbVeggies.SetItemCheckState(3, CheckState.Checked)
```

This selects the check box for the fourth item in the list. Other valid entries in the second parameter include *CheckState.Indeterminate*, which grays out the check box, and *CheckState.Unchecked*, which clears it.

Adding and Removing ListBox Entries From Code

The values in a *ListBox* reside in an *Items* collection. If a *ListBox* control named *lstStates* contained 50 choices, then the *lstStates.Items* collection would contain 50 members. The expression *lstStates.Items.Count* would return the number of items in the collection (50). The expression *lstStates.Items(0)* would return the first value; expression *lstStates.Items(2)* would return the second value, and so forth.

The *Add* method of a *ListBox.Items* collection adds a value to the list box. The new value appears at the end of the list unless the *Sorted* property is *True*; in that case, the new items appear in sequence. Here's an example.

```
lstStates.Items.Add("DC")
```

To add several objects to the list at once, assign an array of object references with the *AddRange* method. Here's an example that adds three items to the end of the *lstStates.Items* list (or in sequence, if the *lstStates.Sorted* property is *True*).

```
lstStates.Items.AddRange(New Object() {"AB", "BC", "MB"})
```

If you want to insert the new value at a specific position, use the *Insert* method instead of the *Add* method. Of course, you must then specify the zero-based position where you want the new value to appear. The following code makes a new value of "BB" appear as the fifth item in the *lstStates* list box:

```
lstStates.Items.Insert(4, "BB")
```

After this statement executes, the value that formerly appeared in position 5 will appear in position 6. The value that formerly appeared in position 6 will appear in position 7, and so forth. Of course, if the *ListBox*'s *Sorted* property is *True*, the new item will appear in sequence no matter what zero-based position you specify.

To remove an item from a *ListBox Items* collection, use either the *Remove* or *RemoveAt* method. The following statements are equivalent:

```
lstStates.Items(4).Remove
lstStates.Items.RemoveAt(4)
```

Responding to Windows Form Control Events

Displaying form controls and working with form control values are both important tasks, but neither addresses the issue of timing. When, for example, should your code process all the values on a form? When should your code check the values of each form field and beep, display a message, or otherwise inform the user that an entry is incorrect? When should your code and the user interact in any other way?

In most programs, the time to interact with the user depends on—surprise!—the user. The most obvious event occurs when the user clicks an OK button, but most controls raise dozens of events during the course of normal use. For example, each control on a form raises an event whenever the mouse passes over it, whenever the mouse leaves it, whenever it gains or loses focus, whenever it receives a keystroke, whenever it receives a mouse click, and so forth. You can make your program respond to any of these events simply by coding an event handler.

As you no doubt recall from Chapter 8, an event handler is simply a subroutine with a declaration that looks like this:

```
Sub <control-name>_<event-name> _
    (sender As Object, e As <argument_type>) _
    Handles <control-name>.<event-name>
```

If your form had a button named *btnOK*, the following subroutine would run whenever the user clicked that button:

```
Sub btnOK_Click _
    (sender As Object, ByVal e As EventArgs) _
    Handles btnOK.Click
'   Code to process button click goes here.
End Sub
```

There are only two tricks to coding an event handler: discovering the event name and discovering the second argument type. Here's how to perform these discoveries:

1   To discover the event name, look up the control type in the MSDN Library. A complete list of events appears in the Members article (in the case of a *TextBox*, for example, in the TextBox Members article).

2   Once you find the correct event, click its name in the members article. The resulting page documents the required argument type.

3   To find out what properties the argument type provides, click its hyperlink and then display its Members page.

The next few sections describe the most common types of Windows form control events and how to handle them. Remember, though, that you have no obligation to write event handlers for events you don't care about. If a particular event has no handler, Windows simply discards the event.

Staging Keyboard Events

Most form controls raise events whenever they have the focus and the user presses a key. Table 10-1 lists these events in the order in which they occur.

Table 10-1   Windows Form Control Keyboard Events

Sequence	Event	Occurs When	Second Argument Type
1	*KeyDown*	The user presses a key while the control has focus.	*KeyEventArgs*
2	*KeyPress*	The user presses a key while the control has focus.	*KeyPressEventArgs*
3	*KeyUp*	The user releases a key while the control has focus.	*KeyEventArgs*

The *KeyPress* event is the easiest of these events to understand. Suppose you have a *TextBox* control named *txtQty* and you define a subroutine like this:

```
Sub txtQty_KeyPress _
        (sender As Object, e As KeyPressEventArgs) _
        Handles txtQty.KeyPress
End Sub
```

Every time the *TextBox* control has focus and the user presses a key, Windows automatically runs the *txtQty_KeyPress* subroutine. The *Sender* argument points to the *txtQty* object. The *e* argument points to a *KeyPressEventArgs* object that provides these properties:

- *e.KeyChar* contains the character code that the user typed, using the operating system's standard character set. If the user typed **A**, the *e.KeyChar* property would contain the ASCII character code for A.

- *e.Handled* is a *Boolean* value that indicates whether your code definitively processed the *KeyPress* event. When your event handler starts to run, this property is always *False*.

  - If you leave this value intact, Windows finishes processing the keystroke. In other words, the character shows up in the text box.

  - If you set *e.Handled* to *True*, Windows discards the event before any other event handler gets to see it. This has the effect of canceling the keystroke.

The following event handler checks each keystroke that the *txtQty* control receives. If the keystroke is neither a digit nor the backspace character, it beeps the PC's speaker and suppresses the keystroke:

```
Sub txtQty_KeyPress _
        (sender As System.Object, e As KeyPressEventArgs) _
        Handles txtQty.KeyPress
    If ((e.KeyChar < "0") Or (e.KeyChar > "9")) _
    And (e.KeyChar <> ChrW(8)) Then
        Beep()
        e.Handled = True
        StatusBar1.Text = "Can't deal with character " & _
                          AscW(e.KeyChar)
    End If
End Sub
```

The *KeyPress* event only occurs when the user generates an ASCII or Unicode character. It provides no way of responding to keys such as Insert, Delete, F1 through F12, and the arrow keys. To deal with such keystrokes, you must use the *KeyDown* and *KeyUp* events.

In the world of *KeyDown* and *KeyUp*, each key on the keyboard has a numeric key code. When the user presses a key, Windows raises the *KeyDown* event and passes the key code as an argument. When the user releases a key, Windows raises the *KeyUp* event and once again identifies the key code.

Key codes are, in general, completely different from character codes. Pressing 0 on the top row of the main keypad and pressing 0 on the numeric keypad generate two different key codes, even though both keys generate a 0 character. Pressing the A key always generates the same key code, no matter the status of the Shift, Ctrl, or Alt keys.

The *KeyDown* and *KeyUp* events both require the usual *Sender As Object* argument and then a second argument of type *KeyEventArgs*. Table 10-2 summarizes the properties this second argument provides.

Table 10-2 *KeyEventArgs* Properties

Property	Type	Description
Alt	*Boolean*	Indicates whether the Alt key is depressed.
Control	*Boolean*	Indicates whether the Ctrl key is depressed.
Shift	*Boolean*	Indicates whether the Shift key is depressed.
Modifiers	*Keys*	Gets the modifier flags for a *KeyDown* or *KeyUp* event. This indicates which combination of modifier keys (Ctrl, Shift, and Alt) is depressed.
KeyCode	*Keys*	Gets the keyboard code for a *KeyDown* or *KeyUp* event.
KeyData	*Keys*	Gets the key data for a *KeyDown* or *KeyUp* event.
KeyValue	*Keys*	Gets the keyboard value for a *KeyDown* or *KeyUp* event.
Handled	*Boolean*	Gets or sets a value indicating whether the event was handled.

The *Alt*, *Control*, and *Shift* properties indicate the state of the corresponding keys when the event occurred. *True* means the key was down and *False* means it was up.

The *KeyCode* and *KeyValue* properties both report the numeric key code of whatever key the user pressed or released. Because memorizing all these codes would be an unpleasant chore, Microsoft provides a named read-only property for each one. You can find the complete list in a MSDN Library article titled "Keys Enumeration," but here are some examples:

Keys.A	The A key
Keys.Alt	The Alt key
Keys.D0	The 0 key on the top row of the main keypad
Keys.NumPad0	The 0 key on the numeric keypad.
Keys.F1	The F1 key

The following event handler would beep the PC speaker every time a *TextBox* named *txtCity* had focus and the user pressed the Caps Lock key:

```
Sub txtCity _
      (sender As Object, e As KeyEventArgs) _
      Handles txtCity.KeyDown
   If e.KeyCode = Keys.CapsLock Then
      Beep()
   End If
End Sub
```

The *Modifiers* property indicates the combined state of the Shift, Ctrl, and Alt keys. Its value will be the sum of the following values, depending on which keys were pressed when the *KeyDown* and *KeyUp* event occurred:

Key	Decimal	Hexadecimal
Shift	65,536	0x10000
Ctrl	131,072	0x20000
Alt	262,144	0x40000

If the user pressed the A key, for example, and the Shift, Ctrl, and Alt keys were all up, *e.KeyCode* would equal *Keys.A* (which is 65) and *e.Modifiers* would equal zero.

If the user pressed A with the Shift key depressed, *e.KeyCode* would still equal *Keys.A* but *e.Modifiers* would equal 65,536. If both Shift and Alt were depressed, *e.Modifiers* would equal 65,536 + 262,144, which is 327,680. This provides an easy way of testing for specific Shift+Ctrl+Alt combinations. The following statements, for example, are equivalent:

```
If e.Shift And (Not e.Ctrl) And e.Alt Then


If e.Modifiers = 327680 Then
```

The *KeyValue* property contains the sum of the *KeyCode* and *Modifiers* properties. Each of the following statements is therefore equivalent; they all test for the Alt+A keystroke:

```
If e.KeyValue = Key.A + 262144 Then


If (e.KeyCode = Key.A) And (e.Modifiers = 262144) Then


If (e.KeyCode = Key.A) And _
   (Not e.Shift) And (Not e.Ctrl) And e.Alt Then
```

The *Handle* property behaves just as it does for the *KeyPress* event. Setting it to *True* stops the event from reaching any more event handlers. In a manner of speaking, it "eats" the keystroke.

Snapshotting Focus Events

As the user enters data and otherwise operates your form, the various controls gain and lose focus. (In simple terms, a control having focus means that anything you type on the keyboard goes to that control.) Table 10-3 lists, in order, the focus events that occur for most controls.

Table 10-3   Focus Events for Windows Form Controls

Sequence	Event	Occurs When	Second Argument Type
1	*Enter* or *Activated*	The control is entered.	*EventArgs*
2	*GotFocus*	The control receives focus.	*EventArgs*
3	*Leave* or *Deactivate*	The input focus leaves the control.	*EventArgs*
4	*Validating*	The control is validating.	*CancelEventArgs*
5	*Validated*	The control is finished validating.	*EventArgs*
6	*LostFocus*	The control loses focus.	*EventArgs*

The *Enter* and *Leave* events for a given control occur when that control gains or loses focus, respectively. The *Enter* event is handy for displaying helpful messages in, for example, a status bar. The *Leave* event is handy for clearing such messages. For *Form* objects, the *Activated* and *Deactivate* events replace *Enter* and *Leave* but operate similarly.

GotFocus and *LostFocus* are low-level events that Windows uses for updating user interface elements. In all normal circumstances, you should ignore these events and use the *Enter* or *Leave* events instead.

The *Validating* and *Validated* events occur only for controls that have a *CausesValidation* property and only if that property is *True*. *True*, however, is the default.

The *Validating* event occurs whenever the user tries to leave the control, but before the control actually loses focus. This is an excellent place to put code that checks the control's content. The following event handler, for example, checks the user's entry in a text box named *txtQty*. If the quantity isn't numeric, the event handler beeps the PC speaker, displays a message box, and then, by setting *e.Cancel* to *True*, prevents the control from losing focus:

Tip   When handling *Validating* events, be cautious about setting the *e.Cancel* property to *True*. This so stringently prevents the control from losing focus that the user can't even click Cancel or the form's Close box.

```
Sub txtQty_Validating(sender As Object, _
    e As System.ComponentModel.CancelEventArgs) _
    Handles txtQty.Validating
```

```
    If Not IsNumeric(txtQty.Text) Then
        Beep()
        MsgBox("The value '" & txtQty.Text & _
            "' isn't numeric.", _
            MsgBoxStyle.Exclamation, _
            Application.ProductName)
        e.Cancel = True
    End If
End Sub
```

The *Validated* event occurs after the *Validating* event, and usually contains any code you want to execute only if the *Validating* event handler didn't set *e.Handled* to *True*.

Try This!   The *ErrorProvider* control offers a handy way to visually identify Windows form controls that contain errors. To use this facility, follow these steps:

1   Display the form in the Windows Form Designer.

2   Double-click the *ErrorProvider* control in the Windows Forms section of the Toolbar window. This creates an invisible object name *ErrorProvider1*.

3   To flag a field in error, code a statement like the following:

```
ErrorProvider1.SetError(txtQty, _
    "The value '" & txtQty.Text & "' isn't numeric.")
```

The first argument is the name of a control on the form and the second is an error message. Altogether, this statement does two things. First, it displays an error icon just to the right of the form control you specify. Second, it establishes the message you specify as a tool tip for that icon. Here's how this looks in a simple application:

To clear the error indication, set the error message to an empty string. Here's an example.

```
ErrorProvider1.SetError(txtQty, "")
```

Listening for Click Events

The events in this class are among the simplest and the most useful Windows has to offer. Table 10-4 lists the most common types.

Table 10-4 Click and Related Events

Event	Occurs When	Second Argument Type
Click	The control is clicked.	EventArgs
Double Click	The control is double-clicked.	EventArgs
CheckedChanged	The Checked property changes	EventArgs
SelectedIndexChanged	The selection in a ListBox changes.	EventArgs
TextChanged	The Text property value changes.	EventArgs

The *Click* event is most useful with *Button* controls. The user clicks the button, the button's *Click* event fires, and your event handler is off to the races. Other controls raise click events as well, but in most cases, those controls also raise specific events that provide more information.

Tip Double-clicking a button in the Windows Form Designer automatically creates a *Click* event handler for that button.

The *DoubleClick* event, of course, occurs when the user double-clicks a control. The need to respond to double-click events doesn't come up frequently, but it's good to know the capability is there.

The *CheckedChanged* event occurs when the user changes the *Checked* property of a *CheckBox* or *RadioButton* control—that is, when the user checks or unchecks the control. The same action generates a *Click* event as well, but it's generally better to use the more specific *CheckedChanged* event.

Tip Double-clicking a *CheckBox* or *RadioButton* control in the Windows Form Designer automatically creates a *CheckedChanged* event handler for that control.

ListBoxes raise a *SelectedIndexChanged* event whenever the user changes the current selection. Again, it's better to rely on this event rather than *Click*.

Making any change to the content of a *TextBox* raises—you probably guessed it—a *TextChanged* event. This event occurs on a keystroke-by-keystroke basis, so you might be inclined to use the *KeyDown* or *KeyPress* event instead. The difference is that *TextChanged* doesn't fire in response to keystrokes like Tab, Enter, and F1 that have no effect on the *TextBox's* value.

Reacting to Mouse Events

Detecting *Click* events is all well and good, but sometimes you just need more information about what the mouse is doing. To handle such occasions, Windows raises the mouse events listed in Table 10-5. These events occur in the sequence shown.

Table 10-5   Mouse Events

Sequence	Event	Occurs When	Second Argument Type
1	*MouseEnter*	The mouse pointer enters the control.	*EventArgs*
2	*MouseMove*	The mouse pointer moves over the control.	*MouseEventArgs*
3	*MouseHover*	The mouse pointer hovers over the control.	*EventArgs*
	MouseDown	The mouse pointer is over the control and the user presses a mouse button.	*MouseEventArgs*
	MouseWheel	The user moves the mouse wheel while the control has focus.	*MouseEventArgs*
4	*MouseUp*	The mouse pointer is over the control and the user releases a mouse button.	*MouseEventArgs*
5	*MouseLeave*	The mouse pointer leaves the control.	*EventArgs*

The *MouseEnter* and *MouseLeave* events are fairly simple; they occur whenever the user moves the mouse pointer into or out of the screen area the control occupies. This is handy if, for example, you want to display a border or a status bar message when the user moves the mouse pointer over a control and remove it when the user takes his or her mouse business elsewhere.

Windows raises a *MouseMove* event every time the position of the mouse pointer changes. This can be a lot of events, so don't display a message box or perform a time-consuming task every time this event occurs.

The event handler for the *MouseMove* event and several others requires a *MouseEventArgs* argument. This has the properties listed in Table 10-6. To determine which mouse button the user clicked, compare *e.Button* to *MouseButtons.Left*, *MouseButtons.Right*, *MouseButtons.Middle*, and so forth. The MSDN Library has a complete list of these values in an article titled "MouseButtons Enumeration."

Table 10-6   MouseEventArgs Properties

Property	Type	Description
Button	*MouseButtons*	Identifies the mouse button the user pressed.
Clicks	*Integer*	Denotes the number of times the user pressed and released the mouse button.
Delta	*Integer*	Denotes a signed count of the number of detents (that is, notches) the user rotated the mouse wheel.

Table 10-6 **MouseEventArgs Properties** *(continued)*

Property	Type	Description
X	*Integer*	Indicates the X coordinate of a mouse click.
Y	*Integer*	Indicates the Y coordinate of a mouse click.

The program in Figure 10-4, for example, uses the following code to display the dialog box shown:

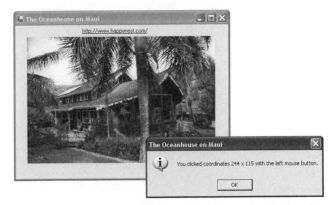

Figure 10-4 A *MouseDown* event handler in this program displays the mouse button and coordinates each time the user clicks on the picture.

```
Private Sub picMain_MouseDown( _
ByVal sender As System.Object, _
ByVal e As System.Windows.Forms.MouseEventArgs) _
Handles picMain.MouseDown
    Dim strButton As String = "Unknown"
    Select Case e.Button
        Case MouseButtons.Left
            strButton = "left"
        Case MouseButtons.Middle
            strButton = "middle"
        Case MouseButtons.None
            strButton = "(none)"
        Case MouseButtons.Right
            strButton = "right"
        Case MouseButtons.XButton1
            strButton = "xButton1"
        Case MouseButtons.XButton2
            strButton = "xButton2"
    End Select
    MsgBox("You clicked coordinates " & _
        e.X & " x " & e.Y & " with the " & _
        strButton & " mouse button.", _
        MsgBoxStyle.Information, _
        Application.ProductName)
End Sub
```

Example: Reporting Crocodiles

To illustrate in a practical way how code and Windows form controls interact, this exercise develops a simple data-entry program that reports crocodile sightings. Figure 10-5 shows the finished result.

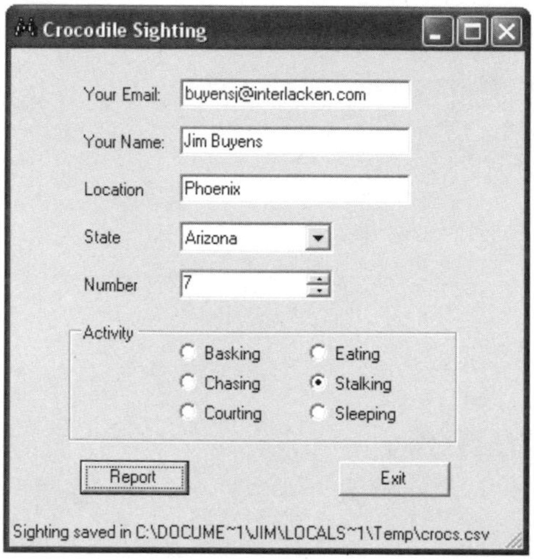

Figure 10-5 This form accepts reports of crocodile sightings and appends each report to a file.

For simplicity, the output file format is comma separated value (CSV). This is a plain text file format that meets these specifications:

- Each line in the file contains one record.

- Each record contains the same combination of fields (although not, of course, the same field values).

- Within each line, commas separate each field value.

- In the first record, each field value is actually the field name.

- If a field value contains any commas, you must surround the value with quotation marks. This keeps a field value that contains a comma from being mistaken for two field values.

- If a field value contains any quotation marks, you must replace each one with two quotation marks. If, for example, you need to record these three values.

```
100

Tom said, "Hello, Judy," and then sat down.

6789
```

the CSV file would need to contain this line:

```
100,"Tom said, ""Hello, Judy,"" and then sat down.",6789
```

The .NET Framework—and therefore Visual Basic .NET—deals with ordinary text files as *streams*. A stream represents any sequence of bytes, such as a file, an input/output device, a Transmission Control Protocol/Internet Protocol (TCP/IP) socket, or any other path between two processes. Using one set of stream objects for all these different types of input and output reduces the learning curve for programmers.

To update the crocodile report file, the example uses these classes from the *System.IO* namespace:

- *FileInfo* provides information about a specific file. It also provides methods for creating, copying, deleting, moving, and opening files, and for creating *FileStream* objects.

- *FileStream* is a *Stream* object that represents a file. It supports both read and write operations.

- *StreamWriter* writes characters into a stream (into a *FileStream* object, for example).

Creating the Crocodile Form

To start creating this program, you need to create a new project and design the form. Here are the steps you need to perform. Don't cheat!

1   Start Visual Studio .NET and create a new Windows Application project named *crocs*.

2   Make sure the *Form1* form is open in the Windows Form Designer, and that the form is selected. Then set the form's *Text* property to Crocodile Sighting. Locate and specify an icon for the form if you wish.

3   Locate the Toolbox window and open the Windows Forms tab. (If the Toolbox window isn't visible, choose Toolbox from the View menu.)

4   Add and arrange the following form controls:

- Five *Label* controls containing the text Your Email, Your Name, Location, State, and Number. You'll find these controls easier to work with if you set their *AutoSize* properties to *True*.

- Three *TextBox* controls named *txtEmail*, *txtName*, and *txtLocation*. Set the *Text* property of each control to an empty string.

- A *ComboBox* control named *cmbState*. Set the *DropDownStyle* property of this control to *DropDownList*.

- A *NumericUpDown* control named *nudNumber*.

- A *GroupBox* control named *grpActivity*. Set the *Text* property to *Activity*.

- Six *RadioButton* controls named *radBasking*, *radChasing*, *radCourting*, *radEating*, *radStalking*, and *radSleeping*. Set their *Text* properties to *Basking*, *Chasing*, *Courting*, *Eating*, *Stalking*, and *Sleeping*.

When you add these controls, make certain that the *grpActivity* group box is selected before you add the control. Otherwise, the RadioButton won't be *inside* the group box; it'll only be near it or on top of it.

- Two *Button* controls named *btnReport* and *btnExit*. Set the *Text* property of these controls to *Report* and *Exit*, respectively.

- A *StatusBar* control having the default name *StatusBar1*. Set this control's *Text* property to *Ready*.

- An *ErrorProvider* control with the default name *ErrorProvider1*.

Figure 10-6 shows how the form should look after you've added these elements. You can safely ignore minor variations in appearance.

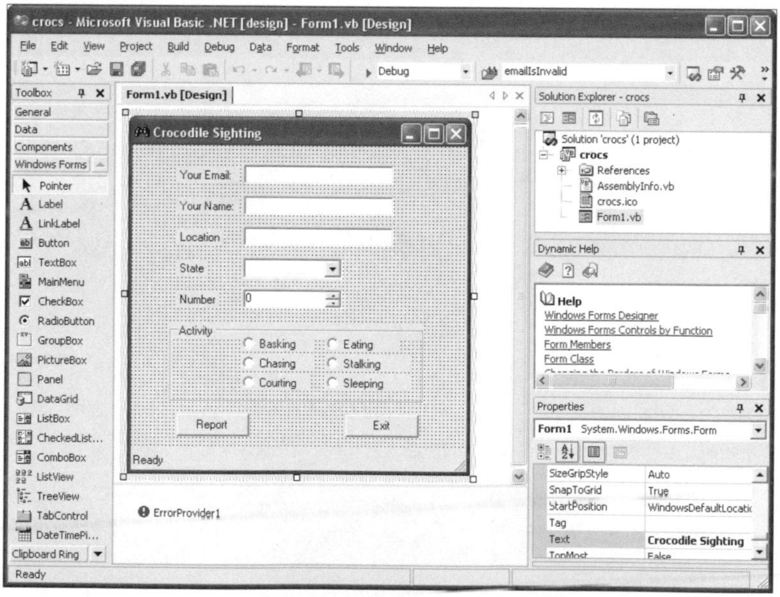

Figure 10-6 This is how the Crocodile Sighting form should look in the Windows Form Designer.

5 Select the *cmbState ComboBox*, then select its *Items* property in the Properties window, then click the ellipsis button that appears as part of the *Property* value. When the String Collection Editor window appears, enter a list of states like the one shown in Figure 10-7. When you're done, click OK.

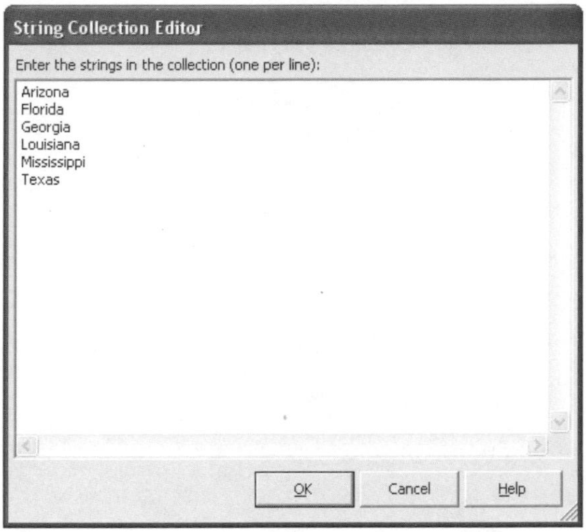

Figure 10-7 This window initializes the entries that will appear in a *ComboBox* control as well as in other controls based on a *ListBox*.

6 Assign the following *TabIndex* values by clicking each control and modifying its *TabIndex* property:

Control	TabIndex
txtEmail	0
txtName	1
txtLocation	2
cmbState	3
nudNumber	4
grpActivity	5
btnReport	6
btnExit	7

7 Using the same procedure, assign these *TabIndex* values to the *RadioButton* controls:

Control	TabIndex
radBasking	0
radChasing	1
radCourting	2
radEating	3
radStalking	4
radSleeping	5

8 Double-click the form background to create a *Form1_Load* subroutine and display it in the code editor.

9 Add the following code to the *Form1_Load* subroutine you created in step 8:

```
Dim intTop As Integer
Dim intLeft As Integer
intLeft = (Screen.PrimaryScreen.WorkingArea.Width _
          - Me.Width) / 2
intTop = (Screen.PrimaryScreen.WorkingArea.Height _
          - Me.Height) / 2
Me.Location = New Point(intLeft, intTop)
```

As you might suspect (but probably wouldn't have guessed) the expression *Screen.PrimaryScreen.WorkingArea.Width* returns the width in pixels of the user's primary display. *Me.Width* returns the width of the form, so the statement on lines 3 and 4 computes the left margin necessary to center the form on the display.

Similarly, the statement on lines 5 and 6 computes the necessary top margin to center the form vertically.

The last statement sets the form's *Location* property to a new *Point* object that contains the calculated margins. This technique positions the form in one movement, avoiding the momentary flash that sometimes results from setting the form's *Top* and *Left* properties in two successive statements.

10 Click the Form1.vb [Design] tab to redisplay the Windows Form Designer, then double-click the *btnExit* button. This creates a *btnExit_Click* subroutine and displays it in the code editor. Add the following statement to this subroutine:

```
Me.Dispose()
```

When the user clicks the *btnExit* button, this statement unloads the form and thereby terminates the program.

11 To save your work, choose Save All from the Visual Studio File menu.

At this point, you should be able to press F5 and see how the form will look to the user. The Your Email text box should have focus when the form first appears and pressing the Tab key should advance smoothly from this control to the one below it or to its right. The Tab key won't stop at the group of *RadioButton* controls, but after clicking one radio button, pressing the Down or Right arrow keys should advance the selection smoothly. Pressing the Up or Left arrow keys should change the selection in the opposite direction.

Clicking the down-pointing arrow on the State box should display a selection list of states. The arrows on the Number box should vary the displayed value from 0 to 100, and selecting any radio button should clear any other radio button that was previously selected.

Clicking Exit should terminate the program. Do so.

Validating the Input Fields

The next task is to verify each of the input fields on the form. With the project still open in Visual Studio.NET, proceed as follows:

1 Click the Form1.vb tab to display the code for the *Form1* form. Then, add the following subroutine after any *End Function* or *End Sub* statement. (To reproduce the example precisely, put it after the *End Sub* statement that marks the end of the *Form1_Load* subroutine.)

```
Private Sub txtEmail_Validating( _
    ByVal sender As Object, _
    ByVal e As System.ComponentModel.CancelEventArgs) _
    Handles txtEmail.Validating
    If EmailIsInvalid() Then
        Beep()
    End If
End Sub
```

The *Handles* clause on line 4 specifies that this subroutine will handle all *Validating* events that the *txtEmail* control raises. The subroutine name on line 1 follows normal conventions, and the argument types on lines 2 and 3 are those required of any *Validating* event handler.

The rest of the subroutine is reasonably trivial. It calls a function named *EmailIsInvalid* that returns *True* if the *txtEmail* control contains an unacceptable value and *False* if the value is acceptable. You'll create this function in the next step.

If the function returns *True*, the code beeps the PC speaker.

2 Add the following function immediately after the subroutine you created in step 1:

```
Function EmailIsInvalid() As Boolean
    txtEmail.Text = Trim(txtEmail.Text)
    If txtEmail.Text = "" Then
        ErrorProvider1.SetError(txtEmail, _
            "You must specify an email address.")
        Return True
    End If
    ErrorProvider1.SetError(txtEmail, "")
    Return False
End Function
```

The first statement inside the function removes any leading or trailing spaces from the value in the *txtEmail* text box. The next statement then determines if the result is an empty string.

- If so, it calls the *SetError* method of the ErrorProvider1 object, specifying *txtEmail* as the control that contains the error and "You Must Specify An Email Address" as the error message. Then, the *Return* statement on line 6 exits the function with a return value of *True*.

- If the result isn't an empty string, the code specifies an empty error message for the *txtEmail* control. This has the effect of clearing any previous error indication. Then, the code exits the function with a return value of *False*.

The reason for putting this code inside a function, by the way, is because you'll need to call it again when the user clicks Report.

3 To check your work, press F5. The *txtEmail* control should have focus as before. If you shift focus out of the *txtEmail* control, however, the PC speaker should beep and a red circle containing a white *i* should appear to the right of the *txtEmail* control. Resting the mouse over the red circle icon should display the message, "You Must Specify An Email Address" as a ToolTip.

To clear the error condition, enter one or more characters in the *txtEmail* text box and then set the focus elsewhere.

Click Exit or the form's Close box to end the program.

4 In the code editor, select the subroutine and function you created in steps 1 and 2, then copy them to the clipboard (press Ctrl+C, for example). Then, set the cursor after the *End Function* from step 3 and paste a second copy of the code back into the program (pressing Ctrl+V does this).

5 In the code you just pasted, change each occurrence of the characters *Email* to the characters *Name*. Then, remove the word *Address* from the error message. The new code should then look like this (occurrences of the new characters *Name* appear in boldface for clarity):

```
Private Sub txtName_Validating( _
    ByVal sender As Object, _
    ByVal e As System.ComponentModel.CancelEventArgs) _
    Handles txtName.Validating
    If NameIsInvalid() Then
        Beep()
    End If
End Sub
```

```
Function NameIsInvalid() As Boolean
    txtName.Text = Trim(txtName.Text)
    If txtName.Text = "" Then
        ErrorProvider1.SetError(txtName, _
            "You must specify a name.")
        Return True
    End If
    ErrorProvider1.SetError(txtName, "")
    Return False
End Function
```

6 As before, use the Copy and Paste commands to create a second copy of the code from step 5. Then, change all occurrences of *Name* to *Location*. Here are the results:

```
Private Sub txtLocation_Validating( _
    ByVal sender As Object, _
    ByVal e As System.ComponentModel.CancelEventArgs) _
    Handles txtLocation.Validating
    If LocationIsInvalid() Then
        Beep()
    End If
End Sub

Function LocationIsInvalid() As Boolean
    txtLocation.Text = Trim(txtLocation.Text)
    If txtLocation.Text - "" Then
        ErrorProvider1.SetError(txtLocation, _
            "You must specify a location.")
        Return True
    End If
    ErrorProvider1.SetError(txtLocation, "")
    Return False
End Function
```

7 The code for validating the *cmbState* box is similar to what you've already seen, but also different because the only invalid selection is no selection at all. Enter this code after the code from step 6:

```
Private Sub cmbState_Validating( _
    ByVal sender As Object, _
    ByVal e As System.ComponentModel.CancelEventArgs) _
    Handles cmbState.Validating
    If StateIsInvalid() Then
        Beep()
    End If
End Sub
```

```
Function StateIsInvalid() As Boolean
    If cmbState.SelectedIndex < 0 Then
        ErrorProvider1.SetError(cmbState, _
            "You must select a state.")
        Return True
    End If
    ErrorProvider1.SetError(cmbState, "")
    Return False
End Function
```

8 Validating the *nudNumber* field once again involves slightly different logic; the *NumericUpDown* control can only return one invalid value, namely zero. To validate this control, add the following code next in line after the code from step 7 (are you starting to see a pattern here?):

```
Private Sub nudNumber_Validating( _
    ByVal sender As Object, _
    ByVal e As System.ComponentModel.CancelEventArgs) _
    Handles nudNumber.Validating
    If NumberIsInvalid() Then
        Beep()
    End If
End Sub

Function NumberIsInvalid() As Boolean
    If nudNumber.Value < 1 Then
        ErrorProvider1.SetError(nudNumber, _
        "You must specify how many crocodiles you saw.")
        Return True
    End If
    ErrorProvider1.SetError(nudNumber, "")
    Return False
End Function
```

9 The last field, *Activity*, involves the greatest wrinkle of all. Because there's no one control that contains an *Activity* value, the code needs to individually check each *RadioButton* control. To do this, add this function next in sequence:

```
Function GetActivity() As String
    If radBasking.Checked Then
        Return "Basking"
    ElseIf radChasing.Checked Then
        Return "Chasing"
    ElseIf radCourting.Checked Then
        Return "Courting"
    ElseIf radEating.Checked Then
        Return "Eating"
    ElseIf radStalking.Checked Then
        Return "Stalking"
```

```
    ElseIf radSleeping.Checked Then
        Return "Sleeping"
    End If
    Return ""
End Function
```

By now you should be able to understand this code just by reading it directly. Basically, though, it checks each *RadioButton* control until it finds one that's selected, and then it returns a corresponding text value. If no *RadioButton* controls are checked, it returns an empty string.

10 To signal an error condition in case no *RadioButton* is checked, add the following function to your code. To reproduce the sample code, place this function just *before* the one you added in step 9:

```
Function ActivityIsInvalid() As Boolean
    If GetActivity() = "" Then
        ErrorProvider1.SetError(grpActivity, _
            "You must specify an activity.")
        Return True
    End If
    ErrorProvider1.SetError(grpActivity, "")
    Return False
End Function
```

Notice that this function tests the value that the *GetActivity* function from step 9 returns, and sets the error indication on the *grpActivity* group box rather than any specific *RadioButton*. It's perfectly acceptable to specify the name of a radio button when you call an *ErrorProvider's Set Error* method, but in this case it makes more sense to flag the whole set of radio buttons rather than any one of them.

Note also that the program doesn't include a *Validating* event handler for the radio buttons. This is because the *grpActivity* group box never gets focus, and therefore never raises a *Validating* event. The next step, however, does use the *ActivityIsInvalid* function.

11 Click the Form1.vb [Design] tag to redisplay the Windows Form Designer, then double-click Report. This creates a *btnReport_Click* subroutine and displays it in the code editor. Add the following statements to this subroutine:

```
Dim booError As Boolean = False
booError = EmailIsInvalid()
booError = booError Or ActivityIsInvalid()
booError = booError Or NameIsInvalid()
booError = booError Or LocationIsInvalid()
booError = booError Or StateIsInvalid()
booError = booError Or NumberIsInvalid()
```

```
booError = booError Or ActivityIsInvalid()
If booError Then
    Beep()
    StatusBar1.Text = "Your last submission had " & _
                      "an error. Nothing was written."
Else
'   WriteOutput()
End If
```

Do you see what this code is doing? First it declares a Boolean variable named *booError*, then it calls the *IsInvalid* function for each field. If any of these functions return *True*, the *booError* variable ends up being *True* as well. (Recall that the *Or* operator returns *True* if its two operands are *True-False, False-True*, or *True-True*.)

If the *booError* variable ends up being *True*, then at least one field is in error. The code therefore beeps the PC speaker and displays a message in the status bar. You could also display a message box at this point, but don't forget that the bad fields will have an error icon and that the speaker will beep. The message box might be overkill.

If the *booError* variable ends up being *False*, it's fine to append a new record to the output file. The next section explains how to write a subroutine named *WriteOutput* that does this but, for now, the statement that invokes it is commented out.

12 To save your work, choose Save All from the Visual Studio File menu.

To test the program, press F5. No error icons should appear immediately, but if you immediately click Report, six error icons should appear: one for each input field because they're all blank. Figure 10-8 shows this result.

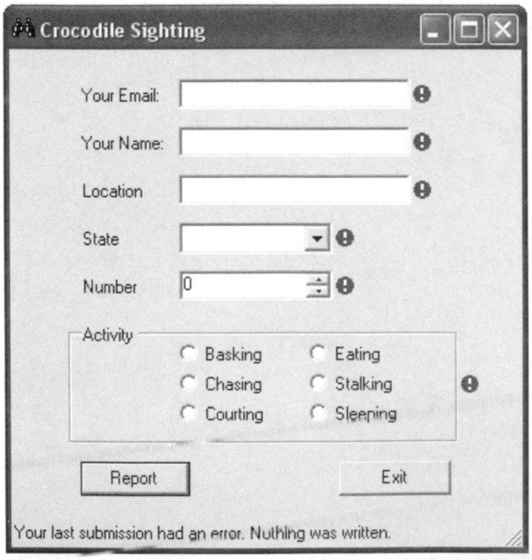

Figure 10-8 An error icon appears near each field for which the code found an error. In this case, all the fields are in error because they're all blank or zero.

To correct the Your Email, Your Name, or Location fields, enter any text and then set the focus elsewhere. The error icon should disappear when the control loses focus. The State, Number, and Activity fields should work the same way except that you resolve the error by making a correct selection.

You should also find that erasing the value in any of the text boxes and then changing the focus results in an immediate error indication.

Writing the Output Record

The last job in completing the crocodile sighting program is to write the subroutine that creates the output file. Proceed as follows:

1 Make sure the *crocs* project is open in Visual Studio and that the program isn't running. Display Form1.vb in the code editor.

2 Because the program will be performing file operations, add the following statement at the very top of the Form1.vb code listing:

```
Imports System.IO
```

This saves you from having to type *System.IO* in front of any class names from this namespace.

3 Add a subroutine named *WriteOutput* to the code. To follow the example, place this subroutine immediately after the *btnReport_Click* subroutine you created in the previous section. The subroutine takes no arguments. Here's the code:

```
Sub WriteOutput()
End Sub
```

4 Declare the following variables inside the subroutine you created in step 3:

```
Dim strFileName As String
Dim booFileExists As Boolean
Dim finFileInfo As FileInfo
Dim fstOut As FileStream
Dim swtOut As StreamWriter
```

Here's how the *WriteOutput* subroutine uses these variables:

● The *strFileName* variable contains the name of the output file.

● The *booFileExists* variable indicates whether a file with this file name already exists.

● The *finFileInfo* variable points to a *FileInfo* object that provides information about the output file.

- The *fstOut* variable points to a *FileStream* object that represents the output file.

- The *swtOut* variable points to a *StreamWriter* object that writes data into the *fstOut* file stream (that is, into the output file).

5 To avoid the complexity of displaying a File Open dialog box that specifies the output file name, the crocodile sighting program always creates a file named Crocs.csv in the current user's temporary file folder. The location of this folder resides in an environment variable named TEMP.

To formulate this file name, add the following statement after the declarations from the previous step:

```
strFileName = _
    Environment.GetEnvironmentVariable("TEMP") & _
    "\crocs.csv"
```

The method in line 2, as you might have surmised, returns the value in the environment variable TEMP.

6 Create a new *FileInfo* object that describes the file named as you determined in step 5. Use the *FileInfo* object's *Exists* property to determine whether this file already exists, and save that result in the *booFileExists* variable. Here's the required code:

```
finFileInfo = New FileInfo(strFileName)
booFileExists = finFileInfo.Exists
```

No error results from creating a *FileInfo* object for a file or path that doesn't exist. In that case, the information is simply that the file or path doesn't exist.

Tip To see what other information a *FileInfo* object provides, locate the article titled "FileInfo Members" in the .NET Framework section of the MSDN Library.

---

7 Create a new *FileStream* object that points to the desired output file. The easiest way of doing this is to use the *OpenWrite* method of the *FileInfo* object you just created. Therefore, add the following statement next in sequence:

```
fstOut = finFileInfo.OpenWrite()
```

8 Create a new *StreamWriter* object that writes into the *FileStream* you just created. This requires the following statement, next in sequence.

```
swtOut = New StreamWriter(fstOut)
```

9 Position the *swtOut* stream writer so that it starts writing at the end of the current file. To do this, append the following statement to the code from the previous step:

```
swtOut.BaseStream.Seek(0, SeekOrigin.End)
```

This is one of those statements that's easier to read than discover. The *swtOut* variable, of course, points to the output stream writer. The *BaseStream* property refers to its underlying stream. *Seek* is a method that positions the stream (in this case, the file) to a specified byte.

The arguments *0* and *SeekOrigin.End* are an offset and an origin, respectively. An origin is a known spot within the file; the expression *SeekOrigin.End* denotes the end of the file. The offset 0 means 0 bytes from the specified origin, in this case, 0 bytes from the end of the file.

10 If the file didn't previously exist (that is, if *booFileExists* is False) write a header line that contains the field names. The *WriteLine* method of a stream writer is perfect for this job: it writes an argument string plus a line ending into the output stream. The following code goes next in sequence:

```
If Not booFileExists Then
    swtOut.WriteLine("Date,Email,Name,Location," & _
                     "State,Number,Activity")
End If
```

11 Write the crocodile report record to the file. This is another job for the stream writer's *WriteLine* method. Each line should contain seven fields separated by commas. These are the current date and time plus the six form field values.

The Your Email, Your Name, and Location fields need special handling because the user might have entered values that include quotation marks or commas. Therefore, run these values through a function named *PrepareText* that adds surrounding quotation marks and doubles up existing quotation marks if necessary. Steps 15 through 17 create this function.

To get the Activity value, call the *GetActivity* function you coded earlier. This function returns a string value that corresponds to the radio button the user selected.

Here's the necessary code. Add it to the code from the previous step:

```
swtOut.WriteLine(Now & "," & _
    PrepareText(txtEmail.Text) & "," & _
    PrepareText(txtName.Text) & "," & _
    PrepareText(txtLocation.Text) & "," & _
    cmbState.SelectedItem & "," & _
    nudNumber.Value & "," & _
    GetActivity())
```

12 Some or all of your stream writer output might still be in memory rather than on disk. To force all the output to disk, call the stream writer's *Flush* method. Then, because there's no more output to write, close the stream writer. To do all this, add the following statements next in sequence:

```
swtOut.Flush()
swtOut.Close()
```

13 It's always a good idea to provide status information to the user. Therefore, complete the *WriteOutput* subroutine by placing a message in the status bar. Here's the required code:

```
StatusBar1.Text = "Sighting saved in " & strFileName
```

14 Now that the *WriteOutput* subroutine exists, you can uncomment the code that calls it from the *btnReport_Click* subroutine. The last three lines of that subroutine should then read as follows:

```
Else
    WriteOutput()
End If
```

15 The only dangling issue is creating the *PrepareText* subroutine. This subroutine receives a string and returns a string, so declare it like this:

```
Function PrepareText(ByVal astrText As String) As String
End Function
```

To follow the example, place this function after the *End Sub* statement that completes the *WriteOutput* subroutine.

16 The *InStr* function that comes with Visual Basic is perfect for searching for one string within another. If the value in its first argument contains the value in its second argument, *InStr* returns the numeric position. Otherwise, it returns zero.

The following code uses the *InStr* function to determine if the *PrepareText* function's *astrText* argument contains a comma or a quotation mark. (The expression *Chr(34)* returns ASCII character 34, which is the quotation mark.) If neither character is present, the code returns the *astrText* value unchanged and exits the function.

Add this code between the statements you entered in step 15:

```
If (InStr(astrText, ",") < 1) _
And (InStr(astrText, Chr(34)) < 1) Then
    Return astrText
End If
```

17 If the code in step 13 did find a comma or quotation mark in the *astrText* value, the *PrepareText* function needs to replace each quotation mark with two quotation marks, surround the result with quotation marks, and return that result to the calling program.

The Visual Basic built-in *Replace* function is perfect for replacing each quotation mark with two. Therefore, add the following statement after the code from step 16:

```
Return Chr(34) & _
    Replace(astrText, Chr(34), Chr(34) & Chr(34)) & _
    Chr(34)
```

18 To save your work, choose Save All from the Visual Studio File menu.

Now, if you press F5 to start the program, enter some data, and click Report, the status bar should display a message such as this:

Sighting Saved In C:\Docume~1\Jim\Locasl~1\Temp\Crocs.csv

The file location in this message uses abbreviated folder names but figuring them out shouldn't be too difficult. The actual path in this case, for example, is

C:\Documents And Settings\Jim\Local Settings\Temp\Crocs.csv

where Jim is the current user name and Local Settings is usually a hidden folder. If Microsoft Excel is installed on your system, double-clicking this file in Windows Explorer should open it in Excel. If Microsoft Access is installed, you should be able to import the file as a database table.

Tip To find a hidden folder such as Local Settings, you might need to activate the Show Hidden Files And Folders option. In Microsoft Windows XP, this is a Windows Explorer option under Tools, Folder Options, View.

Here's a complete listing of the code for the project's Form1.vb form. As usual, the actual placement of functions and subroutines doesn't matter, nor does the exact location of line breaks and continuations.

Form1.vb

```vb
Imports System.IO
Public Class Form1
    Inherits System.Windows.Forms.Form

+ Windows Form Designer generated code

Private Sub Form1_Load( _
    ByVal sender As System.Object, _
    ByVal e As System.EventArgs) _
    Handles MyBase.Load
    Dim intTop As Integer
    Dim intLeft As Integer
    intLeft = (Screen.PrimaryScreen.WorkingArea.Width _
            - Me.Width) / 2
    intTop = (Screen.PrimaryScreen.WorkingArea.Height _
            - Me.Height) / 2
    Me.Location = New Point(intLeft, intTop)

End Sub

Private Sub txtEmail_Validating( _
    ByVal sender As Object, _
    ByVal e As System.ComponentModel.CancelEventArgs) _
    Handles txtEmail.Validating
    If EmailIsInvalid() Then
        Beep()
    End If
End Sub

Function EmailIsInvalid() As Boolean
    txtEmail.Text = Trim(txtEmail.Text)
    If txtEmail.Text = "" Then
        ErrorProvider1.SetError(txtEmail, _
            "You must specify an email address.")
        Return True
    End If
    ErrorProvider1.SetError(txtEmail, "")
    Return False
End Function

Private Sub txtName_Validating( _
ByVal sender As Object, _
ByVal e As System.ComponentModel.CancelEventArgs) _
Handles txtName.Validating
    If NameIsInvalid() Then
        Beep()
    End If
End Sub
```

```vb
Function NameIsInvalid() As Boolean
    txtName.Text = Trim(txtName.Text)
    If txtName.Text = "" Then
        ErrorProvider1.SetError(txtName, _
            "You must specify a name.")
        Return True
    End If
    ErrorProvider1.SetError(txtName, "")
    Return False
End Function


Private Sub txtLocation_Validating( _
    ByVal sender As Object, _
    ByVal e As System.ComponentModel.CancelEventArgs) _
    Handles txtLocation.Validating
    If LocationIsInvalid() Then
        Beep()
    End If
End Sub


Function LocationIsInvalid() As Boolean
    txtLocation.Text = Trim(txtLocation.Text)
    If txtLocation.Text = "" Then
        ErrorProvider1.SetError(txtLocation, _
            "You must specify a location.")
        Return True
    End If
    ErrorProvider1.SetError(txtLocation, "")
    Return False
End Function


Private Sub cmbState_Validating( _
    ByVal sender As Object, _
    ByVal e As System.ComponentModel.CancelEventArgs) _
    Handles cmbState.Validating
    If StateIsInvalid() Then
        Beep()
    End If
End Sub


Function StateIsInvalid() As Boolean
    If cmbState.SelectedIndex < 0 Then
        ErrorProvider1.SetError(cmbState, _
        "You must select a state.")
        Return True
    End If
    ErrorProvider1.SetError(cmbState, "")
    Return False
End Function
```

```
Private Sub nudNumber_Validating( _
    ByVal sender As Object, _
    ByVal e As System.ComponentModel.CancelEventArgs) _
    Handles nudNumber.Validating
    If NumberIsInvalid() Then
        Beep()
    End If
End Sub

Function NumberIsInvalid() As Boolean
    If nudNumber.Value < 1 Then
        ErrorProvider1.SetError(nudNumber, _
            "You must specify how many crocodiles you saw.")
        Return True
    End If
    ErrorProvider1.SetError(nudNumber, "")
    Return False
End Function

Function ActivityIsInvalid() As Boolean
    If GetActivity() = "" Then
        ErrorProvider1.SetError(grpActivity, _
            "You must specify an activity.")
        Return True
    End If
    ErrorProvider1.SetError(grpActivity, "")
    Return False
End Function

Function GetActivity() As String
    If radBasking.Checked Then
        Return "Basking"
    ElseIf radChasing.Checked Then
        Return "Chasing"
    ElseIf radCourting.Checked Then
        Return "Courting"
    ElseIf radEating.Checked Then
        Return "Eating"
    ElseIf radStalking.Checked Then
        Return "Stalking"
    ElseIf radSleeping.Checked Then
        Return "Sleeping"
    End If
    Return ""
End Function

Private Sub btnReport_Click( _
    ByVal sender As System.Object, _
    ByVal e As System.EventArgs) _
    Handles btnReport.Click
```

```
        Dim booError As Boolean = False
        booError = EmailIsInvalid()
        booError = booError Or ActivityIsInvalid()
        booError = booError Or NameIsInvalid()
        booError = booError Or LocationIsInvalid()
        booError = booError Or StateIsInvalid()
        booError = booError Or NumberIsInvalid()
        booError = booError Or ActivityIsInvalid()
        If booError Then
            Beep()
            StatusBar1.Text = "Your last submission had an " & _
                              "error. Nothing was written."
        Else
            WriteOutput()
        End If
    End Sub

    Sub WriteOutput()
        Dim strFileName As String
        Dim booFileExists As Boolean
        Dim finFileInfo As FileInfo
        Dim fstOut As FileStream
        Dim swtOut As StreamWriter

        strFileName = _
            Environment.GetEnvironmentVariable("TEMP") & _
            "\crocs.csv"
        finFileInfo = New FileInfo(strFileName)
        booFileExists = finFileInfo.Exists

        fstOut = finFileInfo.OpenWrite()
        swtOut = New StreamWriter(fstOut)
        swtOut.BaseStream.Seek(0, SeekOrigin.End)
        If Not booFileExists Then
            swtOut.WriteLine("Date,Email,Name,Location," & _
                              "State,Number,Activity")
        End If
        swtOut.WriteLine(Now & "," & _
            PrepareText(txtEmail.Text) & "," & _
            PrepareText(txtName.Text) & "," & _
            PrepareText(txtLocation.Text) & "," & _
            cmbState.SelectedItem & "," & _
            nudNumber.Value & "," & _
            GetActivity())
        swtOut.Flush()
        swtOut.Close()
        StatusBar1.Text = "Sighting saved in " & strFileName
    End Sub
```

```
Function PrepareText(ByVal astrText As String) As String
    If (InStr(astrText, ",") < 1) _
    And (InStr(astrText, Chr(34)) < 1) Then
        Return astrText
    End If
    Return Chr(34) & _
        Replace(astrText, Chr(34), Chr(34) & Chr(34)) & _
        Chr(34)
End Function

Private Sub btnExit_Click( _
    ByVal sender As System.Object, _
    ByVal e As System.EventArgs) _
    Handles btnExit.Click
    Me.Dispose()
End Sub

End Class
```

Key Points

- The .NET Framework—and therefore Visual Basic .NET as well—provides a wide assortment of controls you can add to a Windows form. Many of these support user interaction and information, but there are other types of controls as well.

- The usual way of adding controls to a form is by double-clicking its entry in the Windows Forms section of the Toolbar window, or by selecting it there and then dragging the mouse across the form background. However, you can also add controls using Copy and Paste commands and from code.

- All visible controls have *Position*, *Size*, *Visible*, *Enabled*, and *TabIndex* properties.

- Text boxes, check boxes, and radio buttons are relatively simple to access from code. This usually involves the *Text* property of a *TextBox* or the *Checked* property of a *CheckBox* or *RadioButton*.

- Working with list boxes is a bit more complicated because they contain multiple items and because of differences among various types of list boxes.

- The time to interact with a form control is usually when the user initiates some event. As a result, most form processing code appears with event handler subroutines.

Chapter 11

Accessing Databases

A database is a collection of data organized so that computer programs can readily access, manage, and update its contents. Although databases physically consist of computer files, applications that use databases don't manipulate these files directly. Instead, applications send commands to and receive responses from a database management system (DBMS) such as Microsoft SQL Server and Microsoft Access. A DBMS relieves the programmer of many tedious and intricate tasks involved in processing the database, and it also guards against the introduction of invalid data.

Nearly all modern databases conform to the so-called relational model and are, therefore, relational databases. The basic unit of organization in any relational database is the table. The columns in a table represent fields, and the rows are records. Table 11-1, for example, shows a table that stores information about the participants in a series of athletic events.

Table 11-1 *Players* Table

playerid	firstname	lastname	wins	pswd
aaron@cohovineyard.com	Aaron	Con	0	caboose
adam@fourthcoffee.com	Adam	Barr	2	bison
alan@tailspintoys.com	Alan	Shen	1	slippery
bob@margiestravel.com	Bob	Hohman	0	horse
buyensj@interlacken.com	Jim	Buyens	1	horse
don@contoso.com	Don	Funk	3	fickle

In this table, the first field in each record contains the same kind of data: a player identification code called *playerid*. The second field contains the player's first name, the third field contains the player's surname, and so on. There's nothing special about the order of the fields; you could rearrange, add, or delete fields without affecting the functionality of the table in any way. However, within the same table, you can't make *playerid* the first field in one record and the second field of another, nor can you make one record contain a field (for example, best friend's license plate number) that another record doesn't.

Every relational DBMS must provide the following three functions for accessing data:

- *SELECT* presents a view of a table showing only those records having specified values in specified fields. In English, the following command would request a *SELECT* operation: "Please retrieve all records from the *Players* table where *firstname* is Aaron."

- *PROJECT* presents a view of a table that doesn't include all its fields. A *PROJECT* command might be, "Please retrieve only the *firstname* and *lastname* fields from the *Players* table."

> **Note** When used as database commands, the words *SELECT*, *PROJECT*, and *JOIN* are all verbs. Therefore, pronounce *PROJECT* like the first two syllables in projector and not like the word *project* in Microsoft Project.

- *JOIN* presents a combined view of two tables as if they were one table. The result is a temporary table that the DBMS builds by matching record values in one table to record values in another and then combining fields from both matching records.

Showing an example of a *JOIN* operation requires a second table, such as Table 11-2, which contains a list of events in which players compete. Notice that the *Players* table and the *Events* table each contain a *playerid* field. You could therefore tell the DBMS, "Match the *Events* table and the *Players* table based on *playerid*, and show me a view that includes *events.eventid, events.description, events.venue, events.playerid, players.firstname,* and *players.lastname*."

Note The notation *players.playerid* means "the *playerid* field from the *Players* table." This is a common notation when working with tables and fields.

Table 11-2 *Events* Table

eventid	description	venue	playerid
2	Minesweeper	Winslow	buyensj@interlacken.com
5	Tennis	New York	bob@margiestravel.com
8	Hockey	Toronto	don@contoso.com
11	Pole Vault	Atlanta	aaron@cohovineyard.com
14	Dominoes	Bullhead City	buyensj@interlacken.com

The results of this *JOIN* operation appear in Table 11-3. Although the result of a *JOIN* consists of rows and columns, it isn't a table in a database sense. Instead, the results are a much more fleeting object called a *result set*. Some of the fields come from the *Events* table and some from the *Players* table, but the source records in each case contain equal values in the *playerid* field. You could use such a result set to produce an on-screen display, a report, or anything else, but you would typically discard the result set when your program ended. The next time you ran the same program, you'd want a new result set that reflected any changes in the source tables.

Table 11-3 *Eventplayers* Query

events. eventid	events. description	events. venue	events. playerid	players. firstname	players. lastname
2	Minesweeper	Winslow	buyensj@interlacken.com	Jim	Buyens
5	Tennis	New York	bob@margiestravel.com	Bob	Hohman
8	Hockey	Toronto	don@contoso.com	Don	Funk
11	Pole Vault	Atlanta	aaron@cohovineyard.com	Aaron	Con
14	Dominoes	Bullhead City	buyensj@interlacken.com	Jim	Buyens

You might have noticed that these *JOIN* results don't show all the fields from both tables—because the query didn't ask for all the fields, even though it could have. In fact, this query joins two tables and projects the results. This is perfectly acceptable; you can combine the *SELECT, PROJECT,* and *JOIN* operations at will.

Note   The result of a *JOIN* is always called a result set, even if it's empty or contains a single record.

SQL Concepts and Syntax

Structured Query Language (SQL) is the way that applications usually send commands to relational databases. SQL is a powerful and complex language deserving of whole books of explanation; the material in this section is just an overview. Table 11-4 lists the most fundamental SQL commands.

Table 11-4   Fundamental SQL Commands

Command	Description
SELECT	Returns a set of all records that match given criteria
INSERT	Adds a new record
UPDATE	Changes the value of specified fields in all records that match given criteria
DELETE	Removes all records matching given criteria

To clarify the *SELECT* statement, consider a simple example that selects events with a venue of Toronto. The *SELECT* statement to perform this query looks like this:

```
SELECT eventid, description, venue, playerid
FROM events
WHERE (venue = "Toronto")
```

This statement selects all records from the *Events* table with a *venue* field of Toronto. For each matching record, it shows the four fields named in the first line.

Queries like this one aren't part of Microsoft Visual Basic .NET or, for that matter, any other .NET programming language. As far as your program is concerned, SQL statements are nothing more than strings of text. You therefore need another piece of software that sends SQL statements to the database system and receives success or failure codes, error messages, and result sets in return. In the case of .NET, this software is ActiveX Data Objects (ADO).NET. Later sections in this chapter explain how to use ADO.NET, but first you need to know a bit more about SQL statements.

Retrieving Data with the *SELECT* Statement

To get information from a database, you must first formulate a query that specifies exactly what you want. In SQL, a *SELECT* statement does this job. Executing a *SELECT* statement produces a result set, or a group of matching records. *SELECT* statements consist of several clauses. Table 11-5 lists the most common clauses and the next few sections explain each one.

Table 11-5 Common *SELECT* Statement Clauses

Clause	Description	Relational Function
SELECT	Specifies which fields should appear in the result set	*PROJECT*
FROM	Specifies which tables will provide data	*JOIN*
WHERE	Limits the result set to rows containing certain data values	*SELECT*
GROUP BY	Aggregates rows with the same value in given fields	
HAVING	Limits the result set to rows containing certain data values after aggregation	
ORDER BY	Specifies the order of the result set	

Coding the *SELECT* Clause

The *SELECT* statement specifies what information you want from a database and how you want to receive it. All *SELECT* statements begin with the word *SELECT* followed by a list of fields. Here's how to code that list:

■ After the word *SELECT*, specify the fields you want to show in the result set. Separate multiple fields with commas, and arrange them in the order in which you want them to appear.

■ If the same field name appears in more than one table mentioned in the *FROM* clause (described in the next section), specify it as *<tablename>.<fieldname>*.

■ If a table name or field name contains spaces or special characters, enclose it in square brackets (for example, *players.[first name]*).

■ To include all fields from a table, use an asterisk (for example, *events.**).

■ To assign a field a different name than it has in the database, code the field's database name, the word *AS*, and then the name you want to query to use. Here's an example.

```
SELECT players.firstname AS givenname, ...
```

> **Note** Spaces, line endings, and other "white space" characters aren't significant in SQL statements except to separate terms. You can include or omit as many white space characters as you like.

Coding the *FROM* Clause

FROM identifies the table or join to use in formulating the result set. To select fields from an existing table, specify the table's name. To select from a join of two tables, specify an expression that looks like this:

```
FROM <left-table> <jointype> <right-table>
ON <left-table>.<joinfield> = <right-table>.<joinfield>
```

That is, for example:

```
FROM events INNER JOIN players
ON events.playerid = players.playerid
```

This statement joins the *events* table to the *players* table by matching the *playerid* field of the *events* table to the *playerid* field of the *players* tables. In fact, there are three common join types:

- ■ **INNER JOIN**   The result set only contains records for which the joined fields in both source tables are equal.

- ■ **LEFT JOIN**   The result set contains all records from the left table and only those records from the right table in which the joined fields are equal. When a record from the left table has no matching record in the right table, the result set contains nulls in any field sourced from the right table.

- ■ **RIGHT JOIN**   The result set contains all records from the right table and only those records from the left table in which the joined fields are equal. When a record from the right table has no matching record in the left table, the result set contains nulls in any field sourced from the left table.

Coding the *WHERE* Clause

WHERE specifies criteria for selecting records. Most criteria have the format *fieldname, operator, value,* as in this example:

```
WHERE players.lastname = 'Shen'
```

As shown in this example, single quotation marks identify text constants. Microsoft Access requires that pound signs (#) identify date constants, as in #12/31/1999#, but SQL Server uses apostrophes. Numeric constants have no surrounding delimiters, as in year = 1950. You can group criteria using parentheses, the *AND* operator, and the *OR* operator.

Coding the *GROUP BY* Clause

GROUP BY, when present, tells the database system to consolidate similar records based on equal values in a supplied list of fields. If you specify *GROUP BY firstname, lastname*, the database system, before presenting the result set, consolidates all records having the same set of values in those fields.

Coding the *HAVING* Clause

HAVING works a lot like *WHERE*, except that it operates after applying the *GROUP BY* clause. Suppose, for example, you code the following *SELECT* statement for the *events* table:

```
SELECT firstname, lastname, SUM(wins) AS totwins
FROM events
GROUP BY firstname, lastname
```

If you coded *HAVING totwins* > 10, the database system would first aggregate all events records by *firstname* and *lastname*, and then, from those results, select any record that had an aggregate *totwins* value greater than 10. (*SUM*, by the way, is a SQL function that adds the values of a named field from all records in a given group.)

Coding the *ORDER BY* Clause

ORDER BY controls the order of records in the result set. You can specify any fields in the result set, separated by commas and in any order, and the database system sorts the result set accordingly: first field first, second field second, and so on. To sort any field in descending sequence, specify the keyword *DESC* after its field name. Here's a typical *ORDER BY* clause:

```
ORDER BY lastname, firstname, wins DESC
```

Adding Data with the *INSERT* Statement

The general form of an *INSERT* statement appears in this example. The order of the fields and values isn't significant, except that you must code both of them in the same order:

```
INSERT tablename (textfield, numfield, datefield)
VALUES ('textval', numval, #dateval#)
```

If you omit the list of field names, the database system expects the value list to contain one value for each field in the database in the same order in which the fields appear in the table definition. This often leads to unexpected consequences when someone adds or rearranges fields. For this reason, coding the field names is usually the safest choice.

A problem arises when you try to insert string values that contain apostrophes. In the following statement, for example:

```
INSERT events (description, venue, playerid)
VALUES ('Can't miss opportunity',
        2500,
        'buyensj@interlacken.com')
```

the DBMS will interpret `'Can'` as a value and `t miss opportunity'` as illegal characters in the SQL statement. To avoid this problem, replace all apostrophes in your data with double apostrophes, as shown in the following example.

```
INSERT events (description, venue, playerid)
VALUES ('Can''t miss opportunity',
        2500,
        'buyensj@interlacken.com')
```

Only one apostrophe will be present when you retrieve the data later.

Many tables contain numeric fields that the database system fills in whenever it adds a record. Microsoft Access calls these *Autonumber* fields and SQL Server calls them *Identity* fields. If you ever insert records into such a table, *don't* try to specify your own value for this type of field. The database system will automatically supply a value that you can't override.

Changing Data with the *UPDATE* Statement

Here's a typical *UPDATE* statement. The name that follows the *UPDATE* command specifies the table you want to update. The *SET* clause specifies the values you want to set, and the *WHERE* clause specifies the records you want to update:

```
UPDATE events
SET events.venue = 'Hoboken', playerid = 'don@contoso.com'
WHERE events.eventid = 1
```

There's no need to include *SET* expressions for fields you don't want to update. The preceding code, for example, makes no change to the *description* field. As with the *INSERT* statement, you must code correct delimiters around any values.

Be careful when coding the *WHERE* clause and especially careful if, for whatever reason, you omit it. There's no limit to the number of records an *UPDATE* statement can affect!

- If you code a *WHERE* clause that matches more records than you want, more records than you want will contain the value you set.

- If you omit the *WHERE* clause entirely, the *UPDATE* statement will affect every record in the given table.

Removing Data with the *DELETE* Statement

The *DELETE* statement is one of the easiest SQL statements to code. All you need to know is the name of the table that contains the data and the field values that identify the records you want to delete. Here's an example.

```
DELETE FROM events WHERE venue = 'Waco'
```

The syntax of the *WHERE* clause is exactly the same as it is for *SELECT* statements. If you omit the *WHERE* clause, a *DELETE* statement deletes every record in the given table. If you want to delete only one record, make sure the *WHERE* clause specifies a unique key.

Introducing ADO.NET

.NET programs need a standard way of accessing, processing, and reporting information in databases and this is exactly what ADO.NET provides. Table 11-6 lists the major ADO.NET objects that provide these functions.

Table 11-6   Important ADO.NET Objects and Functions

Operating Mode	Object Name		Function
	SQL Server	**All Other DBMSs**	
All	*SqlConnection*	*OleDbConnection*	Opens a connection (that is, a pathway) to a DBMS
Individual commands	*SqlCommand*	*OleDbCommand*	Stores and executes a SQL statement
One-time read	*SqlDataReader*	*OleDbDataReader*	Runs a query and provides one-time, read-only access to the results
Read into memory Update in memory Analyze and incorporate changes	*SqlDataAdapter*	*OleDbDataAdapter*	Runs a query and stores results in a *DataTable*
	DataSet		Contains one or more *DataTables*
	DataTable		Stores data in database-style row-and-column format
	DataRelation		Defines a logical relationship between two *DataTables*
	DataView		Provides a sorted or filtered view of the contents of a *DataTable*

Notice that the *SqlConnection, SqlCommand, SqlDataReader*, and *SqlDataAdapter* objects each have counterparts with names beginning with *OleDb*. The objects that begin with *Sql* use proprietary, high-speed protocols that communicate only with SQL Server. If your program will use these objects, you should add the following statements at the top of the file:

```
Imports System.Data
Imports System.Data.SqlClient
```

The *OleDb* objects communicate with Microsoft Access, Oracle, and other databases for which Object Linking and Embedding database (OLE DB) drivers exist. Programs that use these objects should include these statements, again at the top of the file:

```
Imports System.Data
Imports System.Data.OleDb
```

There are two fundamentally different ways to add ADO.NET objects to your program:

- You can add them through the Microsoft Visual Studio.NET graphic user interface. This constitutes adding the controls at design time.

- You can add them from code; that is, you can add them at run time.

Using the Visual Studio interface to add ADO.NET controls might seem a little easier at first, but adding them from code offers more flexibility. Either way, you still must understand how the objects work and you still have to add some code. The rest of the chapter describes both approaches.

Opening and Closing ADO.NET Connections

To create a connection string at design time, display your form in the Windows Form Designer, click the Data tab of the Toolbox window, and double-click either *SqlConnection* (for SQL Server databases) or *OleDbConnection* (for all others). This adds the corresponding object to the bottom pane of the Windows Form Designer window. This is a good time to rename the object something meaningful, such as the prefix *con* followed by a short name for the database. To specify the details of a connection, follow these steps:

1 Select the connection object and then, in the Properties window, click the drop-down arrow for the *ConnectionString* property. If this displays an entry for the database you want, select it. Otherwise, select <New Connection...> and wait for the Data Link Properties dialog box shown in Figure 11-1 to appear.

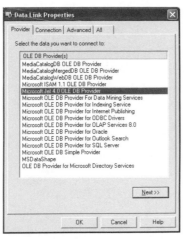

Figure 11-1 This dialog box collects and saves database connection settings. The Connection tab appears by default.

2 When this dialog box first appears, the Connection tab will be selected. To configure a new connection, however, you should begin with the Provider tab. On that tab, select the provider your database requires. For example:

If your database is:	Select provider:
SQL Server	Microsoft OLE DB Provider for SQL Server
Microsoft Access	Microsoft JET 4.0 OLE DB Provider

3 Click the Connection tab. This displays a different collection of fields depending on the provider you specified. For SQL Server databases, you must enter a server name, login credentials such as a user name and password, and the name of the database. For Microsoft Access, you must enter the database file and any user name and password the Microsoft Access database requires.

4 To check your work, click Test Connection. This should display a message box stating Text Connection Succeeded or words to that effect. If you get a failure message, review the entries you made in steps 2 and 3.

5 Click OK to close the Data Link Properties dialog box.

Try This! After you use the Data Link Properties dialog box to configure a set of database connection properties, that database appears in the Server Explorer window. If this window isn't visible, choose Server Explorer from the View menu of Visual Studio .NET. To view the content or properties of the database, click the plus sign icon that precedes it. To create additional connections to the same database (in another program, for example) drag the database out of the Server Explorer window and drop it onto your form.

To create a connection at run time, declare a variable of type *SqlConnection* or *OleDbConnection*, provide a connection string, and then call the object's *Open* method. Here, for example, are some statements that create an ADO.NET connection to a Microsoft Access database. The first statement defines an *OleDbConnection* variable, the second defines a *String* variable to hold the connection string, and the third (which spans two lines) actually constructs the connection string:

```
Dim conGames As OleDbConnection
Dim strGames As String
strGames = "Provider=Microsoft.Jet.OLEDB.4.0;" & _
    "Data Source=C:\databases\games.mdb"
conGames = New OleDbConnection(strGames)
conGames.Open()
```

The fourth statement, which appears on line 5, creates the *OleDbConnection* object, and the last statement opens it. To close the connection, you would code *conGames.Close()* before the program exits.

A connection string is simply a line of text that specifies one or more name=value parameters. Semicolons separate adjacent parameters. Table 11-7 lists the most frequently used parameters and some typical values. You shouldn't code a *Provider* setting for the *SqlConnection* object, nor *Integrated Security* or *Initial Catalog* settings for an *OleDbConnection* object. Otherwise, the *OleDbConnection* and *SqlConnection* objects both expect the same parameters.

Table 11-7   Common ADO.NET Connection String Parameters

Parameter	Typical Values	
	Microsoft Access	**SQL Server**
Provider	Microsoft.Jet.OLEDB.4.0	n/a
Data Source	whatever.mdb	localhost
User ID	Jim	Jim
Password	Sesame	sesame
Integrated Security	n/a	SSPI
Initial Catalog	n/a	Pubs

- *Provider* specifies the name of the database driver. Code this value exactly as shown in the table unless the connection string is for a *SqlConnection* object; in that case, omit it.

- *Data Source* specifies the physical location of the database. The required value varies by database system.

  - Microsoft Access requires the physical path and file name of the .mdb file.

- SQL Server requires the name of the computer running SQL Server and, if applicable, the instance ID. If a computer named HONKER is running two copies of SQL Server and you want the instance called SQL2K, code as follows:

```
Data Source=HONKER\SQL2K
```

■ *User ID* specifies a user name required to open the database. If opening the database doesn't require a user name, omit this parameter completely.

■ *Password* specifies a password required to open the database. If opening the database doesn't require a password, omit this parameter completely.

■ *Integrated Security*, if set to Security Support Provider Interface (SSPI), specifies that a SQL Server database should use the current user's Windows logon ID for access. Don't code this parameter for Microsoft Access databases or when you code the *User ID* and *Password* parameters.

■ *Initial Catalog* specifies the name of the SQL Server database you want. This is the default catalog used when connecting to a data source. Don't code this for Microsoft Access databases.

Using Command Objects

Whenever you need to process a SQL statement, you'll need a *SqlCommand* or *OleDbCommand* object to complete the work. You create these objects just as you would any other, then you set their properties and call the method that does the type of work you require. Table 11-8 lists the most common command object properties.

Table 11-8 Common *SqlCommand* or *OleDbCommand* Properties

Property	Required	Description	
CommandText	Yes	Gets or sets the command you want the data source to execute.	
Connection	Yes	Gets or sets the connection object to use for this command.	
CommandType	No	Tells the data source how to interpret the command. The permissible values are as follows:	
		CommandType.StoredProcedure	The command invokes a stored procedure.
		CommandType.TableDirect	The command is a table name.
		CommandType.Text	The command is a SQL statement. This is the default.

You don't need to set the *Command*.Type property unless the command is something other than a SQL statement. If the command is the name of a stored procedure or table, you must code one of the following statements before you call the *Execute* method:

```
<command object>.CommandType = CommandType.StoredProcedure
<command object>.CommandType = CommandType.TableDirect
```

Table 11-9 lists the *SqlCommand* and *OleDbCommand* methods you're most likely to use.

Table 11-9   Common *SqlCommand* and *OleDbCommand* Methods

Method	Description
ExecuteNonQuery	Executes a SQL statement and returns the number of rows affected
ExecuteReader	Sends the command through the connection and returns the results in a new *DataReader* object
ExecuteScalar	Sends the command through the connection and returns the value in column one, row one of the result set

When you call the *ExecuteNonQuery* method, the command object sends the command to the given database and returns the number of the database table rows that the command affected. Suppose that *conGames* is an open database connection, *strSQL* contains the command you want to execute, and *intRowsAff* is a variable you declared as *Integer*. The following code would then run the command in *strSQL*:

```
Dim cmdPlayer As OleDbCommand
cmdPlayer = New OleDbCommand(strSQL, conGames)
intRowsAff = cmdPlayer.ExecuteNonQuery()
```

The *ExecuteReader* and *ExecuteScalar* methods return data from the database. *ExecuteReader* returns a *DataReader* object, and *ExecuteScalar* returns the elementary value of the first field of the first record.

No matter which one of a command object's *Execute* methods you call, there are several things that can go wrong. You can (and should) detect many of these possible problems by checking the number of affected records. If, for example, you expected to delete or modify one record and the *ExecuteNonQuery* method reports that it affected 0 or 500 records, you have a problem.

Many other kinds of problems cause exceptions. If it isn't acceptable to let these errors bomb your program (and it usually won't be), you'll need to code the *Execute* method within a *Try...Catch...End Try* block and write code that deals with the error.

Using Data Readers

Whenever you execute a SQL command that returns data (i.e., a *SELECT* command), you need to provide an object that receives the results. ADO.NET provides two kinds.

You can use a *DataReader*, which involves the following steps:

1 Load a command object with a SQL statement that runs a query.

2 Call the command object's *ExecuteReader* method to create an *SqlDataReader* or *OleDbDataReader* object.

3 Use the data reader to retrieve the query results.

The *SqlDataReader* and *OleDbDataReader* objects both provide one-time, forward, read-only access to the data. These are serious limitations, but in fact, this type of access will probably satisfy a high percentage of your data needs and it's very fast. The rest of this section explains how to use data readers.

The second approach is to use a *DataAdapter* object, which involves a much different procedure:

1 Create an *OleDbDataAdapter* or *SqlDataAdapter* object and load it with a *SELECT* statement.

2 Create a *DataSet* object, which can hold one or more *DataTables* in memory.

3 Use the *DataAdapter's Fill* method to run the query and store the results as a *DataTable* object within the *DataSet* object.

4 Use the *DataTable's* properties and methods to retrieve the query results.

This second approach has many advantages. You can access the contents of a *DataTable* any way you want: forward, backward, by given row, and so on. You can also insert, update, and delete rows and then write your changes back to the database. You can even create new views of a *DataTable* that sort the data, filter it, or relate it to other *DataTables*.

Of course, the added features of *DataAdapters*, *DataSets*, and *DataTables* come at a price. A program that uses these objects is both tougher to code and slower to run than a program that uses command objects and data readers. The next section explains how to use *DataAdapters*, *DataSets*, and *DataTables*.

Visual Studio.NET doesn't provide a graphical way to create and use data readers. Fortunately, however, creating and using data reader objects in code is fairly simple. First, create a SQL statement that runs a query. Here's an example.

```
strSQL = "SELECT * " & _
         "FROM players " & _
         "WHERE firstname = 'Don' " & _
     "ORDER BY lastname "
```

Next, specify this statement and an open database connection as properties of an *OleDbCommand* or *SqlCommand* object, just as you did in the previous section. Here's an example.

```
Dim cmdPlayer As OleDbCommand
cmdPlayer = New OleDbCommand(strSQL, conGames)
```

To run the query, invoke the command object's *ExecuteReader* method and assign the results to a variable you declared as a data reader:

```
Dim rdrPlayers As OleDbDataReader
rdrPlayers = cmdPlayer.ExecuteReader
```

To process each row of the results, call the data reader's *Read* method until it returns *False*. Here's an example.

```
While rdrPlayers.Read
' Code to process each row of query results goes here.
End While
```

Inside this loop, the expression *rdrPlayers.Item(<field-id>)* returns the value of the given field for the current row. Instead of *<field-id>*, you should supply either the name of the field (such as *"firstname"*) or its numeric position (such as zero for the first field).

Using the *DataAdapter*, *DataSet*, and *DataTable* Objects

A *DataTable* is an object that stores data in columns and rows, just as a database system does. Columns, which are comparable to fields, have names and data types. Rows are comparable to records. A *DataTable*, however, exists only in memory and only for the life of your program.

DataTables don't necessarily exist on their own. A *DataTable* can exist within another in-memory object called a *DataSet*. A *DataSet* contains one or more *DataTables*, just as a database contains one or more tables. To load a *DataTable* from a database table or query, you must do the following:

1   Create and configure a connection object to access the database.

2   Create and configure a *DataAdapter* object to query the database. (The *DataAdapter* passes the SQL statement and connection object you specify to a command object that the *DataAdapter* internally creates and manages.)

3   Call the *DataAdapter's Fill* method to run the query and store the results in the *DataTable* object. The *Fill* method retrieves not only the data, but also the field name, data type, maximum length, and other properties of each field.

At this point, all the methods of the *DataTable* object are available for moving through the result set and retrieving whatever field values or schema information you want. The *DataTable*, however, is only an in-memory copy of the data and doesn't remain connected to the database. If you copy some information into a *DataTable* and then change it, you must explicitly push the information back into the database. Otherwise, your changes will vanish when the program ends.

In practice, this needn't be as complicated as it seems. In Visual Studio, for example, you can add a *SqlDataAdapter* or *OleDbDataAdapter* to your form just by double-clicking the object on the Data tab of the Toolbox window and then following the wizard. To create a *DataSet* and *DataTable*, do either of the following:

■   Double-click *DataSet* in the *Data* Tab of the Toolbox window and then follow the wizard.

■   Right-click the *DataAdapter* that will fill the *DataTable* and choose Generate Dataset from the shortcut menu.

For an example that perform these steps, refer to the example at the end of this chapter. The following is some sample code that creates and loads a *DataAdapter* and a *DataTable*:

```
dapPlayers = New OleDbDataAdapter( _
    "SELECT * FROM players Order By playerid ", _
    conGames)
dstPlayers = New DataSet()
dapPlayers.Fill(dstPlayers, "Players")
```

Here are the significant points of this code:

■   The first statement creates an *OleDbDataAdapter* object. The constructor method for this object automatically creates an *OleDbCommand* object that contains the given SQL statement and refers to the given connection.

■ The second statement, which begins on line 4, creates a new *DataSet* object. Notice that this isn't an *OleDbDataSet* or *SqlDataSet* object. *DataSet*, *DataTable*, *DataRelation*, and *DataView* objects have no direct connection to any database system. This means, among other things, that there aren't separate versions for SQL Server and OLE DB.

■ The third statement runs the command that the first statement stored in the data adapter *dapPlayers*, and then it stores the results in the dataset *dstPlayers*. Within *dapPlayers*, the data will reside in a *DataTable* object named *Players*. The *DataSet* object creates the *DataTable* object automatically.

Once this code has executed, the following statement would load a *DataGrid* object with the contents of the *Players* table. The first statement sets the data source of a *DataGrid* object named *grdPlayers* to be the *Players* table in the *dstPlayers* dataset. The second fills the grid with data:

```
grdPlayers.DataSource = dstPlayers.Tables("Players")
grdPlayers.DataBind
```

To inspect the contents of a data table programmatically, use either a numeric subscript or a *For Each* loop to access its *Rows* collection. The following expression, for example, returns the value of the *lastname* field from row 3 of the *players* table. Row subscripts are zero-based and have a valid range from 0 to *<table-name>.Rows.Count−1*:

```
dstPlayers.Tables("Players").Rows(2).Item("lastname")
```

To insert a row, you must first create a new *DataRow* object, fill it with data, and then add the row to the table. Here's some code that does this. Invoking the *NewRow* method of the *players DataTable* creates a disconnected row with the same field names, data types, and constraints as the *Players DataTable*. The *Add* method on the last line adds the new row to the data table (but not to the database).

```
Dim rowPlayers As DataRow
rowPlayers = dstPlayers.Tables("Players").NewRow()
rowPlayers("playerid") = "ted@treyresearch.net"
rowPlayers("firstname") = "Ted"
rowPlayers("lastname") = "Bremer"
rowPlayers("pswd") = "bricks"
rowPlayers("wins") = 0
dstPlayers.Tables("Players").Rows.Add(rowPlayers)
```

To modify the contents of any row, simply assign a new value to any of its fields. Here's an example.

```
dstPlayers.Tables("Players").Rows(2).Item("firstname") = "John"
```

To delete a row, call either its *Delete* method or its *Remove* method like this:

```
dstPlayers.Tables("Players").Rows(2).Delete
dstPlayers.Tables("Players").Rows.Remove(2)
```

These two statements are decidedly not equivalent.

■ The *Delete* method removes the row from the active view but remembers that the row formerly existed. If you delete a row and then tell the *DataAdapter* to write the data table back into the database, the *DataAdapter* deletes the row from the database.

■ The *Remove* method deletes the row completely, including any record that it ever existed. If you remove a row and then tell the *DataAdapter* to write the data table back into the database, the *DataAdapter* won't delete the row, because the *Remove* method discards the fact that the row ever existed.

When you add rows, update fields, and delete rows in a *DataSet*, your changes affect only the in-memory data. You can write your changes back to the database, but only if all the following are true:

■ You loaded the *DataTable* from a single table. If you loaded the *DataTable* from a query that combined the contents of two or more tables, you can't send updates back into the database.

■ The database table has a primary key that uniquely identifies each record.

■ You retrieved all the fields that make up the primary key and included them in the *DataTable*.

■ You supplied the data adapter with command objects that contain model *INSERT*, *UPDATE*, and *DELETE* statements. ADO.NET provides *OleDbCommandBuilder* and *SqlCommandBuilder* objects that can build these command objects and model statements for you, but it's still your responsibility to call the *CommandBuilder* object.

Once you've satisfied all these conditions, writing changes back to the database is as simple as calling the data adapter's *Update* method and passing as arguments the name of the dataset and the name of the data table. In the following code, line 1 declares an *OleDbCommandBuilder* object named *bldPlayers*. Line 2 actually creates the object and associates it with the *dapPlayers* data adapter. The next three lines create model *INSERT*, *UPDATE*, and *DELETE* commands, and the last statement tells the data adapter to update the database in accordance with all changes made in memory to the *Players DataTable*:

```
Dim bldPlayers As OleDbCommandBuilder
bldPlayers = New OleDbCommandBuilder(dapPlayers)
dapPlayers.InsertCommand = bldPlayers.GetInsertCommand()
dapPlayers.UpdateCommand = bldPlayers.GetUpdateCommand()
dapPlayers.DeleteCommand = bldPlayers.GetDeleteCommand()
dapPlayers.Update(dstPlayers, "Players")
```

If you know the *Update* method won't use a given model statement, there's no point in creating one. If all your changes were deletions, for example, you don't need to create *Insert* and *Update* command objects.

Also, keep in mind that after filling the *DataTable*, the data adapter disconnects from the database. The original database records aren't locked and someone else could update them before you issue the *Update* method. If this happens, the *Update* method throws an exception. It's therefore a very good idea to enclose all calls to a data adapter's *Update* method within *Try ... Catch ... End Try* blocks and recover gracefully.

Displaying and Updating a Database

This example displays and updates the *players* table you've already seen several times in this chapter. To create this program, follow these steps:

1 In Microsoft Access, open a new blank database named Games.mdb. When the Games: Database window appears, select Tables in the Objects bar. On the right, click Create Table In Design View, then specify the table properties you see in Figure 11-2. Don't forget to right-click the *playerid* field and mark it as the primary key.

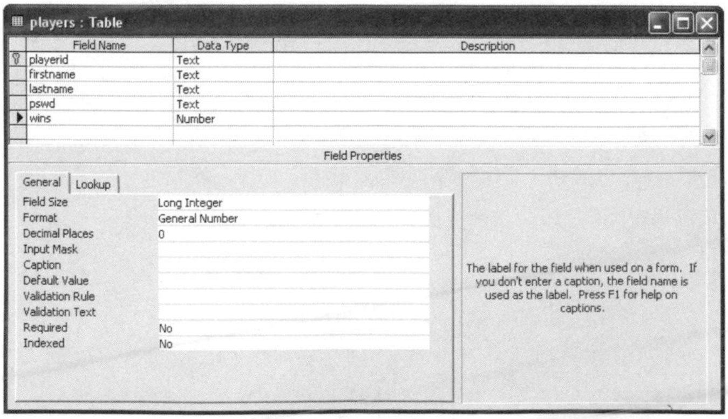

Figure 11-2 Here are the properties of the Players table as Microsoft Access displays them.

Once you have all the fields defined, choose Save As from the File menu and specify a Table Name of *players*. Then, click Open in the Games: Database window and enter the data from Table 11-1. Finally, save everything and quit Microsoft Access.

2 Launch Visual Studio .NET and create a new Windows Application project named *games*.

3 Make sure the *Form1* form is open in the Windows Form Designer, and that the form is selected. Then set the form's *Text* property to *Update Players Table*.

4 Open the Toolbox window's Data tab and drag an *OleDbDataAdapter* object onto the form. This creates an object named *OleDbDataAdapter1* and starts the Data Adapter Configuration Wizard.

5 Review the information in the first page of the wizard and then click Next. When the Choose Your Data Connection page appears, click New Connection.

6 When the DataLink Properties dialog box appears, click the Provider tab and choose Microsoft Jet 4.0 OLE DB Provider. Figure 11-1 pictured this earlier in the chapter.

7 Click the Connection tab to display the dialog box you see in Figure 11-3. Then click the ellipsis button under Select Or Enter A Database Name. This displays a standard File Open dialog box titled Select Access Database. Locate the database you created in step 1 and then click OK.

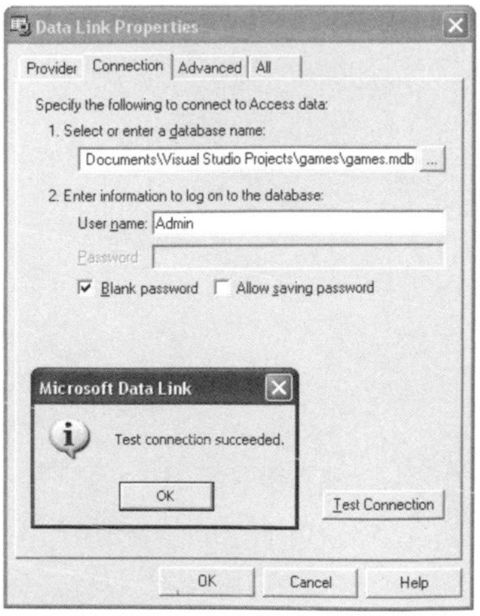

Figure 11-3 When you choose the Microsoft Jet 4.0 OLE DB provider, these connection properties are available.

8 In the Data Link Properties dialog box, click Test Connection and verify that you get the message Test Connection Succeeded. If not, check your work in steps 6 and 7. Verify also that the database is no longer open in Access.

9 Click OK to close the Data Link Properties dialog box, then click Next to move to the next step in the wizard.

10 When the Choose A Query Type page appears, select Use SQL Statements and then click Next.

11 When the Generate SQL Statements page appears, click Query Builder.

12 When the Add Table dialog box appears, select Players, then click Add and then Close.

13 A window titled Query Builder should now be active. In the Players box, select the check boxes in front of the following fields. To reproduce the example you must click these fields in the order shown:

lastname, firstname, playerid, wins, pswd.

14 To the right of the *lastname* field, in the Sort Type column, select Ascending. The window should now resemble Figure 11-4. Make any necessary corrections and then click OK.

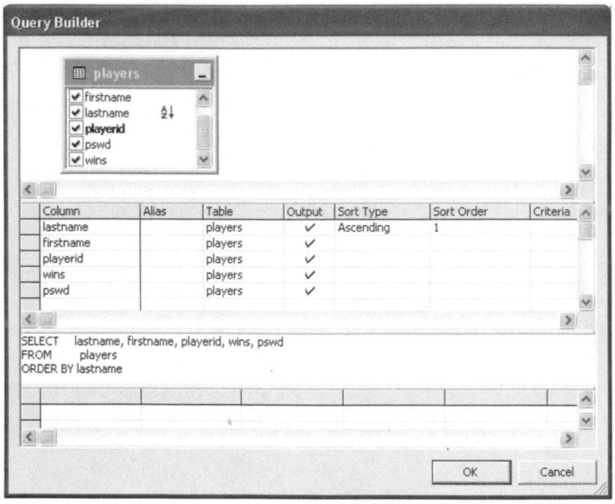

Figure 11-4 Visual Studio's query builder makes it easy to construct SQL statements.

15 Click Next and Finish to complete the Data Adapter Configuration Wizard.

16 Select the *OleDbDataAdapter1* object in Windows Form Designer and then, in the Property window, rename it *dapPlayers*. Similarly, rename the *OleDbConnection1* object *conGames*.

17 Right-click the *dapPlayers* data adapter and choose Generate Dataset from the shortcut menu. When the Generate Dataset dialog box shown in Figure 11-5 appears, perform the following steps:

● Click New and specify a name of *dstPlayers*.

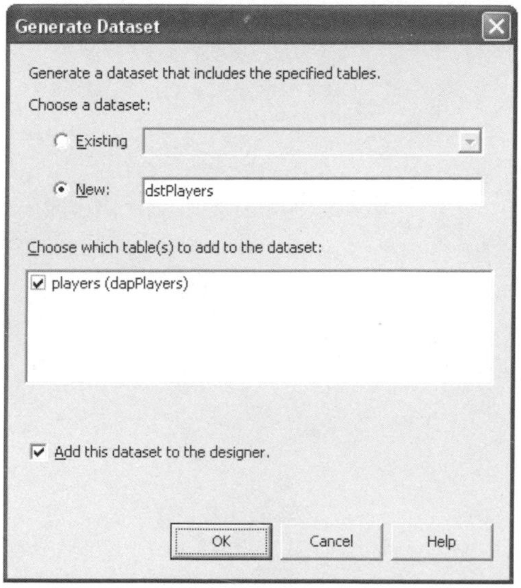

Figure 11-5 This dialog box creates a *DataSet* object that receives one or more tables from a *DataAdapter*.

● Under Choose Which Table(s) To Add To The Dataset, make sure Players(dapPlayers) is selected.

● Make sure Add This Dataset To The Designer is selected.

● Click OK.

● Despite your selection in the first step, Visual Studio names the new dataset *DstPlayers1*. Select this object and then, in the Properties window, rename it to *dstPlayers*.

18 Click the Windows Forms tab in the toolbox and then double-click the *DataGrid* object. Position this object on the form so there's a reasonable top and left margin and then, in the Properties window, rename the grid *grdPlayers*.

19 Still in the Properties window, scroll down to the *DataSource* property, select it, and choose *dstPlayers.players* from the drop-down list. The field names from the *players* table should now appear in the *grdPlayers* data grid. If you can't see them all, enlarge the form and the grid as necessary.

20 Double-click the form background to create a *Form1_Load* subroutine and display it in the code editor. To fill the *DataSet* with data, add the following statement to this subroutine:

```
dapPlayers.Fill(dstPlayers)
```

21 To save your work, select Save All from Visual Studio's File menu. Then, press F5 to run the program. The data from the *players* table should appear in the data grid. Note that you can resize the form but not the data grid.

Notice as well that any changes you make to the grid don't show up in the database. For example, if you make a change, quit the program, and then restart the program, your changes won't appear.

Quit the program when you're done experimenting.

22 To make the program resize the data grid whenever the user resizes the form, add the following event handler after the *End* Sub statement that marks the end of the *Form1_Load* subroutine:

```
Sub Form1_Resize(ByVal sender As Object, _
    ByVal e As EventArgs) _
    Handles MyBase.Resize
    grdPlayers.Width = Me.DisplayRectangle.Width _
                    - (2 * grdPlayers.Left)
    grdPlayers.Height = Me.DisplayRectangle.Height _
                    - (2 * grdPlayers.Top)
End Sub
```

The *Handles* clause of the *Sub* statement, which appears on the third line, tells Windows to run this subroutine whenever the size of the form changes. This includes when the program starts up.

The first statement inside the subroutine sets the width of the *grdPlayers* grid to the inside width of the form minus twice the grid's left margin. This makes the grid fill the form except for equal left and right margins. The second statement plays the same trick in a vertical dimension.

23 To detect and save any grid updates when the program ends, add the following event hander after the one from step 22:

```
Sub Form1_Closing(ByVal sender As Object, _
    ByVal e As System.ComponentModel.CancelEventArgs) _
    Handles MyBase.Closing
    If dstPlayers.HasChanges Then
        Select Case MsgBox( _
                "Do you wish to save these changes?", _
                MsgBoxStyle.Question + _
```

```
                    MsgBoxStyle.YesNoCancel, _
                    Me.Text)
                Case MsgBoxResult.Yes
                    Try
                        dapPlayers.Update(dstPlayers)
                    Catch Ex as Exception
                        e.Cancel = True
                        MsgBox(Ex.Message, _
                            MsgBoxStyle.Critical, _
                            Me.Text)
                    End Try
                Case MsgBoxResult.Cancel
                    e.Cancel = True
            End Select
        End If
End Sub
```

Because of the *Handles MyBase.Closing* clause on line 3, this sub-routine will run whenever the user tries to close the form. Event handlers of this type receive a *System.ComponentModel.CancelEventArgs* argument that has a *Cancel* property. Setting this property to *True* cancels the event; that is, it cancels the form closure.

The *If* statement checks the *HasChanges* property of the *dstPlayers* dataset. If this is *True*, the user has made changes to the data so the code displays a message box with a question mark and Yes, No, and Cancel buttons. A *Select Case* statement determines which of these buttons the user clicked:

- If the user clicked Yes (that is, if the *MsgBox* function returned the value in *MsgBoxResult.Yes*) the code calls the *Update* method of the *dapPlayers* data adapter, specifying the *dstPlayers* dataset as an argument. This (hopefully) updates the database. If updating the database is impossible, a *Try...Catch* block intercepts the exception, cancels the form closure, and displays a message box containing the exception message.

- If the user clicked Cancel, the code sets *e.Cancel* to *True*, thereby canceling the form closure.

- Otherwise, the user must have clicked No. In this case, no further action is necessary. The program ends and the updates vanish.

24 To save your work, choose Save All from Visual Studio's File menu. Press F5 to run the program again. Resizing the form should now resize the data grid. Also, if you make changes to the data grid, move to a different record, and then try to close the form, you should get the

Yes/No/Cancel dialog box. Clicking Yes should save your changes and then quit the program. Clicking No should end the program without saving. Clicking Cancel should keep the program running.

Note   When you enter new values into a *DataGrid* control, the control doesn't update the underplaying data source until you change the focus to a different row in the grid. Until you move away from a row, the grid doesn't know you're finished updating it.

Key Points

■   A database is a collection of data organized so that computer programs can readily access, manage, and update its contents.

■   Most modern databases consist of tables. The rows in each table act as records and the columns as fields. Databases of this type are relational databases.

■   Relational databases receive commands in a syntax called Structured Query Language (SQL).

■   The most common types of SQL statements are:

- *SELECT* (for retrieving data)
- *INSERT* (for creating a new row)
- *UPDATE* (for updating one or more rows)
- *DELETE* (for deleting one or more rows)

■   ActiveX Data Object (ADO).NET is the component most .NET programs use for accessing databases.

■   ADO.NET requires a connection object for each database it accesses.

■   ADO command objects store SQL statements and send them through a database connection for execution.

■   A *DataReader* receives the result of a *SELECT* statement and provides one-time, sequential, read-only access to the result set. *DataReaders* are simple and fast but limited.

■   A *DataTable* stores the result of a *SELECT* statement in such a way that you can read or update any field of any record at will. *DataTables*, however, are more complex than *DataReaders*.

■   *DataTables* typically reside within a *DataSet* object. A *DataAdapter* object loads data into the *DataSet* and sends changes back to the database.

Chapter 12

Programming Web Forms

To call the Web trendy is certainly an understatement. The World Wide Web is just about the hottest thing to hit computing since the bit. Web technologies permeate every facet of computing from the power switch to the eyeball and everything in between.

If you've created Web pages but never done programming, then your pages must have been ordinary Hypertext Markup Language (HTML) files. You type whatever you want the page to say, add some formatting, toss in some pictures and hyperlinks, and end up with a page that never changes until you or your distinguished associates repeat the process. Creating Web pages this way is useful and rewarding, but it only scratches the surface of what the Web can do.

Today's Web developers still create visually stunning designs (usually in a positive sense), but these pages usually aren't the final product; instead, they serve as templates that programs on the Web server will fill with data as the situation requires. This is just as true for textual pages containing, say, press releases, as it is for on-line shopping and other business systems.

The ASP.NET component of the Microsoft .NET Framework provides the features and services you need to program Web applications of all kinds and all complexities. What's more, it does so using the same programming languages and many of the same techniques you've already seen for Microsoft Windows desktop programs. Now really, what could be more interesting than that?

The material in this chapter assumes you have a basic understanding of HTML and that you understand the basics of how Web servers interact with browsers. If you feel a bit light on those topics, you should probably do some outside reading before tackling this chapter.

Introducing the Web

The Web is a client-server system where clients send *requests* to Web servers and Web servers send *responses* back to the clients. The client software is usually a Web browser like Microsoft Internet Explorer or Netscape Navigator. The Web server software is usually Microsoft Internet Information Services (IIS) or an open source program called Apache that runs on UNIX.

The simplest Web requests are those that specify a computer name, a folder path, and a file name. The browser connects to the named computer and transmits the path and file names. The Web server responds by transmitting the file that the browser requested. This is the process for ordinary HTML files, GIF and JPEG pictures, and all other files types that the Web server can keep on hand and deliver without modification.

What, though, if responses from the Web server require customization? It simply isn't practical for, say, a large Internet search engine to prepare Web pages ahead of time for each possible combination of search terms, or for an online retailer to maintain a separate Web page for each salable item. The only practical way to create such sites is to have a program inspect each incoming request and customize each outgoing response. Two things trigger a Web server to run a program rather than deliver an ordinary Web page:

- First, the request must specify a file name extension that the Web server recognizes as a program: .dll or .exe, for example. The list of extensions that the Web server recognizes as programs is part of the Web server's configuration.

- Second, the Web server's configuration must indicate that it's okay to run programs in the folder where the specified file resides. This is a security measure.

The .NET Framework provides excellent support for creating programs that run on a Web server, respond to incoming requests, and create customized responses. The collective name for all these Web-based features is ASP.NET.

ASP.NET takes a somewhat different approach to Web page programming than that of its predecessor, Active Server Pages (ASP), and most other Web programming systems. Specifically, ASP.NET strives to imitate the experience of programming Windows forms, except that the form appears in the Web visitor's browser. In this spirit, the official name for a Web page that includes ASP.NET programming is a *Web form*.

Note   Although in many ways ASP.NET tries to unify the experience of programming Web forms with that of programming Windows forms, Web forms and Windows forms don't look very much alike because ASP.NET displays Web forms using HTML only.

A Web form typically consists of two parts: visual elements and pro-grammed logic. Microsoft Visual Studio stores each of these components in a separate file. The visual elements reside in a text file with an .aspx file name extension, and the code resides in a so-called *code-behind* class with a file name extension of .vb, .cs, or whatever corresponds to the programming language in use. Visual Studio compiles the code-behind file into a dynamic link library (DLL) that runs whenever the Web visitor requests the .aspx file.

Note   If the term *code-behind* seems confusing, consider that a Web form's .vb or .cs file pro-vides the code behind the visual display

---

It is also possible for a Web form's visual elements and program code to reside in the same file. The official term for this arrangement is a *single-file* Web form. Programmers who create ASP.NET pages in Microsoft FrontPage, Notepad, or some other editor usually prefer single-file Web forms, but Visual Studio sup-ports such files in only a limited way. For that reason, this chapter deals exclu-sively with separate .aspx and code-behind files.

No matter where you put the code, remember that it only runs during the brief instant after the Web server receives the visitor's request and before the server sends its response. After that, the code terminates. The browser displays the form but maintains no connection to the Web server and certainly doesn't stay connected to your code. If the form requests any additional processing from the Web server, it gets a new copy of the program for each request.

Creating Web Projects

The procedure for creating a new ASP.NET Web application begins much like that for creating a new Windows application. Simply follow these steps:

1   Launch Visual Studio.NET.

2   Click Get Started on Visual Studio's Start page and then click New Project. (Alternatively, choose New from the Start menu and then choose Project.)

3   When the New Project dialog box appears, select the ASP.NET Web Application template as shown in Figure 12-1, then pause and reflect on the Location box (which defaults to a Web server address).

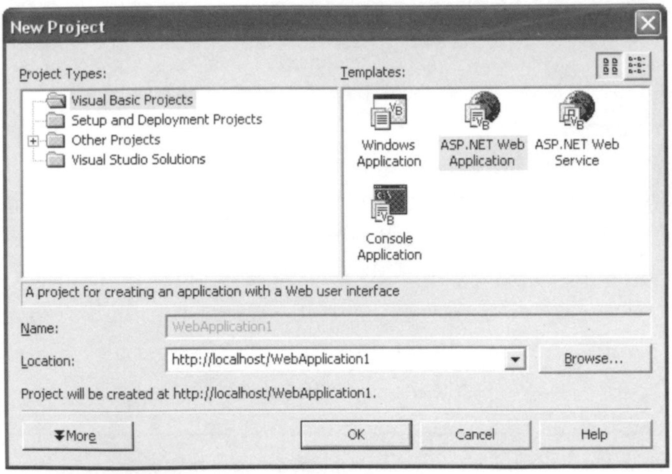

Figure 12-1 To create an ASP.NET Web application, create a new project using the template of that name.

In fact, you *must* enter a Web server location in the Location box whenever you create an ASP.NET Web Application, and that location must satisfy these requirements:

- The Web server must be Microsoft IIS running on Microsoft Windows 2000, Microsoft Windows XP Professional, or a newer version.

- The Web server must be running the FrontPage server extensions, or must have a share name that provides physical access to the Web server location.

- The .NET Framework Software Development Kit must be installed on the Web server.

- You must have certain administrative rights on the Web server. Specifically:

  - If you're accessing the Web server through the FrontPage Server extensions, you must have authority to create a new FrontPage web.

  - If you're accessing the Web server through a share name, you must have authority to create, read, and modify files and folders.

  - In either case, you must have authority to designate folders on the Web servers as application roots.

If you've never administered a Microsoft Web server before, some of these requirements will be puzzling. If a copy of IIS is running on your own PC, and if you're an administrator of your own PC, then you probably won't encounter any difficulties. If you're using a copy of IIS on some other computer, then you might have to contact that computer's administrator to get the necessary permissions or to get the administrator to initialize the new project for you.

If IIS is running on your own PC, then you would generally specify a location like *http://localhost/<projectname>* or *http://127.0.0.1/<projectname>*, where *<projectname>* is the name you want your project to have. If you're going to use a Web server that runs on a different computer, then you would specify the server name just as you would for browsing Web pages on that server.

Tip   The server name *localhost* and the Internet Protocol (IP) address 127.0.0.1 are special values that always refer to the local computer.

If all this seems complicated compared to developing Windows desktop applications, then you're gaining the proper perspective. Developing an application that runs on one computer and displays its user interface on another computer (perhaps running a different operating system) will never be a simple as developing a strictly local application.

The payback, of course, comes from availability. When you create a Windows desktop application, it's only available to people who have the proper operating system and run an installation program. When you create an ASP.NET Web application, it's available to hundreds, thousands, or millions of people anywhere in your company or planet.

Examining a New ASP.NET Web Application

Figure 12-2 shows how Visual Studio displays a new ASP.NET Web application. The exact combination and arrangement of windows on your computer will almost certainly be different, but the Solution Explorer window merits special attention.

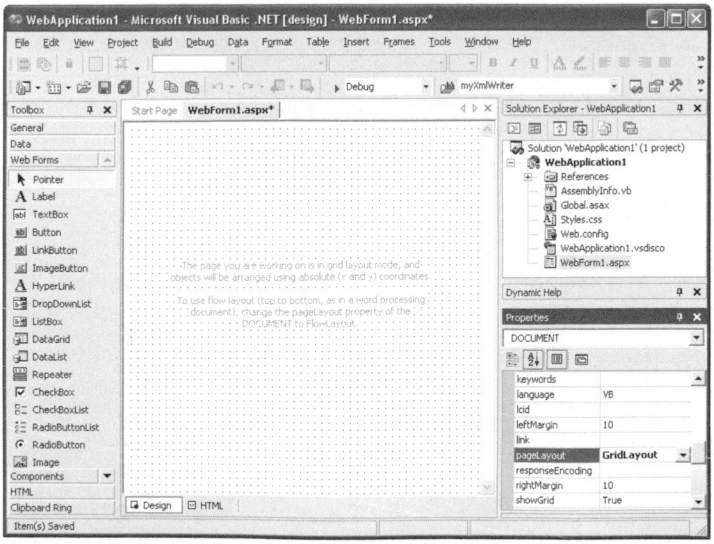

Figure 12-2 Visual Studio displays Web projects in much the same way as Windows forms projects. However, note the Global.asax, Styles.css, and Web.config files.

Try This! Each ASP.NET project you create on a FrontPage Web server will be a FrontPage web. This means that if you're so inclined, you can use FrontPage to open and modify files in an ASP.NET project. If you decide to do this, keep these precautions in mind:

- Use the most current version of FrontPage available. Versions older than Microsoft FrontPage 2002 might disturb the special Extensible Markup Language (XML) tags that ASP.NET pages uses.

- Avoid the use of FrontPage components, especially those related to forms, databases, and saving form results.

- With the project open in Visual Studio, choose Options from the Tools menu, open the Projects category (located in the left pane), and then select Web Settings. Then make sure the following settings are in effect: Set the Preferred Access Method setting to FrontPage Extensions and Select the Repair Links When Web Files Are Moved Or Renamed setting.

Finally, be aware that many files you see in FrontPage won't be visible in Visual Studio. Some of these are files that Visual Studio maintains automatically but others are ordinary Web pages, folders, or pictures. To make these ordinary files appear in Visual Studio's Solution Explorer, follow these steps:

1 Choose Add Existing Item from the File menu.

2 When the Add Existing Item dialog box appears, select the file or folder you want to appear in Solution Explorer.

3 Click Open.

When you create a Web project, Visual Studio constructs a project structure on your local computer and a Web application directory structure on the Web server. The project structure on your computer contains the files that define a solution (a solution, in this case, being a list of projects and settings that you prefer to work with as a unit).

The directory structure that Visual Studio creates on the Web server contains one and only one Web project. A single project, however, can contain any number of Web forms, ordinary HTML files, picture files, or other files that your Web pages use. Table 12-1 lists the files that Visual Studio adds to each new Web project.

Table 12-1   Files in a New ASP.NET Web Application

File Name	Contents
WebForm1.aspx	The visual elements of a blank, default Web forms page.
WebForm1.aspx.vb	The code behind the WebForm1.aspx page. Although this file is present, Solution Explorer hides it.
AssemblyInfo.vb	Information about the assemblies in a project, such as name, version, and culture information.
Web.config	Web server configuration data for the project. This is an XML file.
Global.asax	Statements that tell the Web server where to find code that handles events that occur at the application or session level.
Global.vb	The code behind the Global.asax file. This is another file that Solution Explorer hides.
Styles.css	Cascading style sheet (CSS) specifications that specify default typography for Web pages in the project.
<project-name>.vsdisco	Links to resources that provide discovery information for any XML Web services in the project. This is another XML file.

To add additional files, right-click the project in Solution Explorer and select Add from the shortcut menu. This displays another menu with commands for adding new or existing folders, pictures, Web forms, or other items to the project. (An existing item, in this sense, is a file you added to the project folder on the Web server but that doesn't appear in Solution Explorer. Such files don't appear in Solution Explorer automatically because they might not be relevant to programming tasks.)

Designing Web Forms

Just as Visual Studio provides Windows Form Designer for developing Windows forms, it provides Web Forms Designer for crafting the visual aspect of a Web page. The Web Forms Designer provides two distinct views of each Web page you open. To switch between these views, click the Design or HTML tab at the bottom of the Web Forms Designer window.

- Design view provides an editable what you see is what you get (WYSIWYG) view of the Web page. This is useful for arranging and formatting the visual elements of the page.

- HTML view provides access to the HTML code and ASP.NET element declarations that make up the page, as well as any JavaScript code that will run on the Web visitor's browser.

You can use HTML view for working with ASP.NET code that will run on the Web server but most developers strongly prefer using the Visual Studio code editor. Just as for Windows forms, the code editor displays your code in color, supports IntelliSense code completion, integrates tightly with the compiler, and so forth. To display the ASP.NET code for a page, right-click the Web Forms Designer and then select View Code from the shortcut menu, or select Code from the View menu.

The Web Forms Designer has two distinct page layout modes:

■   Grid layout uses CSS positioning to position each element precisely on the page. This provides almost the same level of positioning control for Web forms that you have with Windows forms. In addition, you can overlap page elements and make them snap to a grid.

    Unfortunately, many browsers don't support CSS positioning very well. Using grid layout mode, therefore, you run the risk that your page will look fine if the Web visitor uses a recent version of Internet Explorer but terrible if not. As a result, very few Web designers use this mode.

■   Flow layout uses the browser's default page layout scheme, which positions elements from left to right within a line, and from bottom to top within the page, in the order in which they appear in the HTML. To position elements spatially on the page, you would typically arrange them in an HTML table.

Any Web browser can display HTML documents that use flow layout mode, and this is the mode Web designers have used effectively for years. As a result, virtually all Web designers prefer flow layout. Unfortunately, grid layout is the default.

To change the layout mode in effect for any page, display the page in the Web Forms Designer, click a blank area at the bottom of the form, and then, in the Properties window, set the *pageLayout* property to the value you want.

Try This!   The fact that grid layout is the default for all Web pages you create in Visual Studio can be a nuisance. To change the default page layout mode for a Web project, follow these steps:

1   Right-click the project name in Solution Explorer.

2   Select Properties from the shortcut menu.

3   When the project's Property Pages dialog box appears, open the Common Properties category and then click Designer Defaults.

4   Under Web Designers, set Page Layout to the mode you want (Grid or Flow).

Unfortunately, Visual Studio provides no way of setting the page layout mode for all new projects to flow. However the following trick seems to work:

1   Locate the Common.js file and open it in any text editor. (The Visual Studio code editor works fine for this, but so does Notepad.) This file usually resides in the following folder, where *d:* is the drive where you installed Visual Studio.

   d:\Program Files\Microsoft Visual Studio .NET\Vb7\VBWizards\1033

2   Find this line of code. It should appear on or about line 249.

```
varprjPageLayout=selProj.Properties("DefaultHTMLPageLayout").Value;
```

3   Just below that line, add this:

```
prjPageLayout = 0;
```

4   Save the Common.js file.

The Life Cycle of an ASP.NET Page

Whenever a Web visitor requests a page with an .aspx file name extension, ASP.NET examines each HTML or XML tag in the page and looks for the attribute *runat="server"*. If this attribute is present, ASP.NET loads the tag into memory as an object called, generically, a *server control*. Otherwise, ASP.NET loads the tag into memory as ordinary text.

After the entire page is loaded into memory, ASP.NET runs any event handlers for which events actually occurred. Some of these events—such as those listed in Table 12-2—occur every time a page executes. Others—such as button clicks—occur only if the Web visitor initiates them.

Table 12-2   Common Page Object Events

Event	Event Handler	Description
Init	*Page_Init*	Occurs when ASP.NET initializes the page. No page elements are available at this time.
Load	*Page_Load*	Occurs when ASP.NET has loaded all server controls into memory.
PreRender	*Page_PreRender*	Occurs when ASP.NET is about to render the page as HTML.
Unload	*Page_Unload*	Occurs after ASP.NET has removed all server controls from memory.
Error	*Page_Error*	Occurs when the page throws an unhandled exception.

Firing a page's event handlers generally sets off a chain reaction of activities. Code in the event handlers typically accesses files, databases, and other resources on the server, then uses the results to update the properties of various server controls. Of course, updating those properties might set off more events. This continues until there are no more events to process, and then ASP.NET sends the resulting page to the Web visitor.

If a given tag in the original .aspx file didn't contain the *runat="server"* attribute, ASP.NET saves it as text and then sends it to the Web visitor verbatim.

A problem occurs when sending tags that contain the *runat="server"* attribute to the Web visitor. ASP.NET loads such tags as server controls, which are objects, but you can't send objects to the Web visitor's browser. You can only send HTML. ASP.NET therefore tells each server control on the page to *render* itself as HTML; that is, to create whatever HTML the server control requires to display itself. If this doesn't seem clear, consider the following example:

```
<a href="smallanimals.htm" runat="server" id="ancSmall">
<img src="mouse.gif">
</a>
```

Because of the *runat="server"* attribute, ASP.NET loads the anchor tag as a server control. The *id* attribute provides a name you can reference in code. Any changes your code makes to the *ancSmall* server control will be in effect when that server control renders itself, and will therefore appear in the HTML that the Web visitor receives. Suppose, for example, that the following statement executed after ASP.NET loaded the *ancSmall* server control and before ASP.NET rendered the page:

```
ancSmall.href = "littlecritters.aspx"
```

The code that the Web visitor receives would then be:

```
<a href="littlecritters.aspx">
<img src="mouse.gif">
</a>
```

Because the image tag doesn't have a *runat="server"* attribute, ASP.NET saves it as text. You can't modify this tag from code, ASP.NET can't modify it, and the tag can't modify itself. What goes in must come out.

Note, however, that when the server control for the anchor tag renders itself, it doesn't bother sending the *runat* and *id* attributes to the Web visitor. These attributes serve no purpose on the Web visitor's browser. In fact, there's no need for the code that creates a server control and the code that the server control sends to the Web visitor to resemble each other in any way. This gives rise to server controls of tremendous power and flexibility, as the next section explains.

Adding Controls to a Web Form

The procedure for adding controls to a Web form is very much like that for adding controls to a Windows form. Follow these steps:

1 Display the page in the Web Forms Designer.

2 If you're working in Flow layout mode, set the cursor where you want the new page element to appear.

3 Double-click the control you want in either the HTML portion or the Web Forms portion of the Toolbox window.

4 To reposition a control on the form, select it and then drag its center. To resize it, drag its handles.

5 Use the Properties window to customize the control's properties.

In addition, Visual Studio displays the following main menu choices whenever the Web Forms Designer is active:

■ **Format** has commands for changing the font, alignment, size, and other visual properties of any Web page element you select.

■ **Table** inserts, deletes, selects, and merges HTML tables, columns, rows, and cells.

■ **Insert** adds forms, spans, divs, images, bookmarks, and hyperlinks to the current page.

■ **Frames** adds, removes, and resizes individual frames in a frameset. (To create a frameset initially, choose Add New Item from the File menu and then choose the Frameset template.)

The Web Forms Designer neither tries nor succeeds in being the world's preeminent artistic design tool for the Web. In fact, you'll probably find that it's a bit klunky. This, however, is one of the reasons that Visual Studio keeps the Web page layout and the code in separate files. With just a little care, you can continue using your favorite design tool for the artistic work and still use Visual Studio for the programming part.

Using HTML Server Controls

The controls in the HTML portion of the Toolbox window are the sort of ordinary HTML objects that Web designers have been using for years. By default, they don't have *runat="server"* attributes, and this means ASP.NET code that runs on the Web server can't modify them. (You *can* modify them to some extent from JavaScript code that runs on the browser, but that's beyond the scope of this book.)

You can, however, convert an HTML control into a server control simply by adding a *runat="server"* attribute. Either of the following procedures does this:

■ Right-click the HTML control and then select Run As Server Control on the shortcut menu. Then, in the Properties window, give the control a meaningful *id* value.

Tip   It's easy to remember that a control named *txtQty* is a text box where the Web visitor will enter a quantity. Remembering what the *Text1* control does isn't so easy.

■ Switch Web Forms Designer to HTML view, locate the tag, and manually enter the *runat="server"* attribute. In addition, enter an *id=* attribute that specifies a meaningful name.

Any HTML control you convert this way becomes an *HTML server control*. You can inspect and modify most attributes of an HTML server control by means of properties named after the corresponding attribute names. The following tag, for example, defines an HTML server control that displays a picture:

```
<img src="abner.jpg" runat="server" id="imgPhoto" />
```

Server Controls and XML Syntax   Although it looks somewhat like HTML, any tag that creates a server control in an .aspx file is actually XML code that must conform to XML syntax. If you always use Web Forms Designer's Design view to create your server controls, this won't be a problem because Visual Studio always creates the XML code correctly. If you ever switch to HTML view and work directly with the code, however, you should be aware that XML requires an ending for every tag. A `<p runat="server">` tag, for example always requires a closing `</p>` tag.

If the opening and closing tags for a control don't need to enclose any content, you can end the opening tag with a slash rather than coding a separate ending tag. In XML lingo, this is *condensed notation*. The following lines of code, for example, are equivalent:

```
<p runat="server" id="prgFirstName"></p>
<p runat="server" id="prgFirstName" />
```

If you forget to close a server control tag, you'll get an error message when you try to run the page. In some cases, ASP.NET complains that the tag containing the *runat="server"* attribute isn't properly ended. In others, the error message states that the HTML following the unclosed tag isn't allowed within that tag.

If you wanted to program this tag so that in the afternoon it displayed the picture Beauregard.jpg, you could code this:

```
If Now.Hour > 12 Then
    imgPhoto.Src = "Beauregard.jpg"
End If
```

In addition, HTML server controls have certain properties that don't correspond directly to normal HTML attributes. There's a *Visible* property, for example, that controls whether or not ASP.NET sends the tag to the browser. If your code sets *imgPhoto.Visible = False*, then as far as the Web visitor was concerned the picture would be completely absent from the Web page.

The similarity between HTML server controls and their ordinary HTML counterparts is both their greatest strength and their greatest limitation. If you already understand ordinary HTML controls, then you already know most of what you need to know about HTML server controls. If you've created existing forms or prefer to create new ones in programs such as FrontPage, you can make their form controls accessible to ASP.NET code by simply right-clicking each control and selecting Run As Server Control from the shortcut menu.

The primary disadvantage of HTML server controls is that they can do no more than ordinary HTML controls. They're not as powerful, for example, as the controls described in the next section.

For a list of all Web server controls, open the Help index and look for the article titled "System.Web.UI.HtmlControls Namespace."

Using Web Server Controls

The controls in the Web Forms portion of the Toolbox window are all Web server controls. Many of these controls functionally resemble HTML server controls, but the underlying code and concepts are quite different. Both of the following tags, for example, create a text box initialized to the word *Hello*:

```
<INPUT type="text" value="Hello" name="txtGreeting"
       runat="server" id="txtGreeting" />

<asp:textbox runat="server" id="txtGreeting">Hello</asp:textbox>
```

Both of these tags send essentially the same HTML to the browser. That code appears here:

```
<input type="text" value="hello" name="txtGreeting" id="txtGreeting" />
```

Note   If you actually try this example, the order of the attributes within the `<input>` tag will be different. This, however, makes no difference in the way the browser displays and processes the control.

Why have two completely different controls that accomplish the same result? Well, the *HtmlInputText* control, as it's called, takes advantage of what you already know about HTML and uses tags that just about any HTML editor in the world understands. The *TextBox* Web server control has properties and methods more like those of a Windows *TextBox* control and more like other Web server controls.

Web server controls are more abstract than HTML server controls. Their object model doesn't necessarily reflect HTML syntax, and the HTML they produce can be completely different from the tags that define them. The *Calendar* Web server control, for example, displays a monthly calendar complete with clickable date numbers for each day, forward and backward buttons, and a heading that shows the month and year. Displaying all these features requires quite a lot of HTML, but the code that makes it happen is simply this:

```
<asp:Calendar id="calStart" runat="server" />
```

The *Literal* and *Label* Web server controls are very handy for displaying variable text on a Web page:

- A *Literal* control sends the browser whatever text you store into its *Text* property, no more and no less. As such, *Literal* controls have no formatting options. They always inherit the appearance of the surrounding Web page.

- A *Label* control also sends the contents of its *Text* property, but surrounded by <span> and </span> tags. The *Label* control therefore supports formatting attributes like *BackColor*, *ForeColor*, and *Font*. If you specify such attributes, the *Label* control adds them to the opening <span> tag.

For a list of all Web server controls, open the Help index and look for the article titled "System.Web.UI.WebControls Namespace."

Responding to Web Form Events

The code behind a Web form can respond to any of the page-level events you saw previously in Table 12-2 as well as to events raised by a specific control.

Page_Load is generally the most useful page-level event because it occurs after ASP.NET loads and initializes all the objects on the page, and before ASP.NET renders the page and transmits it to the Web visitor. Visual Studio creates this event handler by default but to create it yourself, you would follow these steps:

1 Open the Web Forms page in Visual Studio.

2 Right-click the page and select View Code from the shortcut menu.

3 In the Class Name drop-down list box (which appears in the top-left corner of the code editor) select Base Class Events.

4 In the Method Name drop-down list (which appears in the top-right corner) select Load.

This creates an empty *Page_Load* subroutine that looks like this (except that the *Sub* statement appears as one long line):

```
Private Sub Page_Load(ByVal sender As Object, _
                     ByVal e As System.EventArgs) _
                     Handles MyBase.Load

End Sub
```

The *Page_Load* event is particularly useful in two situations. The first occurs when the Web page runs because the Web visitor clicked a hyperlink in another page or typed the page's Uniform Resource Locator (URL) in the browser's Address box. In this situation, code in the *Page_Load* event handler typically initializes form field values and other aspects of the page.

The second situation occurs when the Web form requests additional processing from the Web server. This is tantamount to the form asking the Web server for another copy of itself, taking into account any changes the Web visitor made or any events the Web visitor initiated.

Do you see the problem here? The *Page_Load* event handler typically needs to run different code for the initial display of a page than it does for subsequent form submissions. This obviously requires some way to distinguish the two situations.

Note In the early days of the Web, the page that displayed an HTML form and the program that processed the form input were usually different. When using ASP.NET, however, the page that displays a form and the page that processes submissions should be one and the same.

ASP.NET provides a property named *Page.IsPostBack* that provides this information. If *Page.IsPostBack* is *True*, you're processing a request from the same form. If it's *False*, you're processing an initial request for the page. Here's some sample code that tests the *Page.IsPostBack* property:

```
If Page.IsPostBack Then
'   Code to process form submission goes here
Else
'   Code to initialize form goes here.
End If
```

To capture other events that occur while the Web form is on display in the visitor's browser, use the code editor's Class Name drop-down list box to select the control that raises the event, and its Method Name drop-down list box to select the specific event. You should be aware, though, that most of these events don't fire immediately.

The interaction between a Web form and your ASP.NET form is much more indirect and sluggish than the interaction between a Windows form and its accompanying code. This is no defect of ASP.NET; it's an inevitable consequence of the way browsers and Web servers interact. The browser sends a request to the Web server, and the Web server sends the browser a whole new Web page.

Typically, this interaction—this *round trip*—akes several seconds to occur and causes the entire Web page to repaint. This is so distracting to the Web visitor that form submissions, hyperlink clicks, and button clicks are the only events that ASP.NET raises immediately. Handlers for other events, such as list box selections, don't run until a form submission occurs. If you want one of these event handlers to run immediately, set the server control's *AutoPostBack* property to *True*.

Exchanging Data with the Web Visitor

Unlike most older technologies for processing Web forms, ASP.NET normally preserves the value of all server controls from one submission to the next. In other words, once your code or the Web visitor enters a value into some control, that value persists through any number of form submissions (unless, of course, your code or the Web visitor explicitly changes it). If you don't want the value of a particular control to persist, select it in Web Forms Designer and set its *EnableViewState* property to *False*.

The property that gets or sets the displayed value of an HTML or Web server control varies with the type of control. Table 12-3 lists some examples:

Table 12-3   **Content Properties of Representative Server Controls**

Control Name	Control Type	Visible Property
HtmlText	HTML server control	Value
HtmlInputCheckBox	HTML server control	Checked
HtmlSelect	HTML server control	SelectedIndex, Value
TextBox	Web server control	Text
CheckBox	Web server control	Checked
DropDownList	Web server control	Selected Index, Selected Item

To find the property that contains the visible value of other server controls, consult the corresponding MSDN Library articles.

ASP.NET pages can also receive values from conventional HTML forms and from the URL that originally invokes the .aspx file.

■ If the `<form>` tag of a conventional HTML form specifies method="post" and its *action* attribute species an ASP.NET page, the ASP.NET page can retrieve form field values from the *Page.Request.Form* collection. Consider, for example, the conventional HTML form that the following code defines:

```
<FORM action="savename.aspx" method="post">
    <INPUT type="text" name="txtName">
    <INPUT type="submit" value="Submit" name="btnSub">
</FORM>
```

The code behind the savename.aspx page would retrieve the value of the *txtName* box by using the expression *Page.Request.Form(txtName)*.

■ If the `<form>` tag of a conventional form doesn't specify a method, or if it specifies method="get", or if the URL that requests an ASP.NET page contains a query string, then the ASP.NET page can retrieve form field values from the *Page.Request.QueryString* collection. Suppose, for example, that the URL that requests the savename.aspx page is:

```
http://localhost/webproj/savename.aspx?txtName=Jim
```

The following expression in the code behind the savename.aspx page would then equal Jim: *Page.Request.QueryString(txtName)*.

Testing Your Web Project

ASP.NET pages can only execute within the environment of a suitably configured Web server. The section entitled "Creating Web Projects" earlier in this chapter listed these configurations.

Given the nature of ASP.NET pages, Visual Studio can't run them directly. It can only tell a browser to request the page from the Web server where the ASP.NET page resides. Of course, if you've changed the .aspx file, you must save it before testing it. Otherwise, the Web server will use the old version that's still on disk. If you've changed the code-behind file, you must recompile it. Otherwise, the Web server will use the last version you did compile.

To compile all code-behind files that have changed since the last compilation, choose Build Solution from Visual Studio's Build menu. To compile all the code-behind files in a project from scratch, choose Rebuild Solution from the Build menu.

To tell Internet Explorer to display any page in your project, right-click the page in Solution Explorer and then select View In Browser from the shortcut menu.

To tell it to display the page currently open in Web Forms Designer, right-click the Web Forms Designer window and select View In Browser from the shortcut menu.

When you tell Visual Studio to display a Web page this way, by default it opens an instance of Internet Explorer as a tabbed choice inside the main Visual Studio window. To display the page in a stand-alone browser window, follow these steps:

1 Right-click the page in Solution Explorer.

2 Select Browse With from the shortcut menu.

3 When the Browse With dialog box shown in Figure 12-3 appears, choose Microsoft Internet Explorer. If you want to make this choice your new default, click Set As Default.

4 Click Browse.

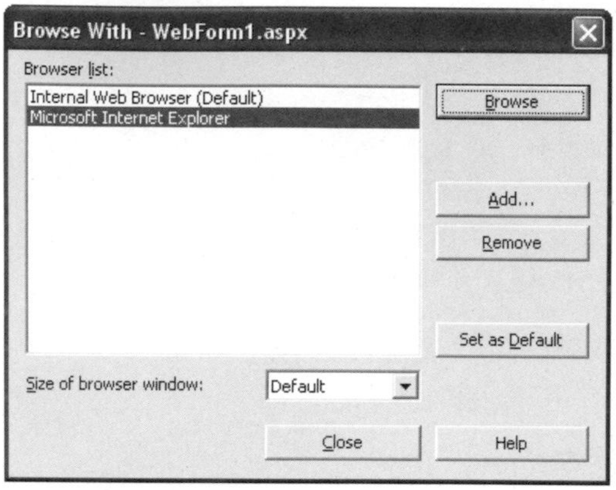

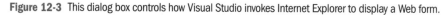

Figure 12-3 This dialog box controls how Visual Studio invokes Internet Explorer to display a Web form.

Visual Studio also supports interactive debugging of ASP.NET pages. This means you can stop the server-side code at specific statements, inspect and modify variables, and so forth. To do this on a Web server that runs on your own PC, follow the instructions in the Visual Studio help article titled "Debugging ASP.NET Web Applications During Development."

It's also possible to debug ASP.NET page on a remote server (meaning a computer other than the one you're using to run Visual Studio). However, these conditions must be met:

- You must be an administrator on the remote server.

- You must be a member of the local group Debugger Users on the remote server.

- Special Visual Studio remote debugging components must be installed on the remote server.

In addition, you should know that debugging ASP.NET pages can noticeably degrade performance of a remote server. Given the requirements and implications of remote debugging, most developers who need to debug an ASP.NET page interactively do so on local Web servers. For more information about debugging ASP.NET pages that run on a computer other than your own PC, refer to the Visual Studio help article titled "Debugging Web Applications on a Remote Server."

Example: Date Evaluator

This example creates an ASP.NET page that calculates the difference in days between two dates. Figure 12-4 shows the finished application in use.

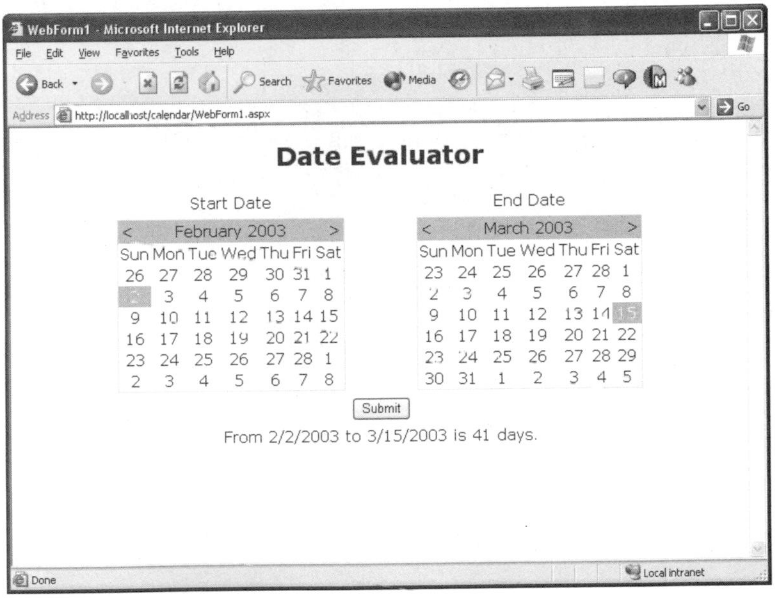

Figure 12-4 This ASP.NET Web application calculates the difference between two dates. The calendar displays are Calendar Web server controls.

Creating a Visual Web Page Design

To create this application, start Visual Studio, close any open projects, and then proceed as follows:

1 Choose New from the File menu and then choose Project.

2 When the New Project dialog box appears, select the ASP.NET Web Application template, specify a location of *http://localhost/DateEval*, and then click OK.

If you need to use a Web server located on some other computer, enter its name in place of *localhost*.

3   When Visual Studio finishes creating the project, select the file WebForm1.aspx in Solution Explorer, press F2, and then change the file's name to DateEval.aspx.

4   Click the Web Form Designer main window, verify that DOCUMENT is selected in the Properties window, and then change the *pageLayout* property to *FlowLayout*.

5   Type the text **Date Evaluator** into the main document window. Then, with the cursor placed anywhere in this text, choose Heading 1 from the Block Format drop-down list box in the Formatting toolbar.

The Block Format list box is the second list box in the Formatting toolbar. If this toolbar isn't visible, choose Toolbars from the View menu and then click Formatting.

6   Set the insertion point at the beginning of a new line below the text Date Evaluator. Then choose Insert from the Table menu and click Table.

7   When the Insert Table dialog box appears, make these entries and then click OK:

Rows:	4
Columns:	3
Width:	(empty)
Border Size:	0
Alignment:	Center
Cell Spacing:	0
Cell Padding:	3

8   Set the insertion point in the top left table cell and then type **Start Date**. Then, in the Properties window, change the *align* property of the <TD> cell to *center*.

9   Set the insertion point in the top right table cell and then type **End Date**. Then, change that cell's *align* property to *center* as well.

10   Set the insertion point in row 2, column 1 of the table, then double-click Calendar in the Web Forms portion of the Toolbox window. With the new *Calendar* control still selected, change the *(ID)* property in the Properties window from *Calendar1* to *calStart*.

11   Just as you did in step 10, add a *Calendar* control named *calEnd* to row 2, column 3 of the table.

12 Set the insertion point in the middle column of row 3, then double-click the *Button* control in the Web Forms portion of the Toolbox window. Then, in the Properties window, change the *(ID)* property from *Button1* to *btnSub* and the *Text* property to *Submit*.

13 Move the mouse pointer over the left edge of table row 4. When the mouse pointer changes to a right-pointing arrow, click the left button to select the entire row. Then, choose Merge Cells from the Table menu.

14 Set the insertion point inside row 4's one and only merged cell, then double-click the Literal control in the Web Forms portion of the Toolbox window. Then, in the Properties window, change the *(ID)* property to from *Literal1* to *litResult*.

15 Click anywhere inside the single merged cell in row 4 except the *litResult* control. Then, in the Properties window, set the <TD> object's *align* property to *center*.

To improve the typographic appearance of the page, do the following:

- Click a blank spot in the Web Forms Designer, then choose Document Styles from the Format menu.

- When the Document Styles window appears, click its Add Style Link toolbar button (third from the left).

- When the Select Style Sheet dialog box appears, select Styles.css in the Contents Of 'DateEval' box and click OK.

- Close the Document Styles window by clicking its close box (that is, the X icon in its top right corner.)

16 To save your work, choose Save All from the File menu.

To see how the page looks in a browser, right-click DateEval.aspx in the Solution Explorer window and select View In Browser from the shortcut menu. The Calendar controls will respond to mouse clicks but the code that makes the Submit button work is missing. The next section provides this.

Add the Code Behind the Date Evaluator Web Page

To write the code that calculates the difference between the two calendar dates, pursue these critical measures.

1 In the Web Forms Designer double-click the page background. This displays the code editor in the main window and creates a subroutine named *Page_Load*.

2   Add the following code inside the *Page_Load* subroutine:

```
If Not Page.IsPostBack Then
    litResult.Text = "Click Submit to calculate the " & _
                     "difference between two dates."
End If
```

   If the page isn't processing a request from its own form (that is, if *Page.IsPostBack* is *False*) the statement on lines 2 and 3 displays initial guidance to the Web visitor.

3   Select *btnSub* in the Class Name drop-down list box and *Click* in the Method Name drop-down list box. (These boxes appear at the top of the code editor window.) A new empty subroutine named *btnSub_Click* should then appear.

4   Within the *btnSub_Click* subroutine, declare a variable named *tspDiff* of type *TimeSpan*. This is a .NET data type designed specifically to store date and time intervals. Here's the required code:

```
Dim tspDiff As TimeSpan
```

5   The *SelectedDate* property of a *Calendar* control contains—guess what—the date that the Web visitor selected! If the visitor didn't select a date, the *SelectedDate* property equals a special value called *DateTime.MinValue*. If either the *calStart* control or the *calEnd* control contains this value, display a message in the *litResult* literal and then exit the subroutine. This requires the code shown here:

```
If calStart.SelectedDate = DateTime.MinValue Then
    litResult.Text = "You must select a start date."
    Exit Sub
End If
If calEnd.SelectedDate = DateTime.MinValue Then
    litResult.Text = "You must select an end date."
    Exit Sub
End If
```

6   Calculate the difference between the dates in the *calStart* and *calEnd* controls. All .NET *TimeDate* objects have a *Subtract* method that's perfect for this job, and returns a *TimeSpan* value. Now you know why you declared the *tspDiff* variable as a *TimeSpan*. Enter this statement after the code from step 5:

```
tspDiff = calEnd.SelectedDate.Subtract(calStart.SelectedDate)
```

7   *TimeSpans* can be positive or negative. (Negative results occur if, for example, you subtract the 15th of some month from the 10th of the same month.) Unfortunately, you can't just compare *TimeSpan* values to zero, nor can you multiply *TimeSpan* values by –1 or use the *Math*.Abs (absolute value) built-in function.

Fortunately, the .NET Framework provides a *TimeSpan.Compare* method that can compare *TimeSpan* values, a *TimeSpan.Zero* value that represents a zero time span, and a *Negate* method that reverses the sign of a *TimeSpan* value. Therefore, to guarantee a positive time span, add the code shown here after the code from step 6:

```
If TimeSpan.Compare(tspDiff, TimeSpan.Zero) = -1 Then
    tspDiff = tspDiff.Negate()
End If
```

8 Now that you have a nice, positive *TimeSpan* value to report, all that remains is displaying it to the Web visitor. This requires the code shown here, which completes the *btnSub_Click* subroutine:

```
litResult.Text = "From " & _
                 calStart.SelectedDate & " to " & _
                 calEnd.SelectedDate & " is " & _
                 tspDiff.Days & " days."
```

The *Days* property of any *TimeSpan* object returns an integer value containing the time interval in days.

9 To save your work, choose Save All from the File menu.

10 Right-click the DateEval.aspx file in Solution Explorer, then select Build And Browse from the shortcut menu.

When the Date Evaluator Web page appears, click a date in the Start Date calendar, click a date in the End Date calendar, and then click Submit. The Web page should respond by displaying the difference in days between the two dates you clicked.

For simplicity, this example didn't access any files, databases, e-mail, or other resources on the server. Rest assured, however, that such access is perfectly possible and, in fact, this is the reason most ASP.NET applications exist. The techniques are essentially the same as those you've seen in earlier Windows forms applications.   •

Key Points

■ The essence of the Web is client-server interaction. Browsers send requests to Web servers, and Web servers send responses to browsers.

■ Creating a new Web project in Visual Studio is largely a matter of selecting the proper template. However, you must provide a location on a suitably configured Web server.

- An ASP.NET Web project is an Internet Information Services (IIS) application on the Web server. If the FrontPage server extensions are installed on the Web server, an ASP.NET Web project is also a FrontPage web.

- Visual Studio provides a Web Forms Designer that's roughly comparable to the Windows Form Designer. The Web Forms Designer, however, works within the confines of HTML.

- Visual Studio stores the HTML layout for a Web form in one file and the code that supports it in a separate code-behind file. This makes it easier for designers and programmers to work on the same application at the same time.

- When a Web visitor requests an ASP.NET page, the Web server loads it into memory, runs any event handlers that respond to standard events or events from the Web visitor, and only then transmits the page to the visitor.

- On the Web server, ASP.NET loads any tag that contains a *runat="server"* attribute as a server control. This exposes properties and methods for working with that tag.

- ASP.NET normally preserves the value of server controls from one form submission to another. In other situations, you might need to read input form values from the *Page.Request.Form* or *Page.Request.QueryString* collection.

- To run the current version of a Web forms page, you must save the .aspx file, compile the code-behind file, and then tell a browser to request a new copy of the page.

For...Next

If you started this book having never written a program, and if you understood the examples in the last few chapters, then you've come a very long way, indeed. Congratulations! You probably now have several thousand questions about additional programming techniques, about running programs in various environments, about the 16,000 classes in the .NET Framework, about files, about databases, and about many others topics as well. If this book has brought you to the point of understanding books or advice about all those other topics, please consider it a success. Good luck with your projects, and I hope we meet again!

Index

Symbols and Numbers

Jim Buyens

Jim Buyens has been professionally involved with the World Wide Web since its inception, having been a server administrator, Web master, content developer, and system architect. He's currently developing Web-based business systems for AG Communications Systems, a provider of advanced telecommunications equipment.

Jim received a Bachelor of Science degree in Computer Science from Purdue University in 1971 and a Master of Business Administration from Arizona State University in 1992. When not enhancing the Web or writing books, he enjoys traveling and attending professional sports events—especially NHL hockey. He resides with his family in Phoenix.

Jim is also the author of numerous books on technology topics. Titles published by Microsoft Press are: *Web Database Development Step by Step .NET Edition* (forthcoming, mid-2003); *Troubleshooting Microsoft FrontPage 2002*; *Microsoft FrontPage Version 2002 Inside Out*; *Web Database Development Step by Step*; *Running Microsoft FrontPage 2000*; *Stupid Web Tricks*; and *Running Microsoft FrontPage 98*. He is also the author of *Building Net Sites with Windows NT— An Internet Services Handbook*, published by Addison-Wesley Developers Press.

The manuscript for this book was prepared and submitted to Microsoft Press in electronic form. The pages were composed by nSight, Inc., using Adobe FrameMaker+SGML for Windows, with text in Garamond and display text in ITC Franklin Gothic Condensed. Composed pages were delivered to the printer as electronic pre-press files.

Cover Designer	Tim Girvin Design
Interior Graphic Designer	James D. Kramer
Compositor	Donald Cowan
Project Manager	Tempe Goodhue
Copy Editor	Teresa Horton
Technical Editor	Bob Hogan
Proofreaders	Jennifer Carr, Katie O'Connell
Indexer	Jack Lewis

Get a **Free**
e-mail newsletter, updates,
special offers, links to related books,
and more when you
register on line!

Register your Microsoft Press® title on our Web site and you'll get a FREE subscription to our e-mail newsletter, *Microsoft Press Book Connections*. You'll find out about newly released and upcoming books and learning tools, online events, software downloads, special offers and coupons for Microsoft Press customers, and information about major Microsoft® product releases. You can also read useful additional information about all the titles we publish, such as detailed book descriptions, tables of contents and indexes, sample chapters, links to related books and book series, author biographies, and reviews by other customers.

Registration is easy. Just visit this Web page and fill in your information:

http://www.microsoft.com/mspress/register

Microsoft®

- -

Proof of Purchase

Use this page as proof of purchase if participating in a promotion or rebate offer on this title. Proof of purchase must be used in conjunction with other proof(s) of payment such as your dated sales receipt—see offer details.

Faster Smarter Beginning Programming
0-7356-1780-5

CUSTOMER NAME

Microsoft Press, PO Box 97017, Redmond, WA 98073-9830